Hellenic Studies 21

THE EPIC CITY

THE EPIC CITY

Urbanism, Utopia, and the Garden in Ancient Greece and Rome

Annette Lucia Giesecke

Center for Hellenic Studies
Trustees for Harvard University
Washington, DC
Distributed by Harvard University Press
Cambridge, Massachusetts, and London, England
2007

The Epic City: Urbanism, Utopia, and the Garden in Ancient Greece and Rome
by Annette Lucia Giesecke
Copyright © 2007 Center for Hellenic Studies, Trustees for Harvard University
Second printing, with errors corrected, 2010
All Rights Reserved.
Published by Center for Hellenic Studies, Trustees for Harvard University,
    Washington, DC
Distributed by Harvard University Press, Cambridge, Massachusetts, and
    London, England
Production Editor: Ivy Livingston
Cover Design and Illustration: Joni Godlove

EDITORIAL TEAM:
Senior Advisors: W. Robert Connor, Gloria Ferrari Pinney, Albert Henrichs,
    James O'Donnell, Bernd Seidensticker
Editorial Board: Gregory Nagy (Editor-in-Chief), Christopher Blackwell,
    Casey Dué (Executive Editor), Mary Ebbott (Executive Editor), Olga
    Levaniouk, Anne Mahoney, Leonard Muellner, Ross Scaife
Production Editors: M. Zoie Lafis, Ivy Livingston, Jennifer Reilly
Web Producer: Mark Tomasko

A revised version of "Homer's Eutopolis: Epic Journeys and the Search for an
    Ideal Society" (*Utopian Studies*, vol. 14, no. 2 [2003], 23–40) is reprinted by
    permission of the publisher.

LIBRARY OF CONGRESS CATALOGING-IN-PUBLICATION DATA

The Epic city: urbanism, utopia, and the garden in ancient Greece and Rome /
    by Annette Lucia Giesecke.
        p. cm. — (Hellenic studies series; 21)
    Includes bibliographical references and index.
    ISBN-13: 978-0-674-02374-1
    ISBN-10: 0-674-02374-9
1. Gardens—Greece—History. 2. Gardens—Symbolic aspects—Greece—
    History. 3. Greece—Antiquities. 4. Gardens—Rome. 5. Gardens—Symbolic
    aspects—Rome. 6. Rome—Antiquities. I. Title. II. Series.
    SB451.36.G8G54 2007
    712.0938—dc22
                                        2007028877

In Memory of Hakapoua, Wes Mere, and Koha

Hēdea Dōra

Contents

Illustrations

Acknowledgments

THIS BOOK STEMS from a sense of lasting awe before the marvels of the natural world. It stems from walks in the woods, along the resounding sea, and through lushly planted gardens. It stems also from the wondrous painted landscapes in Roman houses and villas on the Bay of Naples, from Lucretius' impassioned, often painterly discourse on Nature, the stark beauty of the Athenian Acropolis, and the timeless allure of the Homeric epics, all vivid expressions of a utopian ideal.

I owe a debt of deepest gratitude to Gregory Nagy for his enthusiastic support of this project. I am grateful also to the many individuals at the Center for Hellenic Studies who had a hand in the shaping of this book, particularly to Leonard Muellner for his generous guidance, Jill Curry Robbins for her efforts in obtaining and assembling illustrations, Ryan Hackney for his apt criticism, and Jennifer Reilly for managing the numerous and complex details of production. To Matthew O'Reilly I owe a growing fascination, as well as continuously evolving understanding, of "the frame" and its properties. Finally, I am grateful beyond words to Donald Dunham for everything.

Prologue

An Afternoon Walk

ONE FINE AFTERNOON IN ATHENS, Cicero, together with his friends Marcus Piso and Titus Pomponius, his brother Quintus, and his first cousin Lucius Cicero, set off on foot through the imposing Dipylon Gate and beyond the city's circuit wall. Their destination was the nearby Academy where they intended to take a relaxing stroll to unwind from a morning spent listening to the philosophical discourse of Antiochus.[1] Upon their arrival, they declared this tranquil spot ideal, its shaded, fragrant walks deservedly famous. Indeed, centuries earlier, Aristophanes had extolled the Academy's plantings of olive, plane, yew, and poplar.[2] The shaded walks and groves of the obscure hero Hekademos had remained an oasis, a pleasant place in which to escape the bustle of inner city life. Here, to their delight, the friends vividly conjured the memory of Plato, who had set up shop in these pleasant, hallowed groves.

However idyllic the Academy may have been, Epicurus, whose Garden the friends passed along the way, eschewed it as a location for his school, taking the radical step of creating a garden oasis for his pupils within the city itself. Just how significant a step it was that Epicurus established his *horti* 'garden(s)' within the city versus in its outlying *suburbium* can be recognized if one recalls that in its prime—as even to this day—Athens was not a garden city. Indeed, the suburban gymnasia provided the closest thing to pleasure gardens, and within the city's walls, gardens of any variety were few and far between. Classical Athens, with scattered intra-mural plantings limited to public spaces such as sanctuaries and the Agora, was testimony of the triumph of human-kind over wild Nature. Girt by the raw beauty of the sea, which was harvested for its wealth of fish, and the mountain triad of Penteli, Parnes, and Hymettos, which yielded marble, game, and pasturage, Athens was secured by its circuit walls against human and animal foe alike. Meanwhile, marking the "urban

---

[1] *De Finibus Bonorum et Malorum* (*On the Ends of Good and Evil*) 5.1.1–3.
[2] *Clouds* 1005–1008.

center," a massive temple dedicated to the city's patron goddess rose from and unabashedly appropriated a colossal rock in the midst of the Attic plain. The message of Athena's temple was unambiguous: the city protected by this goddess had fought against and prevailed over the bestial, the monstrous, the barbarian—in short, every potential threat to a perfect, civilized, anthropocentric order.

Athens' exclusion of "menacing" Nature from the city's heart was a phenomenon mirrored by the dwelling house. Closely clustered along narrow, labyrinthine roads, Athenian houses presented a blank, fortress-like façade to the outside world. Their source of light and air was an interior courtyard, which served as a space for work, play, and worship, but not as a place to test one's green thumb. Inner city, domestic gardens were limited, in the main, to ephemeral container plantings perched on rooftops and displayed in honor of Aphrodite's beloved Adonis. In Classical Athens, the ideal garden was extramural and utilitarian. Outside the fortified urban center lay market gardens in which fruit, vegetables, herbs, and flowers were grown. Here too were orchards, vineyards, and fields of grain, and, beyond them, pasturelands.

Beginning with Homer's *Iliad* and *Odyssey*, the pages that follow will examine the impulse underlying the development of the particular and carefully designed anthropocentric order that would become pivotal in the ideological self-fashioning of the Athenians and the Hellenes more generally. These pages will also address the causes underlying the "retreat" into the garden—first into groves that lay beyond the city walls and then into inner city gardens—as a vantage point from which to reflect on the optimal ordering of society. Why did Epicurus subvert the age-old order by bringing Nature within the city's walls, and why had Plato before him established his school in the groves of the Academy? Why, in turn, was the Roman sensibility towards Nature that emerged as the Republic set out to dominate the world so very different from that of Classical Greece? It is true that early Roman houses had garden spaces at their rear, evidence of an innate affinity for, or acknowledged dependence on, Nature, but the garden would eventually become a key feature fully integrated into the fabric of the Roman house. Exposure to the Hellenized East in the last centuries before the Common Era was attended by the assimilation of peristyle courts, but unlike their Greek counterparts, these peristyles were lushly planted. Outfitted with statuary and splashing fountains, the peristyle garden became the focal point of the Roman house. Now Nature was center stage. Planted gardens were "expanded" by paintings that mimicked their ornate hedges and bright blooms, and garden scenes, illusionistically painted, even appeared on the walls of interior living spaces. In short, the garden became a ubiquitous presence in the Roman house.

As for the city of Rome itself, peri-urban market gardens gave way to luxurious and expansive estates. These villas and their grounds, together with the "urbane" villas in outlying hills or in coveted coastal regions, set the precedent for the domestication of Nature evidenced on a smaller scale by "peristyle" houses as well as by apartments that boasted diminutive gardens in their window boxes. Both from "within" and from "without," Rome gradually became a garden city, its defensive walls breached by garden estates such as those of the illustrious Maecenas, whose Esquiline gardens spilled over, and thus appropriated, the Servian Wall.[3] By the age of Augustus, such blurring of distinctions between country and city, the intra- and extra-mural, manifested itself not only in and through the private gardens of villas and smaller dwellings but also through the proliferation of public parks, the first of which was established by none other than Pompey the Great, Caesar's foremost rival. The Porticus Pompeiana, as this park was called, featured a theater as well as shady walks, fountains, a sculpture collection, and a museum gallery displaying paintings by Greek masters. In close proximity to the Porticus Pompeiana were the Horti of Agrippa, an estate with lavish gardens, baths, and stunning water features, all bequeathed upon his passing to the Roman people. Also nearby were the gardens of Augustus' mausoleum, which were closely associated with the Ara Pacis, the stately "altar" commemorating peace in the Empire and adorned with a profusion of sculpted plant and animal life, the earthly bounty of the new Golden Age.

It has been said of Pompey's *porticus* that it was above all a "strategic display of political as well as military power," "a place both of dedication to Venus and a display of the *manubiae*, or booty, acquired under her protection."[4] Similarly, the Augustan Ara Pacis is certainly a memorial to the *Princeps'* military conquests, as a result of which peace in the Empire could be achieved. Domestic gardens, both the planted and the illusionistically painted, have likewise been characterized as a means of publicizing their owners' wealth, power, taste, and ingenuity, all evidence of Roman world dominion. Certainly, the grandest gardens evoked the pleasure parks, *paradeisoi*, of Persian and Hellenistic monarchs in their lives of absolute, godlike luxury. They evoked too the sanctuaries and gymnasia of Greece, public places drawn into the

---

[3] Purcell 2001:553 notes this "breach" of the city's first stone circuit-wall.
[4] Gleason 1994:13, 19.

private sphere. Was Nature just another vanquished enemy? Were ornamental plants and exotic animals merely trophies uprooted from native habitats and proudly displayed by their new Roman masters and commanders? The Elder Pliny, for his part, reports that trees from the far reaches of the Empire were led as captives in triumphal processions, subsequently becoming tribute-paying subjects of Rome.[5] Was it the not-so-secret aim of every garden-owning Roman to be a togate Xerxes, their founts and pools a reflection of the tamed Hellespont?[6] Or did the Roman garden impulse stem from a deep-seated desire to recapture the "primitive" lifestyle of virtuous Cincinnatus, recalled from the plow to serve his country, or of the herdsman Romulus?[7] Was the garden a sanctuary from the cacophony of smithies, bakers, peddlers, money-changers, and beggars who swarmed the streets of Rome even before Martial bewailed their insalubrious presence?[8] Was immersing oneself in the garden's delights a means by which to experience first hand, free from inhibitions occasioned by a sense of superiority or fear, the primal unity of life? Was it an expression of humanity's utopian propensity?[9] On all of these questions the works of Homer and Virgil, the "national epics" of Classical Greece and Rome, must reasonably shed light. Fundamental to the *Iliad*, *Odyssey*, and *Aeneid* alike are "the city," whether "cities" generally or a particular city, and, consequently, the dialectic between Nature and culture that urbanism engenders.

---

[5] *Natural History* 12.54.111–112 (*... a Pompeio Magno in triumpho arbores quoque duximus. servit nunc haec ac tributa pendit cum sua gente ...*), where reference is made specifically to the balsam tree. The text is from Mayhoff's 1909 Teubner edition. Unless otherwise specified (as in the case of the *Natural History*), Oxford Classical Texts furnished the editions upon which quotations in this text are based. For the sake of internal consistency, "v" appears for "u-consonant" in quotations of all Latin texts.

[6] This is a reference to the extravagant Lucullus and his massive earthworks on the shore near Naples that earned him the nickname of "Xerxes." Here, as reported by Plutarch, he carved tunnels through the hills to fill his fish ponds, surrounded parts of his villa with zones of salt and fresh water, and set suites of rooms afloat in the sea (Plutarch *Life of Lucullus* 39.3).

[7] See Percival 1996:65–66.

[8] *Epigrams* 12.57.

[9] See Finley 1967:3, who observes that it is characteristic of humankind to "yearn for a better life and a better world."

Introduction

Seeds of Perfection

IN THE COURSE OF THE SO-CALLED HEROIC AGE, the Greeks mustered a fleet of a thousand ships and sailed to Troy in order to retrieve the radiant Helen, wife of the Spartan king, as well as to avenge the Trojan prince's breach of the sacrosanct relationship between guest and host.[1] Thus it was, as Homer recounts, that hostilities between the Greeks and the Trojans began. The story of the Trojan War and its greatest heroes, Achilles and Odysseus, is, of course, extremely well known, while concrete facts regarding the story's origin still remain largely shrouded in mystery. The usual questions posed by scholars about the Trojan War and the *Iliad* and *Odyssey*, our primary sources of information about that event and its participants, are as follows: Was there a historical Trojan War? Was there, in actual fact, a bard called Homer, and did he compose the *Iliad* and *Odyssey*? Do the *Iliad* and *Odyssey* in any way accurately reflect Greek society at any historical period, or is the social background against which the epic heroes act out the drama of their lives entirely a fictional construct? To these compelling questions, I would like to add another. Could the *Iliad* and *Odyssey* both be counted among those literary works that are fundamentally utopian in outlook? On the grounds that they strongly manifest the dream of a society for a better life, I will argue that they should.[2] The *Iliad* and *Odyssey* both "pursue the prospect of recasting a political

---

[1] The Introduction and Chapter 1 reproduce and build upon material originally published in Giesecke 2003. In the course of this discussion, "Heroic Age" and "Bronze Age" will be used interchangeably. As has become common usage, the term "Mycenaean Period" will refer to the Bronze Age in mainland Greece specifically, and the adjective "Mycenaean" will be employed in reference to mainland Bronze Age culture and civilization.

[2] It is not my intention to argue here that the *Iliad* and *Odyssey* should be classed as formal literary utopias but rather that the works are utopian in nature and that they are manifestations of a contemporary utopian propensity. As Sargent 2000:8 argues: "Although the word *utopia* and the literary genre resulted from the book now known as *Utopia* by Thomas More, the phenomenon long predated the book." The definition adopted here of utopianism as "social dreaming" is likewise Sargent's 1994:3. The utopian content question itself

and social order" in the best possible way, and as such they should be viewed as "pre-texts" or "hypo-texts" of the utopian genre in literature.[3] Specifically, these epic tales "frame a value system that sustains and ... educates a society" by presenting societal evolution from village to *polis* as an ideal.[4] Through the words of the epic Muse, both the *Iliad* and *Odyssey*, each in its unique way, illustrate the post-Mycenaean Greek faith in urbanism as the optimum vehicle of human advancement, spiritual, ethical, intellectual, and technological alike; the form and institutions of the *polis*, it was thought, could best negotiate a place for humanity in Nature. Indeed, more than three centuries after the time of Homer, when the *polis* was well established as the characteristic social and political organization of the Greeks, it would remain Aristotle's opinion that the person who forms no part of the *polis* must be either beast or god, a creature well below or well above the human level.[5]

In regarding the Homeric poems from a utopian vantage point, I am making a series of assumptions that will necessarily influence the course of my argument. First, it is my opinion that there was a Trojan War—or wars—dating to the thirteenth century BCE and that there is accordingly a historical core to the poems.[6] Further, I believe that the Trojan saga was handed down orally from generation to generation, being creatively "re-fashioned" with every re-telling, and that the Homeric poems represent the culmination of this oral transmission.[7] Whether Homer was a historical figure and a poet trained in the oral tradition who, either himself or via scribe, recorded the poems in writing, or whether Homer is a fabricated "culture hero ... retrojected as the original genius of epic" and the embodiment of "a single pan-Hellenic tradition of epic" remains a singularly thorny question.[8] While various iden-

---

is a natural appendage to the "Homeric Question," for determining the purpose of these epics is surely as weighty a scholarly concern as their authorship and dating.

[3] For the extended quote, see Schaer 2000:4. Pradeau 2000:83 applies the tag of utopian "pre-text" and "hypo-text" to Plato's *Critias*, specifically the Atlantis myth.

[4] Nagy 1990:34.

[5] *Politics* 1253a1–4.

[6] For detailed and, at the same time, readable summaries and evaluations of the evidence regarding the historicity of the Trojan War see Latacz 2001 and Wood 1987.

[7] On the workings of oral poetics and the "identity" of Homer, see the persuasive arguments of Nagy. The arguments set forth in *Homeric Questions, Greek Mythology and Poetics,* and, more recently, in *Homeric Responses* (Nagy 1990, 1996, and 2003) have heavily influenced the perspective adopted here.

[8] For the quotations, see Nagy 1996:21 and 40 respectively. Nagy, for example 2003:2–3, continues to re-evaluate and re-synthesize the fundamental work of Milman Parry and Albert Lord and argues convincingly against the eighth-century dictation model in favor of consecutive periods of transmission, a movement from fluidity through transcription to

tifications of Homer continue to be argued persuasively yet, ultimately, still indecisively, it is my belief that the *Iliad* and *Odyssey* reached a critical juncture in their generation, a point of relative stability and substantial completion, in the latter half of the eighth century BCE.[9]

The dating of the poems is critical because the eighth century was a time of tremendous change and evolution in the Greek world, both socially and politically. Greece had only just emerged from the so-called Dark Age, roughly 1150–800 BCE, a period in which the art of writing had been lost; in which monumental architecture (or anything that could be considered "art") was no longer produced; and in which, generally speaking, people in the Greek world seem to have been reduced to a more or less nomadic, subsistence existence. Archaeological evidence reveals that this time of "material poverty and social insecurity on a grand scale" was attended by a dramatic decline in population and a nearly complete loss of foreign contact.[10] However, the passage of time has revealed that social and political crisis, upheaval, and conflict constitute the very seeds of perfection. Dissatisfaction is the most potent catalyst of speculation about modes of social improvement; it is crisis, not contentment, that breeds utopias and utopian thought.[11] The Greeks' emergence from Dark Age regionalism and isolationism was marked by a new and growing social consciousness and a desire to define "what it was to be Greek."[12] The eighth century saw the re-introduction of an alphabet, now borrowed from the Phoenicians, the organization of pan-Hellenic institutions such as the Olympic Games and the Delphic oracle, the expansion of colonization, and, most critically for my purposes, the appearance of the *polis* 'city-state' as a distinct form

---

ultimate textual crystallization in the second century BCE. Scholars who espouse and also persuasively argue the dictation and/or written composition theories include the following: Janko 1982, Jensen 1980, West 1990, Whitman 1958, and Powell 2002. Others would identify Homer as the first "singer" of these particular heroic lays or, alternatively, the most prestigious/influential (and not necessarily the last).

[9] The dating of the Homeric poems is, of course, no less hotly debated than the identity of Homer. Currently, most scholars lean towards the eighth century date for the significant shaping of the poems. See, for example, Hammer 2002, Langdon 1993, Osborne 1996:137–156, and Sherratt 1990 for the "textbook" view. My argument will be somewhat, though not entirely, at odds with Van Wees 2002 and Nagy 2003. Van Wees 2002 argues for a date between 735 and 640 BCE, entailing a forward dating-shift that I think my theory can sustain. On the other hand, while Nagy 2003:2–3 argues for a very late fixation date for the Homeric texts, he does designate the eighth (through sixth) century as a "more formative or 'Pan-Hellenic' period" in the poems' evolutionary history.

[10] Langdon 1993:9. See also Thomas and Conant 1999:58.

[11] For the observation that utopian thinking is prompted by specific crises and social problems, see Manuel and Manuel 1979:23–24.

[12] Hurwit 1985:83–84.

of social organization.[13] This time of recovery and change was ideal for the flourishing of utopian speculation.

If the Homeric poems are products of the very-formative eighth century, it stands to reason that the social conditions and material culture in which the poems began to take their ultimate form should somehow be reflected in the fabric of the poems themselves. As products of an oral tradition, the poems needed to be "modern enough to be understandable, but archaic enough to be believable."[14] So, for instance, artifacts such as the tower shield, boar's tusk helmet, and silver-riveted sword, all unlikely to have been used in the Dark Age or thereafter, are now understood as devices employed to lend the poems a convincingly antiquated cast rather than as evidence of the poems' crystallization in the Bronze Age. At the same time, the elaborate bureaucracies and highly stratified social and political systems of the palaces that sustained the warrior elite of Bronze Age Greece are at most reflected in traces.[15] The relative impotence, as well as the sheer numbers, of kings, *wanakes* and *basileis*, together with the importance and recurrence of assemblies of the People, is particularly telling. Any reader of the *Iliad* will observe that Agamemnon, while commander-in-chief of the expedition to Troy, is not actually able to assert himself over Achilles or the rest of the Greek contingent. Odysseus, for his part, prevails over the heinous threat of the suitors in Ithaka by means not only of cleverness and physical prowess but also of brute force. It has been noted that political influence in the Homeric poems is determined less by the official position an individual holds than by his "social standing," "rhetorical abilities," and "personal charisma."[16] Further, the succession of kingship is far from clear. For instance, Odysseus has succeeded his father Laertes in the kingship, but in Odysseus' absence, Laertes, having chosen what is tantamount to exile, has no say whatsoever politically; political activity has, in fact, ceased altogether. Meanwhile Telemachus, Odysseus' son, has not automatically assumed his father's position, nor is he guaranteed this position if his father should ultimately fail to return.[17] What emerges from the Homeric poems is,

---

[13] For a discussion of the emergence of pan-Hellenism at this time, see Nagy 1990:passim and 1979:7–8, Osborne 1996:70–156, and Hammer 2002:30–33.

[14] Raaflaub 1997:628. This point is also made in Redfield 1994:35–39. Foley 1997 provides a sweeping history of scholarly advances towards gaining an understanding of orality and the oral tradition.

[15] A full discussion of Bronze Age and Dark Age material in Homer can be found in Luce 1975: passim and in Sherratt 1990.

[16] Osborne 1996:150, pointing to Agamemnon and Odysseus as prime exemplars.

[17] These examples, all recounted by Osborne 1996:150–151, are contained also in Finley's discussion 1970:84–86.

accordingly, not the picture of a typically dynastic, absolute kingship. Power is not firmly in the hands of a single ruler.

The general lack of clarity regarding the authority and prerogatives of Homeric kings corresponds much more credibly to the changeable conditions of the Dark Age and the opening of the subsequent Archaic period than it does to the late Bronze Age. The Dark Age brought with it, or rather was ushered in by, the collapse of the palaces and, consequently, of the elaborate political and social systems they had sustained; "the powerful kings and their small armies of officials, scribes, and workers that supported the elaborate redistribution system were gone forever."[18] The villages and territories formerly under the control of the Mycenaean palaces did, however, continue to be "governed" by *basileis*. These were not kings but rather chieftains or strongmen, most likely the heads of the most powerful families in a given region. Their precarious position depended on the consent and support of other local chiefs who served as an advisory "council." It is likely too that as populations grew and administrative duties became more complex, the chieftains deferred increasingly to their councils. The ever more powerful council eclipsed the power of the chieftains, who were themselves replaced by elected magistrates. In the course of the eighth century BCE, the chieftainship would disappear almost everywhere in Greece, and where the office of *basileus* was retained, it was transformed into a magistracy almost exclusively religious in nature.[19]

The transformation and hegemonic devolution of the chieftainship went hand-in-hand with the birth and development of the Greek *polis*. A definition of the mature *polis* can be variously conceived, as usage of this term by ancient authors has proven to be remarkably fluid, ranging in meaning from "stronghold" to a "totality of town and hinterland."[20] For example, the *polis*, which Aristotle believed to have evolved organically from a partnership of villages, is spoken of by Thucydides not as a physical construct but as a community of men; "men," he says, "make the *polis*, not empty walls or ships" (*Peloponnesian War* 7.77.7).[21] A conception of the *polis* similar to that of Thucydides may be found also in Alcaeus and Aeschylus, while in Herodotus' *Histories*, the urban sense of the word is more common than the communal or political.[22] Pausanias,

---

[18] Pomeroy et al. 1999:43.

[19] This account is a summary of fuller discussions in Fine 1983:53–57, Langdon 1993:9–36, Osborne 1996:3–102, Thomas and Conant 1999:passim, and Pomeroy et al. 1999:43–59, 87–89.

[20] Hansen 1997:15. See also Hansen and Nielsen 2004:12–150.

[21] See Aristotle *Politics* especially 1252b16–1253b1.

[22] For the sentiment that the inhabitants "make" the *polis*, see Alcaeus Z103 and Aeschylus *Persians* 348–349. The observation regarding Herodotus' use of the term is Hansen's 1997:15.

again, describes the *polis* in purely physical terms when he remarks that the city of Panopeus in Phokis lacks the accoutrements of a proper *polis*, namely civic buildings, gymnasia, theaters, a marketplace, and a spring to supply the city with fresh water.[23] Likewise adopting a "structural" and physical perspective, Aristotle envisions the ideal *polis* as a walled city that is easily defensible and has sufficient territory, good port access, healthful air and water, a restricted population, and purposefully placed temples, public buildings, and *agorai* 'places of gathering'.[24] Based on the most prevalent applications and usages of the term, the *polis* may be understood as minimally comprising "a community of persons, of place or territory, of cults, customs and laws, and capable of (full or partial) self-administration (which presupposes institutions and meeting places)."[25]

Naturally, one would be hard pressed to find an equivalent of the fully evolved *polis* of Classical times in Homer's works, as the *polis* itself existed only in nascent form in the latter half of the eighth century. In contrast to its Classical counterpart, the Homeric *polis* is characterized by the "informal and somewhat rudimentary nature of its political organization and legal system," as well as a relative lack of interest in or awareness of the notion of citizenship.[26] Still, the existence and prominence of *poleis* in Homer cannot be overlooked.[27] The "*polis*" (and its Homeric synonym, *astu*) pervades the fabric of the Homeric poems. The word for "village," on the other hand, does not appear, for the *polis* is presented "as the typical form of human community."[28]

The tremendous significance in Homer of the *polis*, this new and evolving "urban" form of social organization, is perhaps most vividly illustrated by the fact that the action of the *Iliad* is located in and around a "*polis*" fighting for its very survival.[29] Likewise in the *Odyssey*, the critical situation that textually and

---

[23] Pausanias *Description of Greece* 10.4.1.

[24] Aristotle *Politics* 1325b34–1331b24. *Agora* appears in the plural here because Aristotle specifies the need for two types of *agora*, one designated for commercial activity and the other precluding it.

[25] Raaflaub 1997:630.

[26] Luce 1978:15.

[27] See Edwards 1993, Raaflaub 1997, and Scully 1981.

[28] Luce 1978:3. For the absence of the word "village" in Homer, see Scully 1981:1.

[29] The Homeric use of the word "*polis*" in tales purportedly set in the Bronze Age, which was a citadel-based, not a *polis*-based, society, has occasioned no small degree of confusion. As Scully 1990:3 remarks, the description of Troy, for instance, "is not a historical portrait of a *polis* at any one period of Greek history but a pastiche of old and new" in which aspects of the Mycenaean citadel are blended with the ideology of the new city-state. The same may be said of Ithaka, whose "actual" evolution from Bronze Age monarchy to *polis* we witness in the *Odyssey* but which is nevertheless referred to throughout as a *polis*. This argument will be elaborated in what follows.

conceptually frames the hero's wanderings is the grievous, looming threat to the very existence of the *"polis"* once governed by Odysseus on the island of Ithaka.[30] In the twenty years that he has been absent, the "city" of Odysseus has progressively ceased to function in anything but the most rudimentary way. No assemblies have been held, and no individual or group of individuals has stepped in to govern, even temporarily, in Odysseus' absence. As a result, lawlessness, as exemplified by the outrageous behavior of Penelope's suitors and those who willingly attend them, is rampant. Further, due to the suitors and their unchecked behavior, the resources of the land are being rapidly depleted. In short, the situation on Ithaka is reminiscent of the post-palatial, pre-*polis* organizational chaos of the Dark Age.

Interestingly, Homer remains tantalizingly vague about the constitution or political organization of Odysseus' *polis* both before and after its reorganization; this is something about which the poem's audience is left to speculate. The *Odyssey* focuses instead on the process by which the hero is equipped to undertake the societal reorganization that is so desperately required, and Homer, not unlike Thomas More in his *Utopia*, employs the literature of travel as a vehicle by which his "political" imagination, "assisted by fiction, can freely roam."[31] While More had not by any means been the first to envision a "better way of living and being," which is the substance of the social dream we call utopian, his sixteenth-century text formalizes the discourse on the good society, relegating it to a didactic frame of narrative fiction.[32] This narrative consists of a journey to a new world and a detailed description of the life, customs, and constitution of its inhabitants.[33] More's new world is at once a place impossible to locate in space (*ou-topos* 'no place') and a good place (*eu-topos*), a foil and corrective model for contemporary society.[34] Notably, More refers directly to Odysseus in casting his explorer Hythlodaeus as "a man superior to Ulysses himself in his knowledge of countries, men, and affairs," and again as a "wide-awake and observant" traveler, not like Palinurus who falls asleep at the helm, but rather like Ulysses or the well-traveled Plato.[35]

---

[30] This basic but profound observation about the critical role of the *polis* in the *Iliad* and *Odyssey* is Scully's 1981:2.

[31] Schaer 2000:4.

[32] Levitas 1990:7 argues that "the desire for a better way of being and living" is the one constant in the diverse corpus of utopian literature.

[33] On the formal elements of a proper (Morean) literary utopia, see Kumar 1991:31.

[34] The pun is More's own from the six-line poem ("Hexastichon in Utopiam Insulam") that forms part of the so-called *parerga* to *Utopia*. See Surtz and Hexter's edition 1965:20.

[35] The quotation is Surtz and Hexter's translation (1965:21) from the original Latin of a sentiment in the letter from Peter Giles to Jerome Busleyden that likewise forms part of the *parerga* to

In shaping his discourse on the good society, More most certainly had the Homeric text in mind. The narrative of travel, for its part, remains the device favored in composing literary utopias precisely because the traveler can witness alternative social orders firsthand in the course of a journey.

Scholars have argued that the wanderings of Odysseus represent the redefinition of what it means to be a hero in the post-palatial world and/or that they symbolize a historical process of enlightenment achieved through de-mythologizing—and therefore more completely understanding and controlling—the workings of the natural world.[36] It has been argued too that the *Odyssey* illustrates the hero's progressive activation of "the unconscious potential of the self."[37] There is ample textual support for all of these readings, but these widely accepted, or at least acknowledged, readings fail to provide a complete answer to a fundamental question that arises at the beginning of the poem. The proem, formal opening, of an epic poem is programmatic; it reveals the themes of greatest import:

> Ἄνδρα μοι ἔννεπε, Μοῦσα, πολύτροπον, ὃς μάλα πολλὰ
> πλάγχθη, ἐπεὶ Τροίης ἱερὸν πτολίεθρον ἔπερσε·
> πολλῶν δ᾽ ἀνθρώπων ἴδεν ἄστεα καὶ νόον ἔγνω,
> πολλὰ δ᾽ ὅ γ᾽ ἐν πόντῳ πάθεν ἄλγεα ὃν κατὰ θυμόν,
> ἀρνύμενος ἥν τε ψυχὴν καὶ νόστον ἑταίρων.

> Tell me, Muse, of a man of many ways, who far and wide
> was driven to wander, when he had sacked Troy's hallowed
>   citadel.
> He saw the cities and came to know the sensibilities of many
>   peoples,
> and many were the pains his heart suffered at sea,
> as he struggled for his life and the homecoming of his
>   companions.

> *Odyssey* 1.1–5[38]

Utopia. The reference to Palinurus, Ulysses, and Plato appears in the first book of *Utopia*, Surtz and Hexter 1965:48. For the description of Hythlodaeus as "wide awake and observant," see Surtz and Hexter 1965:301 *ad loc.*

[36] The former argument underlies the text of Whitman 1958 and the latter that of Horkheimer and Adorno 1993.

[37] Segal 1994:14.

[38] Unless otherwise noted, all translations of ancient texts are my own. The translations provided here are not intended to be particularly artful in and of themselves. Rather, my intention has been to render in English each line and each word therein as literally as possible for the purpose of supporting my arguments.

Homer states at the outset that Odysseus is a man of the greatest intelligence and endurance, and as such, he is ideally suited to travel extensively and gather information of an "ethnographic," socio-political nature.[39] But why precisely, one wonders, does the poet introduce his hero to many cities and many societies? Why, again, would Augustan Rome rehearse the wanderings of Odysseus anew in the figure of Aeneas?

[39] Dougherty 2001 explores the notion of Odysseus as ideal "ethnographer" and the *Odyssey* as a direct reflection of the colonizing spirit of the eighth century BCE.

1

Homer's Eutopolis

FOR TEN LONG YEARS after the fall of Troy, Odysseus endures one hardship after another as his ships are driven over the ominous, wine-dark sea, but his sufferings are not in vain. In the course of his wanderings, Odysseus sees many cities and intimately comes to know many ways of life. The intelligence he gathers will be of the utmost importance to him if and when he achieves his own *nostos* 'homecoming'. Upon his return, he will find his household and his city in shambles. Yet equipped with the knowledge of other cities and other societies of people, divinities, or monsters that he has encountered during his protracted travels, he will now have the resources, physical and intellectual alike, to restore everything to order.

However, it would be imprudent at best to assume that the restoration would not involve a major reorganization. A leader absent for some twenty years could not honestly expect to resume precisely where he left off. This is *the* fatal mistake Agamemnon makes in Aeschylus' tragic trilogy the *Oresteia*: upon his return to Argos after a ten-year absence as the leader of the Greek contingent at Troy, Agamemnon fails to heed the elders' advice that he make inquiries regarding the fidelity of the kingdom's remaining citizenry. As a result of his failure to gather this information, he walks directly into the lethal bath prepared for him by his unfaithful wife Clytaemnestra, who, in his absence, had become the city's acting regent. While Homer's Agamemnon, like Aeschylus', is not remarkable for the power of his mental faculties, Odysseus *is*. When Odysseus returns home and subsequently reorganizes his city, he will presumably aim to do so in the best possible way, to create the best possible society. Ithaka's pre-Trojan War political "state" is not germane to this endeavor, hence Homer's relative disinterest in the island's former social order. Again, it would be imprudent to try to turn back the clock. Utter chaos is Odysseus' starting point. Therefore, Homer's purpose would be, at least to some significant extent, to present his audience with the picture of what constitutes an ideal society via the encounters that will inform and guide the hero's new political settlement (Figure 1). The *Odyssey* must, in turn, be considered utopian. Moreover, it would not seem inappropriate to view Odysseus' reorganization as a metaphorical, mythological re-enactment of Greece's historical evolution from the order of Mycenaean palace-based society through the chaos of the Dark Age to an urban, *polis*-based society.

Figure 1. Mapping utopia. Map of the wanderings of Odysseus, after Otho Cushing in Charles Lamb, *The Adventures of Ulysses* (Boston: Ginn & Company, 1894, 1917), frontispiece.

What Odysseus' *polis* at home in Ithaka should *not* strive to emulate is fairly plain. The outstanding example is the apolitical, dystopian "society" of the Cyclopes:

> Κυκλώπων δ' ἐς γαῖαν ὑπερφιάλων ἀθεμίστων
> ἱκόμεθ', οἵ ῥα θεοῖσι πεποιθότες ἀθανάτοισιν

οὔτε φυτεύουσιν χερσὶν φυτὸν οὔτ᾽ ἀρόωσιν,
ἀλλὰ τά γ᾽ ἄσπαρτα καὶ ἀνήροτα πάντα φύονται,
110 πυροὶ καὶ κριθαὶ ἠδ᾽ ἄμπελοι, αἵ τε φέρουσιν
οἶνον ἐρισταφυλον, καί σφιν Διὸς ὄμβρος ἀέξει.
τοῖσιν δ᾽ οὔτ᾽ ἀγοραὶ βουληφόροι οὔτε θέμιστες,
ἀλλ᾽ οἵ γ᾽ ὑψηλῶν ὀρέων ναίουσι κάρηνα
ἐν σπέσσι γλαφυροῖσι, θεμιστεύει δὲ ἕκαστος
115 παίδων ἠδ᾽ ἀλόχων, οὐδ᾽ ἀλλήλων ἀλέγουσι.

The land of the insolent, lawless Cyclopes
did we reach. They, trusting in the immortal gods,
neither plant crops with their hands, nor do they plow;
rather, everything grows without sowing and cultivation,
110 wheat, barley, and grapevines, which yield
wine full-bodied, nourished by Zeus' rain.
For them there are neither deliberating assemblies nor
        precedents of law;
rather they inhabit the peaks of lofty mountains
in hollow caves, and each makes his own law
115 over his children and wives, and for one another they have
        no regard.

Odyssey 9.106–115

Homer is at pains to inform his audience that these monsters do not practice agriculture; they leave almost everything in the hands of the immortals. The Cyclopes' choice of habitation, namely caverns hollowed among the peaks of the high mountains, likewise demonstrates their inability, or lack of desire, to create order out of natural forms. Ultimately, they acknowledge no separation between themselves and the natural or animal world. The Cyclopes have neither institutions nor meetings for counsels. There is no body of law, divinely ordained or otherwise, that governs the Cyclopes' behavior; rather, each creates laws for his own wife and children. *Xenia* 'guest friendship/hospitality', which was so much part of the "civilized" Greek "way" that its breach precipitated the Trojan War, is certainly not a concept for the Cyclopes. A host would never eat his guests. Indeed the Cyclopes' entire existence may be described as insular; they care nothing about each other nor, apparently, are they curious about much apart from what readily presents itself on their (is)land.[1] There is an island of great fertility with a large population of goats

---

[1] Although Homer designates neither the land of the Cyclopes nor Phaiakian Scheria as an island,

in what would seem tantalizing proximity to the Cyclopes' own territory, yet they lack the necessary navigation skills to avail themselves of its endless potential. They could never even fathom that this is an island ripe for settlement, a notion precisely rendered by Odysseus (*Odyssey* 9.130). He describes an island affording a landscape ideally suited to the needs of civilized humanity, providing a wilderness for hunting, ample land for grazing, and farmland, as well as a site for a city complete with spring and harbor.[2]

To give the Cyclopes some credit, they are apparently quite good at making cheese and keeping track of the sheep on their own land. Nevertheless, it is evident that they lack "all forms of communal or non-tribal organization."[3] Technology, commerce, and communication, all of which the *polis* fosters and which are the veritable underpinnings of civilization, are nowhere in evidence among them.[4] It is telling, of course, that Aristotle names the Cyclops as the outstanding exemplar of an apolitical being:

> ... ὁ ἄνθρωπος φύσει πολιτικὸν ζῷον, καὶ ὁ ἄπολις διὰ φύσιν καὶ οὐ διὰ τύχην ἤτοι φαῦλός ἐστιν, ἢ κρείττων ἢ ἄνθρωπος· ὥσπερ καὶ ὁ ὑφ᾽ Ὁμήρου λοιδορηθεὶς "ἀφρήτωρ ἀθέμιστος ἀνέστιος"· ἅμα γὰρ φύσει τοιοῦτος καὶ πολέμου ἐπιθυμητής, ἅτε περ ἄζυξ ὢν ὥσπερ ἐν πεττοῖς.

> ... a human being is by nature a creature of the *polis*, and he who is no part of a *polis* due to natural inclination and not due to a stroke of fortune is, indeed, either inferior or superior to a human being—just like the one reviled by Homer as having no brotherhood, no divinely appointed ordinances, and no hearth, for being thus by nature, he also is eager for war—in as much as he is like an isolated game piece at draughts.

> *Politics* 1253a2–7

It is the Cyclopes' lack of social ties, their lack of divinely and culturally sanctioned ordinances or codes of behavior, and their lack, even, of a hearth that Aristotle points to specifically in order to mark them as inhuman, bestial, and, therefore, not suited to the life of the *polis*.[5] In truth, the hearth's impor-

---

the tendency to identify these lands as islands dates back at least to the fifth century BCE. So, for instance, Thucydides *Peloponnesian War* 6.2.1 and 1.25.4 respectively.

[2] Edwards 1993:28.

[3] Scully 1981:4.

[4] Observed also by Scully 1981:4.

[5] For the observation that the hearth represents the security of the home, see Nagler 1977:85n22.

tance to human civilization would be difficult to overstate. For the Greeks, the hearth represented and ensured the physical security and continuity of the family unit and, by extension, of any "political" union of families. The hearth was life-giving and life-sustaining, a source of stability in a mutable universe and a necessary link between the vulnerable human and the invulnerable, immutable divine.[6] Accordingly, the hearthless, lawless Cyclopes, privileged brutes living amidst a Golden Age abundance of natural resources, have nothing positive to offer Odysseus in terms of progressive social organization. Adopting their lifestyle would entail a massive step backwards to a time before humankind had emerged from the cave. Theirs is a lifestyle, Aristotle affirms, characterizing *the unenlightened times of old* (οὕτω τὸ ἀρχαῖον ᾤκουν, *Politics* 1252b23–24).

In the case of Calypso, Odysseus encounters another cave dweller, again surrounded by preternatural fecundity, but this encounter affords a glimpse into a lifestyle of an altogether different sort. On Calypso's lovely island Odysseus comes face to face with one of several fully animate manifestations of the myth of matriarchy. We, the audience, first experience Calypso's island from Hermes' vantage point as he wings his way across the heavens.

> 55 ἀλλ' ὅτε δὴ τὴν νῆσον ἀφίκετο τηλόθ' ἐοῦσαν,
> ἔνθ' ἐκ πόντου βὰς ἰοειδέος ἤπειρόνδε
> ἤϊεν, ὄφρα μέγα σπέος ἵκετο, τῷ ἔνι νύμφη
> ναῖεν ἐϋπλόκαμος· τὴν δ' ἔνδοθι τέτμεν ἐοῦσαν.
> πῦρ μὲν ἐπ' ἐσχαρόφιν μέγα καίετο, τηλόθι δ' ὀδμὴ
> 60 κέδρου τ' εὐκεάτοιο θύου τ' ἀνὰ νῆσον ὀδώδει
> δαιομένων· ἡ δ' ἔνδον ἀοιδιάουσ' ὀπὶ καλῇ
> ἱστὸν ἐποιχομένη χρυσείῃ κερκίδ' ὕφαινεν.
> ὕλη δὲ σπέος ἀμφὶ πεφύκει τηλεθόωσα,
> κλήθρη τ' αἴγειρός τε καὶ εὐώδης κυπάρισσος.
> 65 ἔνθα δέ τ' ὄρνιθες τανυσίπτεροι εὐνάζοντο,
> σκῶπές τ' ἴρηκές τε τανύγλωσσοί τε κορῶναι
> εἰνάλιαι, τῇσίν τε θαλάσσια ἔργα μέμηλεν.
> ἡ δ' αὐτοῦ τετάνυστο περὶ σπείους γλαφυροῖο
> ἡμερὶς ἡβώωσα, τεθήλει δὲ σταφυλῇσι·
> 70 κρῆναι δ' ἑξείης πίσυρες ῥέον ὕδατι λευκῷ,

For a discussion of the importance of fire in the creation of a human culture separated from the animal world, see Betsky 1995:9.

[6] See Vernant 1983:127–175.

πλησίαι ἀλλήλων τετραμμέναι ἄλλυδις ἄλλη.
ἀμφὶ δὲ λειμῶνες μαλακοὶ ἴου ἠδὲ σελίνου
θήλεον· ἔνθα κ' ἔπειτα καὶ ἀθάνατός περ ἐπελθὼν
θηήσαιτο ἰδὼν καὶ τερφθείη φρεσὶν ᾗσιν.
75 ἔνθα στὰς θηεῖτο διάκτορος ἀργειφόντης.

55 But when he came to the remote island,
then, stepping from the violet-colored sea, onto the land
he made his way, until he came to a huge cave, in which a
nymph
lovely-haired made her home. And her he found within.
A large fire was burning in the hearth, and far did the
fragrance
60 of split cedar and citronwood waft over the island
as it burned. And she, singing in a beautiful voice
as she went back and forth before the loom, was weaving
with a golden shuttle.
And a luxuriant forest was growing around the cave,
alders, and poplars, and fragrant cypresses.
65 And there long-winged birds had their resting places,
owls, and hawks, and loud-crying gulls
from the sea, who busy themselves with tasks supplied by
the ocean.
And around the hollow cave itself had spread a
burgeoning vine, and it was flourishing with clustering
grapes.
70 And four fountains in formation flowed with clear water
nearby each other, one in one direction and another in
another.
Around it soft meadows of violets and celery
were blooming. There even one of the immortals, happening
upon the place,
would marvel as he beheld it and would rejoice in his heart.
75 There, coming to a halt, the messenger Argeiphontes gazed
with admiration.

Odyssey 5.55–75

The description of Calypso's island veritably confounds the senses. There are sweet smells, soft meadows, refreshing fountains, chattering birds, and an abundance of plant life, including flowers, trees, and grapevines, that of themselves would make the island irresistible. Still, this lush beauty is merely the backdrop for the most alluring of the island's treasures, the fair woman, singing sweetly as she works at her loom to the light of a blazing fire. The allure of the place and of the woman is ultimately too much for Odysseus to resist, but this, at first glance perhaps surprisingly, is less the result of Odysseus' overwhelming desire than of Calypso's ability to manipulate him into submissiveness. It is out of compulsion, *anagkēi* (ἀνάγκῃ, *Odyssey* 5.154), the poet tells us, that Odysseus unwillingly sleeps with Calypso, who is willing (παρ' οὐκ ἐθέλων ἐθελούσῃ, *Odyssey* 5.155). In Calypso, Odysseus faces a fantastic illusion. The goddess has the semblance of a proper wife safely contained in a proper, though primitive, home; at least *her* cave, unlike that of the Cyclops, contains a hearth.[7] Here, it seems, a paradisiacal existence is within the hero's reach. No ordinary woman, however, Calypso is a *deinē theos* 'dread goddess' (δεινὴ θεός, *Odyssey* 7.246, 255) likely of Indo-European and Near Eastern origin, and her cave is not a safe, primitive relic from a lost Golden Age.[8]

Ironically, the source of Calypso's sensual appeal constitutes the essence of the threat she embodies. Who and what Calypso is—and what her particular allure—emerges from the manifold symbolic resonances of her cave. As traditional haunt of nymphs, the cave partakes of the divine, but viewed from a human evolutionary perspective, it is "the natural womb out of which man set forth to conquer the world."[9] Caves are both the source and safeguard of life, and as such they are refractions of Earth herself. So too is Calypso. The fecundity of the wilderness that surrounds her is not something the goddess passively enjoys; rather, she is its source and mistress. There is certainly no question of her comfort in this setting. Nothing here threatens her existence, whereas the security of a mortal settlement would necessitate a substantial, intrusive curbing of Nature. In truth, the proximity of a forest, regarded as Nature at her most intimidating, would suffice to fill the hearts of humanity with profoundest trepidation.

Notably, this island wilderness does not grow unchecked in spite of the lack of walls or barriers keeping it at bay, and a very real sense of order to the landscape is obscured somewhat by the fluidity of the poet's description.[10] The Earth goddess, it appears, is firmly in control. One who has attempted to

---

[7] Nagler 1977:85n20 notes that the weaving of both Calypso and Circe provides Odysseus with the false impression of a potential home.

[8] For the Indo-European origins of and Near Eastern influences in the Calypso episode, see Nagler 1977 (especially 79–81).

[9] Betsky 1995:xviii.

[10] As noted also by Austin 1975:149.

create a garden in the forest knows that woodland trees or weeds will soon encroach on and engulf an untended meadow. A tenacious vine too will spread extensively and bury everything in its path. Here, however, meadow and forest have remained distinct, and Calypso's cave has not succumbed to the strangling intrusion of the vine. The orderliness of this "wilderness" extends even to the presence of four fountains providing fresh water to all parts of the island. These fountains, a small-scale replica of the four waters that nourish life and divide the Earth, must also, one suspects, have issued from some form of artful manipulation.[11]

That Calypso is one with and empowered by the hallowed, generative Earth she inhabits is further expressed by her weaving, that feminine *tekhnē* 'skill' through which "women could weave nature together into clothes, baskets, and tools."[12] Weaving is a means by which to control Nature and by which, simultaneously, to create. It is also a metaphor for intellectual process; a capable weaver possesses a pliant mind.[13] Calypso possesses what might, from a male perspective, be viewed as a surprising range of creative, craftsmanly skills and knowledge. It is she, for instance, who instructs Odysseus on how to construct the raft that will carry him to the island of the Phaiakians, and she is well aware that the optimum material for building the raft is the buoyant wood of trees whose precise location she had previously mapped.[14]

To the Greek mind, Earth was "self-sufficient" and "self-generating," qualities that engendered in men no small degree of ambivalence.[15] That which is parthenogenic has no need for sexual reproduction. Calypso, the Earth goddess, has no need of a masculine presence to secure her life and livelihood, since she can seemingly create anything that she might require. Becoming part of her world would be disastrous for Odysseus, and the transference of her world order to patriarchal Greece would be a terrifying pros-

---

[11] On the Near Eastern notion of four rivers that sustain life on Earth and divide her territory into quadrants, as well as the "imitation" of these rivers in Persian gardens, see Moynihan 1979:8–9 and King 1979:21–31.

[12] Betsky 1995:10.

[13] On the metaphorical meaning of "weaving," see Snyder 1981 (especially 194) and also Scheid and Svenbro 1996:passim.

[14] In this particular context, Homer informs his audience that Odysseus is a skilled craftsman, but a craftsman, however skilled, does not necessarily know how to build every given structure. It is Calypso who provides him with tools, material, and, perhaps most importantly, a "plan": "But come now, cutting long planks with an axe, fit together a wide raft; and firmly set platforms upon it of good height so that it may carry you over the misty sea" (*Odyssey* 5.162–164).

[15] duBois 1988:57.

pect. Odysseus' requiring Calypso to "swear a great oath" (*Odyssey* 5.178–179) that her help in securing his escape is no lethal ruse is evidence enough of the extremity of his anxiety.

There are numerous additional indications that it will be necessary for Odysseus to exercise the greatest caution in order to survive his encounter with Calypso, a Creator with the prerogative also to destroy. Caves such as that of Calypso, for example, are certainly shelters and womb-like sources of life, but they are simultaneously passages to the underworld, the realm of the dead. They are *thēsauroi* 'treasuries' that may refuse to yield their treasure. Of this fact the cave-dwelling goddess' name, derived as it is from *kaluptein* 'to hide/conceal', serves as a vivid reminder. While Calypso does undeniably rescue and nurture Odysseus, the hero would lose the opportunity to end his life as a mortal among mortals, his potency as a man and a human drained, if he were to remain engulfed in her embrace.

Calypso's sinister aspect resonates through her physical environment. Her island's burgeoning flora, for all their lush beauty, include the cypress, alder, and black poplar, all plants that had funerary associations for the Greeks.[16] It is curious that there appear to be no fauna on this island except birds, but it is outright foreboding that the resident population of birds, consisting of owls, hawks, and gulls, all eaters of flesh, are associated with evil omens.[17] Even Calypso's soft, verdant meadows are not without their latent dangers. In Greek mythology, meadows, like caves, are common settings for sexual encounters, a good many of which result from rape.[18] Moreover, the sexual act itself was viewed as potentially lethal, particularly if engaged in with females, whether god or mortal, due to their "biologically" determined participation both in the workings of untamed Nature, constituting the savage, un-socialized world, and in the occult.[19]

Similar meadows appear in the landscapes of the dead and on the island of the fearsome, man-eating Sirens who, together with Scylla and Charybdis, exemplify the essence of the matriarchal threat, the threat of Nature unbri-

---

[16] In a full discussion of Calypso's cave, Weinberg 1986:21 notes that the alder was sacred to Cronos and the black poplar to Persephone. The cypress, meanwhile, was sacred to Dis.

[17] The dearth of wildlife on Ogygia apart from birds is observed by Louden 1999:107, and Weinberg 1986:21–22 remarks on the ominous aspect of Calypso's birds. Crane 1988:15–18, who discusses the funerary aspects of the island, does not, however, emphasize them to the extent that Weinberg does.

[18] See Crane 1988:17.

[19] For further discussion of the ambiguous position of women in the Greek world because of their latent savagery and inherent pollution, see Zaidman 1992:338–376 and also Arthur 1973. On sex and death in particular, see Vermeule 1979:145–177.

dled.[20] Of these the whirlpool Charybdis, fully elemental in her "being," constitutes the most basic sort of danger to the survival of humankind. She is no
sea monster but rather the sea at her most monstrous. More precisely, she is
the sea's ravening maw. Seafaring was always a risky business in antiquity,
and the sea, though abounding with life, presented the possibility of a death
more frightening than the most horrible demise on land. Even a relatively
calm sea could literally swallow those who fell victim to her, and their remains
would likely never be recovered for a proper burial.[21] Those who died at sea
thus risked finding their souls condemned to eternal wandering. Such is the
peril faced by those unlucky enough to encounter either Charybdis or Scylla,
who is, like the Cyclops, a cave-dwelling anthropophage. Scylla, with her six
necks and ravening canine heads, may be physiologically more "evolved"
than Charybdis, but her instincts are no less primal. She is a predator pure
and simple, fishing for any life form that approaches within striking distance
(*Odyssey* 12.94–97). Foolishly, the Greeks themselves attempt to assume the
role of predator immediately on the heels of their Scylla *Abenteur*. Emerging
from the cave that had become their shelter, they prey on the sacred cattle
of Helios. The result is predictably disastrous. Unless one has no need of the
gods—and no need to worry about divine retribution—one may not, as it turns
out, slaughter, eat, and sacrifice as domesticated those animals not raised and
tended by oneself or one's community.[22]

As for the Sirens, their predatory response is more sophisticated than
that of their monstrous "cousin" Scylla. Whether or not Homer's Sirens are
biform with human and avian physical characteristics is impossible to know,
though biformality was certainly the consensus amongst Greek artists.[23]
Homer does, however, tell us that the Sirens had sweet singing voices clearly
intelligible to the Greeks. Remarkably, their diction is specifically "epic" and,
more specifically, Iliadic.[24] Later testimonies clearly associate the Sirens not
only with the Earth, who is named as their mother, but also with Persephone
in the underworld.[25] Among the Earth's many powers is her ability to emanate

---

[20] Gresseth 1970:208–209 points to the meadows of asphodel in the realm of the dead (*Odyssey*
11.539 and *Odyssey* 24.13), the Elysian plain (*Odyssey* 4.563), and the island of the Sirens (*Odyssey*
12.45, 159).

[21] Vermeule 1979:185.

[22] Vidal-Naquet 1970:1288–1289.

[23] The literature on the Sirens consulted here includes: Buitron-Oliver and Cohen 1995, Buschor
1944, Doherty 1995a and 1995b, Hofstetter 1990, Gresseth 1970, Gropengiesser 1977, Pucci 1979
and 1998, and Vermeule 1979:75.

[24] Pucci 1979.

[25] Gresseth 1970:212 cites Euripides' *Helen* (168) for the notion that Earth is the Sirens' mother,

prophecies in the form of dreams. She is accordingly the treasure house not only of life and death but also of all knowledge. Thus the Sirens, the so-called Muses of the Afterlife, combine sexual allure, symbolized by their meadow, with the promise of possessing the most perfect knowledge, knowledge of all things that have occurred or will occur in the world.[26] Those who succumb to their temptation will meet a certain, instant death. In one way or another the Sirens, Scylla, and Charybdis all embody characteristics of the "Earth" goddess Calypso and also of Circe, her matriarchal counterpart.[27]

When Odysseus and his men pull their ship into a safe harbor at Circe's island Aeaea, they hope desperately that they will somewhere glimpse the works of humans, *erga brotōn* (ἔργα βροτῶν, *Odyssey* 10.147), and hear human voices, both relatively certain indicators, under "normal" circumstances, of a civilized culture and a hospitable reception. Their hopes are not utterly vain, since Odysseus discerns smoke rising in the distance. By now, however, Odysseus has learned to be very, very circumspect in his approach to the inhabitants of such unknown places, and his precautionary measure in sending out a scouting party is definitely in order. Smoke rising from a dwelling in the midst of densely growing woods and thickets signals that the Greeks will likely encounter something unexpected. Certainly "works of humans" such as cultivated fields would have been more comforting than a structure engulfed by forest.[28] It is thus hardly surprising that the inhabitant of this dwelling is a witch, partly a creature of folklore and partly Indo-European/Near-Eastern Nature goddess.[29] Unlike Calypso, who is attended merely by a few handmaids, Circe presides over what might be described as a small community, or, at least, an extensive household consisting both of female servants, some of whom are nymphs of the water and woods, and of wild animals. The attitude of these creatures of the wild is significant; these woodland wolves and lions are described as fawning about Odysseus' men like dogs greeting their master.[30] The effect Circe has on

---

and *Hecuba* (70–71) for the Sirens' association with Persephone. Vermeule 1979:75 derives them from the Egyptian ba-soul.

[26] "Muses of the Afterlife" is Buschor's description (1944). As remarked by Graham 1995:21, the sexual allure of the Sirens is also implied by the verbs *thelgein* (θέλγειν, *Odyssey* 12.44) and *terpesthai* (τέρπεσθαι, *Odyssey* 12.188), both verbs meaning 'to delight' and both commonly found in amorous contexts.

[27] See Louden 1999 (especially 105–117) for an extended comparison between the two goddesses.

[28] Circe's house is described as being located in a clearing, or, more properly, *periskeptōi eni khōrōi* 'in a place visible from all sides' (περισκέπτῳ ἐνὶ χώρῳ, *Odyssey* 10.211), but that is the extent of "earthworks" here.

[29] See Carpenter 1956:passim, Crane 1988:31–85, Dyck 1981, and Segal 1968 (especially 440).

[30] *Odyssey* 10.212–215.

the animals is precisely that of Aphrodite on the wolves, bears, lions, and leopards of Mount Ida, which are described as fawning around her in the so-called Homeric hymn composed in her honor.[31] Both Circe and Aphrodite have about them something of the *Potnia Th.ērōn*, the Mistress of Animals known in Greece at least as early as the Bronze Age. If, however, Circe can tame these animals, she could certainly—and easily—incite them to fury. The control she exercises over both the animals in her kingdom and the men whom she has either transformed, or is about to transform into animals, stems from qualities that she shares with Calypso and the Sirens. These attributes include the possession of an agile, scheming, "mantic" intellect and the powerful abilities to seduce and beguile.[32] Fortunately for him, Odysseus receives assistance from the divine sphere that enables him to resist Circe's manifold threat.

What sets Odysseus' encounter with Circe apart from those with Calypso, the Sirens, and all his other female foes is the explicitness of the ideological male/female conflict in this passage. Only in this portion of his adventures does Odysseus openly reveal the fear of being emasculated, *anēnōr* (ἀνήνωρ, *Odyssey* 10.301, 341), and sword in hand, he overpowers the Earth goddess with a weapon that is an extension of the warrior "self." Circe is the only female adversary whom Odysseus feels the need to attack physically, and the extremity of the measures he takes to defend himself against her results not only from the fact that she poses a physical threat to himself and his companions, a threat to their survival, but also from the fact that she represents the greatest threat of all to "evolved" patriarchal civilization. In the case of Calypso, the prototypical Greek faces the danger of being eternally confined in a quasi-paradisiacal, matriarchal Paleolithic, but Circe's architectonic faculties suggest that she has progressed well into the province that Western culture has claimed as masculine. Where Circe lives is not a cave, a natural orifice within the Earth herself, but rather in a house crafted from polished stone (τετυγμένα δώματα Κίρκης / ξεστοῖσιν λάεσσι, *Odyssey* 10.210–211). This finely constructed house comprises the true peril of Circe.

---

[31] *Homeric Hymn to Aphrodite* 69–72.

[32] Both Calypso and Circe (technically, her island) are described as *doloessa* 'deceitful' (δολόεσσα, *Odyssey* 7.245 and *Odyssey* 9.32 respectively). The verb *thelgein* 'to beguile/charm' (θέλγειν) is used of Calypso (*Odyssey* 1.57), Circe (*Odyssey* 10.213), and the Sirens (*Odyssey* 12.40, 44). Part of the allure of the Sirens, Circe, and Calypso is their mantic faculty which, in the case of Calypso and Circe, is suggested by their designation as *deinē theos audēessa* 'dread goddess endowed with speech' (δεινὴ θεὸς αὐδήεσσα, *Odyssey* 10.136; *Odyssey* 11.8; and *Odyssey* 12.150, 449), indicating that the goddesses possess speech that is like that of mortals in sound and also, more significantly, prophetic in nature. For this interpretation, see Nagler 1977.

Circe's peril is directly linked to the theoretical debate regarding the "sex" of architecture that scholars have traced back to Vitruvius but that clearly comes into play in this very much older Greek text. The conceptual gender crisis that has long occupied architectural theorists is perhaps best expressed in the words of fifteenth-century architectural utopian Antonio Averlino, more commonly known as Filarete:[33]

> ... the building is constructed as a simile for the human figure. You see that I have shown you by means of a simile that a building is derived from man, that is, from his form, members, and measure... You perhaps could say, you have told me that the building is similar to man. Therefore, if this is so it needs to be conceived and then born. As with man himself, so with the Building ... Since no one can conceive himself without a woman, by another simile, the building cannot be conceived by one man alone. As it cannot be done without woman, so he who wishes to build needs an architect. He conceives it with him and then the architect carries it. When the architect has given birth he becomes the mother of the building.
>
> *Treatise on Architecture* 12–16

Filarete's stumbling block was the Vitruvian idea that a building is based on the proportions of a man and is a male entity. A building, however, must be created, and creation is by nature the province of the feminine. Filarete's solution was a sort of "transsexual operation" whereby the architect is transformed functionally into a woman while remaining male in gender.[34] In the case of Circe, there is no indication that a male has created her dwelling. Furthermore, this structure is described in terms that clearly suggest a high level of craftsmanship and technical skill. While Homer has not explicitly stated that Circe built it with her own hands, the ability to have done so is certainly within her reach. Like Calypso, Circe is a skilled weaver. Indeed, she is more than simply skilled; her work is not only technically proficient, delicate, but also exquisitely beautiful, lovely and radiant (λεπτά τε καὶ χαρίεντα καὶ ἀγλαὰ ἔργα, *Odyssey* 10.223). Weaving, as evidenced by Calypso's tectonic abilities, is a form of creation that stems from *mētis* 'knowledge', which "embraces both mental and manual prowess."[35] Simply put, weaving is "an architecture."[36] One very basic and

---

[33] As cited in Agrest 1991:173–195.

[34] Agrest 1991:182.

[35] Bergren 1993:8.

[36] Betsky 1995:40. As Scheid and Svenbro 1996:25 note, Plato himself described weaving as yielding a form of "housing," namely a product that defends and protects (*Statesman* 279d).

important manifestation of weaving's architecture is clothing, the original fabricated shelter enabling humanity to emerge from the cave and brave the elements. The hut or tent, and ultimately the house, are therefore extensions or elaborations of the original, intimate, body shelter. More specifically, tent, hut, and house are modeled on, or are reflections of, the protective umbrella of the maternal skirt.[37] On Aeaea, an island inhabited only by women, it would appear that the creation of all forms of shelter rests in the hands of the current population, a condition consistent with the inherently feminine nature of shelter fabrication. Controlling "space" and creating a culture outside of the house through construction of buildings in the environment constitutes a manifest subversion of the patriarchal order shown to exist in the Hellenic world of Homer's poems. In the end, Circe's entrancing small community denies male autonomy on every level.

Lessons regarding the nature and perils of matriarchy learned on Aeaea as well as on Ogygia, Calypso's fair island, will serve Odysseus well upon his return.[38] What he will find in Ithaka are the seeds of matriarchy, for his house and kingdom had been left by default in the hands of Penelope. In intellect and clever deceitfulness she is a match for Odysseus, and her skill in weaving is such that it permits her to control the passage of time and, thereby, the fate of Ithaka.[39] During the protracted Ithakan crisis, the progress of Penelope's weaving constitutes the sole constraint of her unruly suitors' willful, outrageous behavior; without the completion of the shroud she is weaving, no man can claim her as his bride, or, through marriage, claim mastery over Odysseus' domestic and political domain. Fortunately for Odysseus, Penelope has no matriarchal aspirations and remains faithful to him in body and soul. She will be his ally in effecting a new social order in which her weaving will presumably continue to serve as a vehicle of social cohesion ensuring a stable union of the sexes within the household, harmonious relations between households,

---

[37] This is vividly illustrated by a ceramic sculpture crafted by Oaxacan folk-artist Josefina Aguilar. The sculpture in question is a self-portrait representing the artist wearing a floor-length skirt. The garment's painted "belt" is a substantial wall with its formidable gate at the figure's navel. Covering the skirt itself are miniature likenesses in high relief of the members of the artist's extended family. Beyond any doubt, this sculpture represents the female, the mother, as the shelter that provides security and sustenance for her family. For the image, see Wasserspring 2000:115.

[38] Convincing arguments countering Bachofen's conclusions (1967) regarding the historical reality of matriarchy may be found in Zeitlin 1978 and duBois 1982, who characterize matriarchal myths as cautionary expressions of the male fear of domination by the irrational second sex.

[39] The inversion of sex roles on Ithaka in Odysseus' absence is discussed by Foley 1978.

and larger unity between collectives of households in the form of villages and *poleis*. Such, at least, would be the "proper" application of weaving in the patriarchal order forged in post-Bronze Age Greece.[40]

Odysseus does, of course, encounter other groups or individuals that provide examples of social organization comparable to the "matriarchies" in their impracticality or Hellenic inadmissibility. The Lotus Eaters, for instance, are seemingly benign and content enough with their way of life, but their existence is in a sense unreal; theirs is not a vital, productive life because it is passed in a drug-induced haze. It "is actually the illusion of happiness, a dull vegetation, as meager as an animal's bare existence, and at best only the absence of the awareness of misfortune."[41] Moreover, succumbing to the temptation of the lotus would be nothing short of "a regression to the phase of collecting the fruits of the earth and of the sea, a stage more ancient than agriculture, cattle-rearing, and even hunting, older, in fact than all production."[42] It can certainly be argued that the Lotus Eaters exemplify a basic sort of utopia, the so-called Cockaigne utopia, which is characterized by the gratification in abundance of the average person's desires. Lands of Cockaigne, in which the populace is devoted to "unrestrained enjoyment and pleasure," are appealing on the surface, but they harbor the potential of deterioration "into excess and satiety, probably also to killing and of riotous disorder."[43] Odysseus, whose intentions are clearly progressive rather than regressive, wisely resists the temptation of this illusory happiness. In the end, this vegetative life has nothing more to offer than Hades, whose realm Odysseus also visits. It is true that the netherworld yields invaluable information regarding the mechanics of his homecoming, the current state of his household, and a premonition of his death from the sea at some point in the more distant future. In the house of Hades, Odysseus is made painfully aware that his family has suffered and that the creation of a new social order in Ithaka must be preceded by a reaffirmation of the bond between himself and his wife, his son, and his father. Still, the dead are disembodied souls, weak, unproductive, and lacking in sensory perception, and there is ultimately nothing within their current social order

---

[40] As Scheid and Svenbro 1996:9–34 indicate, the political application of weaving as a vehicle and reflection of civic harmony is vividly demonstrated by the Athenians' ritualized fabrication and dedication of a robe to their patron goddess at the Panathenaia and, additionally, by the collaboration of women from once-dissenting Elean cities in weaving a robe for the Olympic Heraea.

[41] Horkheimer and Adorno 1993:63.

[42] Horkheimer and Adorno 1993:63.

[43] Kumar 1991:18.

that Odysseus can practically apply to his reformative efforts in the world of the living except, perhaps, their sense of justice.[44] Homer's dead are not, as they will later be, characterized as *makares* 'happy', and the House of Hades itself has been seen as resembling a Bronze Age kingdom with a walled, central palace containing a lordly hall.[45] Odysseus will return to this largely joyless, retrospective place soon enough, and there is certainly no reason to aspire to recreate Hell on Earth.

The dead, the Lotus Eaters, the Cyclopes, Circe, and Calypso all exemplify or offer "lifestyles," however superficially appealing, that Odysseus could not or would not actually want to adopt, and all can exist in their respective "worlds" without the organization and security provided by a city. They require no urban defense because, in various ways, they are impervious to the threats of wild Nature, some rendered invulnerable by the permanent or temporary loss of vital functions, others through a kinship with the Elemental. Odysseus does, however, encounter beings more like himself, more vulnerable in the face of menacing Nature, and these inhabit *poleis*. Apart from the city of the Kikones, who are firmly of this world, there are three other-worldly *poleis* that Odysseus and his men come upon. These are the cities of Aeolus, the Laestrygonians, and the Phaiakians. Not all cities, to be sure, are equal, and the impressively fortified, exceptionally well-ordered city of the Phaiakians will prove to be the only positive model that Odysseus encounters. In the case of Aeolus' city, there may be formidable fortifications made of unbreakable bronze, but there appears to be no *agora* and, therefore, no public business.[46] In fact, the only activities on Aeolus' island about which we hear are feasting, sleeping, and the dispensation of *xenia*. Strangest of all, Aeolus, his wife, and his children form the only social unit on this island, which leads inevitably to the practice of incest.[47] The Laestrygonians, for their part, seem diverse enough as a population. They have a king and a queen, and they possess a functioning *agora* from which the king is summoned upon the Greeks' arrival.

---

[44] Odysseus characterizes the dead as "powerless" (ἀμενηνὰ κάρηνα, *Odyssey* 11.29), and Achilles speaks of them as "senseless" and "finished with/worn out by the work of mortals" (ἀφραδέες … βροτῶν εἴδωλα καμόντων, *Odyssey* 11.476).

[45] The realization that the House of Hades resembles a Mycenaean palace is elaborated in Vermeule 1979:35, where the author points specifically to the evidence of *Iliad* 23.71 and 76. The concept of the "happy dead" and its history is examined in Vermeule 1979:73.

[46] Lowenstam (1993) focuses on the presence or absence of a *megaron*, a rectangular room containing a central hearth and entered from one side through one or more antechambers and a porch, and *agora* (as well as activities related to the *megaron* and *agora*) as he evaluates the relevance of these various cities and settlements to the Greek experience.

[47] See also Clay 1983:129.

Their city has a good, safe harbor, and there is a stream nearby to provide water. Nevertheless, other typical *polis* components, such as city walls and the works of oxen and men, are missing. It is soon revealed that these "omissions" result from the Laestrygonians' greater proximity to the bestial than the divine. Like the Cyclopes, they are anthropophages, albeit more advanced in social organization.

The Phaiakian *polis*, by contrast, is everything these other cities are not. On the way to the king's palace, Odysseus beholds the harbors, walls, and meeting place of the city (*Odyssey* 6.261–267). This is clearly a well-developed *polis*. Unlike the loose society of Cyclopes, this city, with its harbor and ships, is at least theoretically open to, rather than sequestered from, the larger world. The city's meeting place, *agora,* by the temple of Poseidon, "provides orderly social, political, and economic communication within, and the city's walls make distinct this order within from the world outside."[48] In terms of social or political organization, the king, Alkinoos, is no absolute, hereditary monarch. Rather, as Alkinoos himself says, he is one of thirteen men with the same title, *basileus*, who hold power as leaders of the people (*Odyssey* 8.390–391). While he is the most powerful of these and his position is inherited, Alkinoos' preeminence is nonetheless precarious. He is really *primus inter pares* 'first among equals', and his status is based at least as much, if not more, upon personal accomplishment and reputation as on descent. Just how well the wise Alkinoos (whose name means "strength of mind") has ordered his *polis* is directly reflected by the order within his neatly fenced garden, which includes both a vineyard and extensive orchard (*Odyssey* 7.112–131). Apparently, the good "politician" must also be a good gardener.

It is not surprising, therefore, that the *Odyssey* closes, and Odysseus' resettlement of the Ithakan *polis* is completed, in the garden. An unmistakable signifier of his return, Odysseus must visit his father in *his* garden and must recall, and in a sense relive, their planting of the garden's orchard together (*Odyssey* 24.336–344). The establishment and existence of the *polis* depends on the containment of Nature. Only after reorganizing or reclaiming the garden can Odysseus hope to make peace with the families of his wife's slain suitors and legitimately resume the position of civic leader. Arguably, the hero's slaying of the suitors and the concomitant execution of a number of handmaids are not actions befitting a utopian venture. However, Homer makes it abundantly clear that the suitors and handmaids are eminently deserving of punishment. It can be no coincidence that the poet applies the same epithets

---

[48] Scully 1981:5.

to the suitors as he does to the Cyclopes. Both are repeatedly described as utterly insolent, lawless, and brimming with *hubris*.[49] The suitors may not always appear to be uniformly heinous, but the undeniable fact remains that all of them, selfishly motivated by the desire to possess Penelope and the household of Odysseus, had readily assisted in the plotting of Telemachus' murder (*Odyssey* 4.673). The handmaids whom Odysseus condemns to hanging are likewise guilty of grievous wrongdoing. They have abused Penelope and slept with the suitors (*Odyssey* 22.417–425). In other words, the handmaids have prostituted themselves for the suitors' amusement, and Homer gives no evidence of their having been forced to do so. Meanwhile, Homer is careful to point out that the singer and herald, both of whom have also served the suitors, are deemed blameless and spared because they *had* been forced to submit to the suitors' will (*Odyssey* 22.340–360). As for the use of violence itself, even Thomas More's Utopians avail themselves thereof in order to preserve the integrity of their own social order when it is deemed absolutely necessary. Wars are undeniably waged and criminals executed in the archetypal literary utopia.

Having survived and successfully navigated the extreme challenges presented by a decade's worth of nomadism and, metaphorically speaking, having first survived the end of the Heroic Age as prefigured by the collapse of Troy, Odysseus ultimately finds himself in a position equivalent to that of the historical, eighth-century Greek. Faced with organizing a civic and administrative unit after what might be described as a period of "Dark Age" unsettlement and chaos, he has much in common with those at the forefront of the societal changes inherent in the fashioning and evolution of the *polis*. Through Odysseus' many adventures, Homer, together with his audience, explores the relative deficiencies and excesses of a variety of "settlements." The model for Odysseus' ideal settlement is clearly the *polis* of the Phaiakians.[50] They alone practice agriculture and viticulture. They alone worship, and build temples for,

---

[49] These adjectives are, respectively: *huperphialos, athemistos, hubristēs* (ὑπερφίαλος, ἀθέμιστος, ὑβριστής). *Hubris*, in the Greek sense, means not so much 'pride' as the failure to recognize the traditionally sanctioned limits placed on human behavior in one's interactions both with the gods and with one's fellow human beings.

[50] That this is the case is further substantiated by the fact that, aside from Penelope, the Phaiakians alone enjoy the privilege of hearing the account of Odysseus' wanderings. Additionally, parallels in plot and structure between the Phaiakian and Ithakan-return episodes abound, which strongly suggests that the Phaiakian adventure is a trial run or preparation for what lies ahead in Ithaka. It is a suitable venue for such preparation, as the Phaiakians possess values most like those to which Odysseus aspires. See, for example, Vidal-Naquet 1970:1292–1297, Segal 1994:12–64, and Doherty 1995b:91–92.

the gods. Theirs is a walled, well-organized, architecturally differentiated city with a just and progressive system of government. Of course, the Phaiakians are also particularly close to the gods. Deities physically attend their feasts, and it is due to the gods' bounty that the Phaiakian crops evince a preternatural fecundity with no dependence whatsoever upon seasonality. In addition, the existence of the Phaiakians is all but free from difficulty and stress. They have a life and lifestyle to which mortals can aspire, but which they can never actually achieve. On the basis of its inimitable perfection Scheria has been viewed by some scholars as the "first surviving Utopia in European literature."[51] Still, while neither Odysseus nor Homer's audience could ever hope to approximate the Phaiakians' closeness to the gods, the Scherian civic organization *can* be emulated, and one expects that this is what the wise Odysseus—and Homer's audience—will do. The fact that Homer does not expound the new Ithakan constitution is testimony of his genius as a storyteller and as a political thinker. He relies instead on the formidable power of suggestion, whereby he can most fully engage his audience in the act of *polis*-building.

As a tale set outside a *polis* besieged, the *Iliad*, like the *Odyssey*, clearly concerns itself with "the city"; however, where the *Odyssey* focuses on fashioning an ideal polity, the *Iliad* works towards defining such a polity's ideal citizen.[52] In order to elucidate this notion, one need merely look at the two most heroic, or larger-than-life, human actors in the Trojan drama. These are Achilles, the foremost warrior among the Greeks, and Hektor, the Trojan prince and staunch defender of his city. Through their dealings with others, it will become clear what values the citizen of a thriving *polis* must hold.

The *Iliad* opens with a quarrel between Achilles and Agamemnon, the leader of the Trojan expedition. The quarrel is over a prize of honor, a young woman whom Agamemnon has decided to take from Achilles although she had been awarded to the latter by the collective armed forces as a symbol of his preeminence in war. Symbolically stripped of an honor that no individual should be able to "remove," Achilles withdraws from the war effort. This benefits Trojan defense efforts and leads to the deaths of countless Greeks. From a social standpoint, removing himself from the fray and becoming a veritable island unto himself (ultimately participating in next to none of the activities that mark one as human—such as eating and sleeping) is the wrong thing to

---

[51] Ferguson 1975:14.

[52] In presenting the *Iliad* as a political drama and Homer as a political thinker, Hammer 2002 supports this notion. Hammer focuses on Homer's concern with defining the relationship between the individual and his or her community as a reflection of real-time politics in the middle of the eighth century BCE.

do. Homer makes this apparent on many levels, but most vividly by likening Achilles to *polis*-destroying fire:[53]

ὡς δ' ὅτε καπνὸς ἰὼν εἰς οὐρανὸν εὐρὺν ἵκηται
ἄστεος αἰθομένοιο, θεῶν δέ ἑ μῆνις ἀνῆκε,
πᾶσι δ' ἔθηκε πόνον, πολλοῖσι δὲ κήδε' ἐφῆκεν,
ὣς Ἀχιλεὺς Τρώεσσι πόνον καὶ κήδε' ἔθηκεν.

As when smoke, rising, reaches the wide heaven
from a city ablaze, and the wrath of the gods has incited it,
to all it brings toil and inflicts sorrows upon many,
thus did Achilles bring toil and sorrow upon the Trojans.

Iliad 21.522–525

Sinking to sub-human cruelty in response to grief over the death of his dearest companion, Achilles becomes the polar opposite of his all too human, family-oriented, Trojan counterpart, Hektor. Likewise influenced by the concerns of a shame culture, Hektor struggles with the issue of what constitutes virtue and honor. Concern for himself, however, readily gives way to his concern for others, for his family and for the welfare of all the citizens of his *polis*. Hektor is the beloved, compassionate city defender; his very name, likely a shorted form of *Ekhepolis* 'city-holder/defender', casts his role in an unmistakable light.[54] He is the life-blood of the city, and his death is inextricably linked with the fall of Troy. The city flourishes and falls with him. Hektor's personality and convictions are "an example of the real-time infiltration of the new ethics of the *polis*," of a concrete social consciousness.[55] In order to redeem himself in the new world order and achieve a meaningful greatness therein, Achilles must not only comprehend Hektor's humanity but also embrace and absorb it. This he does in the poem's climactic scene. It is only when he is able to forgive his friend's slayer—who happened to be Hektor—and feel compassion for the latter's bereaved father, that he reaches truly heroic heights. This capacity for compassion, which Achilles has in reality always possessed, is activated by the realization of the senselessness of war and of the inevitability of death that unites all humanity in a common fate.[56] Through Achilles' realization,

---

[53] On the bestiality of Achilles as well as the impropriety and senselessness of his removing himself from the fabric of culture (and entering the realm of wild Nature), see Kim 2000:141 and Redfield 1994 (especially 104).

[54] For this derivation of "Hektor," see Nagy 1979:146–147.

[55] Jaeger 1966:121.

[56] Kim 2000:10, 57, and passim, points out that that Achilles' compassion or pity stems from his

the individualistic heroic code of old is proven irrelevant and outdated in the *Iliad*. A new heroism of social responsibility has been born. The Achilles who emerges at the close of the poem is an individual suited to leadership in the sort of social order he has, previously uncomprehendingly, carried with him on the emblem of his shield.

Depicted on the Shield is the Cosmos: the heavens, the constellations, the sun, and, at its very heart, the Earth. The central tableau, the image of Earth, is dominated by a fully animated representation of two beautiful cities (*poleis kalas, Iliad* 18.490–491). The prominent position of the cities in the picture field is an unambiguous signifier: the *polis* is central to the human experience. Further, the Shield's cities and their inhabitants convey a socio-political message of the greatest importance. A wedding and its attendant festivities open the description of the first city. Simultaneously, a very different event, a court trial for murder, is taking place in the *agora*. In this proceeding the people, in addition to the judges, have a significant voice, and for this reason, both the accused and the accuser are at pains to sway the people's opinion with their arguments:

> λαοὶ δ' εἰν ἀγορῇ ἔσαν ἀθρόοι· ἔνθα δὲ νεῖκος
> ὠρώρει, δύο δ' ἄνδρες ἐνείκεον εἴνεκα ποινῆς
> ἀνδρὸς ἀποφθιμένου· ὁ μὲν εὔχετο παντ' ἀποδοῦναι
> 500 δήμῳ πιφαύσκων, ὁ δ' ἀναίνετο μηδὲν ἑλέσθαι·
> ἄμφω δ' ἱέσθην ἐπὶ ἴστορι πεῖραρ ἑλέσθαι.
> λαοὶ δ' ἀμφοτέροισιν ἐπήπυον, ἀμφὶς ἀρωγοί·
> κήρυκες δ' ἄρα λαὸν ἐρήτυον· οἱ δὲ γέροντες
> ἥατ' ἐπὶ ξεστοῖσι λίθοις ἱερῷ ἐνὶ κύκλῳ,
> 505 σκῆπτρα δὲ κηρύκων ἐν χέρσ' ἔχον ἠεροφώνων·
> τοῖσιν ἔπειτ' ἤϊσσον, ἀμοιβηδὶς δὲ δίκαζον.
> κεῖτο δ' ἄρ' ἐν μέσσοισι δύω χρυσοῖο τάλαντα,
> τῷ δόμεν ὃς μετὰ τοῖσι δίκην ἰθύντατα εἴποι.

> The people were gathered in the place of assembly. There a dispute
> had arisen, and two men were contending over the penalty
> for a man who had been killed. The one made a claim to pay back in full,

---

ability to see Priam as a *philos* 'friend', a capacity that he has always had, for the ransom and return of Hektor's body is foreshadowed throughout the poem.

31

500 stating his case to the community, but the other was refusing
　　　to accept anything.
　　Both were heading for an arbitrator to set a limit;
　　and the people voiced their approval of both, as supporters
　　　on both sides.
　　But the heralds held the people in check, and the elders
　　were seated on seats of carved stone in the sacred circle
505 and held in their hands the scepters of the loud-voiced
　　　heralds.
　　With these in hand they leapt to their feet and cast judgment
　　　in turns,
　　and in their midst lay two talents of gold
　　to give to that man amongst them who should utter the
　　　fairest judgment.

　　　　　　　　　　　　　　　　　　　　　　　Iliad 18.497–508[57]

Clearly, the meting out of justice in this blood feud, traditionally a family matter, has been taken out of the hands of the individual. This system of justice has advanced immeasurably beyond that of the Cyclopes, where each is a law unto himself. It is also more institutionalized and democratic than what is believed to have existed in Bronze and Dark Age Greece, when the dispensation of justice was the personal province of the king or chieftain. In fact, the concern with publicly sanctioned justice on the Shield is so pronounced that the court vignette concludes with the promise of a substantial monetary reward to the judge whose verdict is deemed the fairest.[58]

At this point the poet turns his attention to the Shield's second city. This is a city at war, and its juxtaposition to the "just" City at Peace is very striking. We, the audience, are not told the reason for the conflict, and the solution chosen is not peaceable arbitration but rather a show of force. In truth, ultimate resolution of the conflict by peaceable means appears unlikely, since the attacking army is itself divided over tactics and issues of booty distribution (*Iliad* 18.510–512). What is at stake, meanwhile, for the besieged army is nothing less than what they love most, their wives and their children (*Iliad* 18.514). If captured, their fate cannot possibly be better than that of the inno-

---

[57] The translation of lines 499 and 501 is taken from Nagy 1997:195–196 (reiterated in 2003:74), and that of line 500 is based on that of Muellner 1976:106.

[58] As Muellner 1976:100–106 has noted, the novelty of the judicial proceedings described on the Shield is all the more pronounced as this passage contains the only literary application of the word εὔχομαι, *eukhomai* 'make a claim', in a legal context (*Iliad* 18.499).

cent herdsmen who are treacherously slain, flocks and all (*Iliad* 18.520–529). The ensuing battle is gory almost beyond belief. Strife and Tumult have joined the fray, and deadly Fate, her flowing garments smeared with blood, drags both the dead and the wounded through the seething masses (*Iliad* 18.535–540). Then the poet seems abruptly to change his focus to things less painful. He describes the plowing of fields, the making of wine, the herding of flocks, and, in conclusion, the rhythmic and joyous dancing of youths and maidens (*Iliad* 18.541–606). With this dance the parade of earthly images has come full circle, for it is with a wedding dance that the cityscapes commence. Represented here are the realities, joys, and necessities of daily life, all of which, in their earthly fragility, will fall victim to the ravages of war when violence is the method chosen to deal with a dispute.

Ironically, it is over a wedding, and a subsequent illicit union, that the Trojan War began. Such was Helen's beauty that a contingent large enough to man a thousand ships was easily assembled, for her numerous suitors had sworn an oath to support whomever she selected if a crisis were to arise. Because Paris, Helen's seducer and abductor, had refused the resolution of the conflict by diplomatic means, the best and bravest of Greece came to the assistance of Helen's legal consort, Menelaos, in an effort to bring Troy to its knees. While the gods' interference saw to it that diplomacy would fail, gods in Homer's portrayal rarely, if ever, cause what human actors would not themselves have occasioned. In the midst of the Trojan drama, surrounded everywhere by the screams of the dying, is Achilles. To *this* war he has lost not only Briseis, the measure of his valor, but also Patroklos, the person whom he loved most. His first response is to become rage incarnate, sinking lower than a beast and combusting into elemental fire. In his rage, he becomes the Lord of Death himself, unmistakably rendered by Homer's proliferation of under-world imagery.[59] Accordingly, when Troy's aged King Priam makes his perilous journey to the underworld of Achilles' camp, it is Hermes, the *Psychopompos* 'conveyor of souls', who leads.

Achilles faces a tremendous challenge. In order to save himself in any meaningful way and rise to truly heroic heights, he must climb from the depths to which he has fallen. On his arm—on his shield—he carries the model for the path he will ultimately choose, the path he presently rejects. The matter of Briseis, which entails making amends with Agamemnon, and the matter of Patroklos, which entails making peace with the father of his friend's slayer, are, in the end, resolved not through continued hostilities but through the

---

[59] For the progressive transformation of Achilles, see Whitman 1958:181–220 and King 1987:1–49.

exchange of words, by diplomacy. Though Achilles will return to the fighting around him, he will do so a greater man, a man shown worthy of belonging wholly in the City at Peace.

Achilles' journey is a search for justice and higher meaning in a rapidly evolving world. Admittedly, Achilles is goddess-born and accordingly functions on a level elevated somewhat above other mortals. He can certainly be more assured of divine assistance when he needs it. Nevertheless, his spiritual quest has a direct bearing on the lives of his audience, whether ancient or modern, in so far as ethical behavior remains among humanity's leading concerns in its eternal quest for betterment. The same can be said of Odysseus, whose many travails have brought the ultimate reward of wisdom commensurate with creating an ideal society; the quest of Odysseus too has remained relevant throughout the ages. Homer has created a "paradigm for seeing and talking about the world" and for exploring the role of humanity in it.[60] More specifically, the Homeric poems present the view that the *polis*, the social order in formation at the time the poems were composed, "represents civilization, progress, community, justice, and openness [while] not to live in a *polis* means primitiveness, isolation, fragmentation, lack of community, and lawlessness."[61] As Aristotle succinctly asserts, the *polis* is an institution that "came into being in order to foster life but exists for the purpose of promoting good living" (*Politics* 1252b29–30).[62] Although Homer was consulted as the authority on religion, philosophy, and pre- (or mythological) history, he was neither a philosopher nor a historian. He was a poet with a grand vision of and for humanity, a eutopian vision realized in the embrace of the *polis*.

---

[60] Dougherty 2001:6.

[61] Raaflaub 1997:648.

[62] Aristotle's wording is as follows: γιγνομένη μὲν τοῦ ζῆν ἕνεκεν, οὖσα δὲ τοῦ εὖ ζῆν, *gignomenē men tou zēn heneken, ousa de tou eu zēn*. It is worthy of note that Aristotle employs the word *eu* 'well/good' in the phrase "good living," the same *eu* that, together with *ou* 'no', is inherent in the naming of More's Utopia. There are certainly other words in Greek to denote 'good', 'just', 'noble', and so forth.

2

Greece and the Garden

I T IS AT DAWN, the time of new beginnings, that the Phaiakian ship, with Odysseus onboard, draws near to the island of Ithaka. There the spectacular harbor of Phorkys, enclosed by two lofty promontories sheltering it from perilous winds and waves, affords all vessels a ready approach. At the head of the harbor, Homer tells us, is a long-leaved olive tree and a cave, lovely and shaded, sacred to the Naiad nymphs (*Odyssey* 13.96–112). The cave, itself a marvel, contains bowls and jars of stone in which bees store their honey, looms upon which the nymphs weave precious cloths dyed purple as the sea, and springs whose water flows without ceasing. The entrances to this cave are two, for immortal and mortal separately. Athena steeps all the harbor's splendor in a thick mist, so that Odysseus will not lapse, in a moment of jubilant weakness, into ill-timed complacency. This seductive landscape is not what it may at first appear; it is no fleeting idyll. Nowhere in Homer is there an unmotivated landscape, natural scenery for its own sake. Lovely though it may be, the natural environment is governed by its own, unpredictable laws. To this extent, the Homeric ideal, which is also the ideal of the nascent *polis*, entails the manipulation and transformation of the landscape by skilled human hands, by *tekhnē*. The belief that the inscription of Nature is fundamental to both the physical and moral constitution of the *polis* would remain prevalent in Greece through the Archaic and Classical periods until the eclipse of Athens and Sparta, the power-*poleis*, by Macedonia and the replacement of the *poleis* by the *megalopolis*.

Returning to the illusory idyll of the Ithakan harbor scene, each of its features, cave, spring, harbor, and olive tree, is inextricably bound to the utopian "blueprint" revealed elsewhere in the course of Odysseus' wanderings. The cave had been previously demonstrated an unsuitable habitat for progressive humanity. It is a cave that the brute Cyclopes, existing in a Neolithic Golden Age, inhabit, and a cave that Calypso calls home. Yet both caves would ultimately have hidden Odysseus entirely from the world of the living, sending him instead along the dark and treacherous path to the House of Hades. Though both caves contain signs of industry well known in the human realm, namely weaving and the making of cheese, these enterprises merely constitute traps or lures for unsuspecting mortal prey. Similarly, the cave of the Naiads is not presented as a potentially fitting human domicile, however appealing it may have been to the weary traveler. It can be no coincidence that the Phaiakians deposit Odysseus outside the cave and not inside it. More appropriately, the cave houses only divinities having nothing to fear from the surrounding wilderness. The nymphs' cave is, to be sure, a site of industry, of weaving and collecting honey, but the nymphs' products are not meant for human consumption. Mortals do, however, have a "safe" designated point of access to the cave as sanctuary, a regulated locus of interface between mortal and divine.[1] Herein the nymphs' abode is a far cry from the gruesomely elemental cavern of Scylla. The cave as sanctuary, appearing on an island on the verge of political revolution, forcefully suggests that in the new, evolving social order of the *Odyssey*, humanity must once and for all leave the comforts of the Earth-womb to the elemental, feminine divine.

The Ithakan harbor's cave sanctuary, together with its spring, harbor, and olive, ultimately resonates with the ideal represented by the Phaiakian island state of Scheria. Removing his people physically and ideologically as far as possible from the overbearing Cyclopes, Nausithoos, the founding father of the Scherian *polis*, carefully structured his new settlement with walls, houses, apportioned fields, and sanctuaries of the gods.[2] However, in addition to human constructs such as those issued by Nausithoos, an optimally ordered and equipped city must have at least one abundant spring. The Laestrygonians, who have a city complete with an *agora*, do possess a spring, but they lack the moral sensibility and intellect required of a model *polis*. Calypso too has access to abundant waters. Her springs, four in number, water every corner of her hyper-naturally fecund island, but on Ogygia Nature serves only Nature. Agriculture, cooking, washing, and sacrifice, all dependent on water, are unnecessary to her apolitical existence. By contrast, such activities form as integral a part of the Phaiakian technological utopia as they presumably will of the new Ithakan *polis*. Scheria has a spring along the road outside the city proper and two springs within that provide water both for Alkinoos' garden and the

---

[1] Suggested by Hoekstra 1989 in his commentary on *Odyssey* 13.104–112. The nymphs' cave on the island of Helios apparently had no provision for cult, thus rendering it a "pure" divine habitation. For a discussion of Porphyry's provocative Neoplatonic reading of this passage, see Weinberg 1986:32–37.

[2] *Odyssey* 6.7–10.

houses of the citizens.[3] Here Nature serves the populace. The Phaiakians had clearly carefully surveyed their landscape in order to exploit its assets to their fullest potential. Famed seafarers, *nausiklutoi andres*, the Phaiakians put their harbors to good use, filling them with well-balanced ships.[4] Notably, Odysseus expresses admiration for these harbors while he merely remarks upon the existence of the safe harbors of Goat Island, lying empty due to the Cyclopes' lack of technological curiosity, and of the Laestrygonian *polis*, serving solely as a locus of extermination rather than fruitful social intercourse.

In every major respect, Ithaka possesses the physical elements requisite for a *polis* on the Scherian model, though necessarily less perfect because it is to be an entirely human creation in the "real" world. These elements include not only sanctuaries, springs, and harbors, but also land suitable for cultivation. Ithaka may be a rugged place, but it is still, in Odysseus' words, a "good nurse of young men."[5] The land's agricultural potential is indicated by the presence of the leafy olive growing by the Naiads' cave. The olive can serve as a shelter, and it is therefore under the tree's spreading canopy that the Phaiakians deposit the sleeping hero. More important, however, than its protective capacity is the fact that the wild olive can be tamed, cultivated to yield a precious harvest. Bread, wine, and olives were the staples of the Greek diet in antiquity. But the olive had always enjoyed particular distinction. Long-lived and tolerant of arid conditions, the olive had come to symbolize the tenacious, immortal spirit of Greece. Victorious athletes in the games at the Panathenaia and at Olympia, mortals at their most divine, were crowned with wreaths of olive. The olive was the gift of the gods, and more than any other tree or plant, it was "specifically human."[6]

With respect to the thematic and symbolic framework of the *Odyssey*, the olive is absolutely central. Odysseus' homecoming, identity, household, and community core all rest securely on the foundation of the great olive tree that he had carved to form his marriage bed. Removed from the cycles of Nature, this olive has become an artifact sustaining human culture and society.[7] In the course of his wanderings too, the olive more than once saves Odysseus from utter disaster. It is olive wood from which he crafts the stake with which to pierce the eye of Polyphemos. Again as a tool, olive wood appears in the

---

[3] *Odyssey* 6.292 and *Odyssey* 7.129–131 respectively.

[4] The Phaiakians are described as famed sailors at the following: *Odyssey* 7.39; *Odyssey* 8.191, 369; *Odyssey* 13.166; and *Odyssey* 16.227.

[5] *agathē kourotrophos* (ἀγαθὴ κουροτρόφος, *Odyssey* 9.27)

[6] Vidal-Naquet 1970:1284.

[7] Cook 1995:154.

form of an exceedingly beautiful axe-handle.[8] With the axe in question he constructs the raft facilitating his passage to Scheria and, at the same time, precipitating the end of his wanderings. On Scheria, the Phaiakians' active cultivation of the olive signals to Odysseus, and to Homer's audience alike, that he has at long last arrived at a place where human, and specifically Greek, values prevail. For instance, it is customary in Homer's world to anoint oneself, one's guest, or one's "charge" with olive oil subsequent to ablutions in order to restore suppleness to skin parched by the Mediterranean sun. This ritual is fundamental to the dispensation of *xenia*; it signifies the establishment of a special bond. While one of Circe's handmaids does perform this kindly service, it is only after Odysseus has tamed the witch by force of his sword.[9] Among the peoples of Odysseus' wanderings, Nausicaa alone offers him a bath and olive oil without compulsion.[10] At home in Ithaka, his washing at the hands of Eurykleia later signifies the absoluteness of his return.

Only on Scheria and Ithaka is the olive specifically described as growing in cultivation, in the gardens of Alkinoos and Laertes.[11] The descriptions of these two gardens are undeniably linked, as it is solely in reference to them that the poet employs terms designating 'garden': *kēpos, orkhatos,* and *aloē.*[12] These are not pleasure gardens but orchards, vineyards, and vegetable gardens, gardens laboriously planted and cared for, even in the case of Scheria where the climate affords constant productivity. The gardens are remarkably similar in what they contain: apples, pears, figs, grapes, olives, and herbs. Only the pomegranate is a plant grown by Alkinoos and not by Laertes.[13] Where the gardens differ most is in their state of completeness or physical condition. The garden of Alkinoos is a model of order and efficiency:

---

[8] Cook 1995:154.

[9] *Odyssey* 10.360–367.

[10] *Odyssey* 6.218–231.

[11] Luxurious olives, figs, pears, apples, and pomegranates are suspended above the head of Tantalus, but his "place" in the underworld is no cultivated garden (*Odyssey* 11.588–590)

[12] The terms *kēpos, orkhatos* (also *orkhos*), and *aloē*, all meaning 'garden/orchard/vineyard', may be used interchangeably in keeping with the mixed-planting nature of utilitarian gardens in rural and suburban areas. All three terms are used to describe the gardens of Laertes and Alkinoos. *Kēpos* (κῆπος): Alkinoos' at *Odyssey* 7.129; Laertes' at *Odyssey* 4.737 and *Odyssey* 24.338. *Orkhatos* (ὄρχατος): Alkinoos' at *Odyssey* 7.112; Laertes' at *Odyssey* 24.222, 245, and 257. *Aloē* (ἀλωή): Alkinoos' at *Odyssey* 6.293 and *Odyssey* 7.122; Laertes' at *Odyssey* 1.193, *Odyssey* 11.193, and *Odyssey* 24. 221, 224, 226, and 336. For gardens in ancient Greece, see Gothein 1909; Carroll-Spillecke 1989, 1992a, and 1992b; and Carroll 2003:1–30. For gardens in Homer specifically, see Ferriolo 1989.

[13] The gardens may, of course, also have grown plants the poet has not specifically mentioned. The correspondence of plants is noted in Hainsworth's commentary (1988:329) on *Odyssey* 7.115–116.

ἔκτοσθεν δ᾽ αὐλῆς μέγας <u>ὄρχατος</u> ἄγχι θυράων
τετράγυος· περὶ δ᾽ <u>ἕρκος</u> ἐλήλαται ἀμφοτέρωθεν.
ἔνθα δὲ δένδρεα μακρὰ πεφύκασι τηλεθόωντα,
115 ὄγχναι καὶ ῥοιαὶ καὶ μηλέαι ἀγλαόκαρποι
συκέαι τε γλυκεραὶ καὶ ἐλαῖαι τηλεθόωσαι.
τάων οὔ ποτε καρπὸς ἀπόλλυται οὐδ᾽ ἀπολείπει
χείματος οὐδὲ θέρευς, ἐπετήσιος· ἀλλὰ μάλ᾽ αἰεὶ
Ζεφυρίη πνείουσα τὰ μὲν φύει, ἄλλα δὲ πέσσει.
120 ὄγχνη ἐπ᾽ ὄγχνη γηράσκει, μῆλον δ᾽ ἐπὶ μήλῳ,
αὐτὰρ ἐπὶ σταφυλῇ σταφυλή, σῦκον δ᾽ ἐπὶ σύκῳ.
ἔνθα δέ οἱ πολύκαρπος <u>ἀλωὴ</u> ἐρρίζωται,
τῆς ἕτερον μὲν θειλόπεδον λευρῷ ἐνὶ χώρῳ
τέρσεται ἠελίῳ, ἑτέρας δ᾽ ἄρα τε τρυγόωσιν,
125 ἄλλας δὲ τραπέουσι· πάροιθε δέ τ᾽ ὄμφακές εἰσιν
ἄνθος ἀφιεῖσαι, ἕτεραι δ᾽ ὑποπερκάζουσιν.
ἔνθα δὲ κοσμηταὶ πρασιαὶ παρὰ νείατον <u>ὄρχον</u>
παντοῖαι πεφύασιν, ἐπηετανὸν γανόωσαι·

And outside the courtyard near the doors lay a vast orchard
  (*orkhatos*)
of four days' plowing, and around it a *fence* (*herkos*) had been
  run in both directions.
And there large trees grow in profusion,
115 pears and pomegranates and apples bearing bright fruit
and both sweet figs and the flourishing olive.
Never does their fruit spoil, nor is it lacking
either in winter or summer, through all the year, but rather
  ever
does the blowing Zephyr cause some to grow and others to
  ripen.
120 Pear after pear mellows, and apple after apple,
also cluster after cluster of grapes and fig after fig.
And there his abundantly productive vineyard (*alōē*) is
  established,
on one side of which in a warm spot on level ground
[the harvest] dries in the sun, others, in turn, they are
  gathering
125 and yet others they trample. And in the foreground are
  unripe grapes

that have cast off their bloom and others that are darkening.
And there at the bottom of the orchard (*orkhos*) well ordered
    herbs
of all sorts grow, green throughout the year.

Odyssey 7.112–128

The garden's orderliness, mirroring the good order and virtuous constitution of Alkinoos' household and *polis* generally, is what makes it so attractive. A fence, *herkos*, has been driven all around it (περὶ δ' ἕρκος ἐλήλαται ἀμφοτέρωθεν, *Odyssey* 7.113), and the plantings within are clearly distinguished from one another. There are separate areas for fruit trees and grapevines, and another, adjacent to the grapes, for herbs laid out in beds. Laertes, while neglecting the care of his own person, has spared no effort in tending the plants in his garden. Odysseus tells us so. Still, there is something in the garden that requires an essential repair: the garden wall, so critical for keeping unwanted Nature out, and tamed, subservient Nature in. When Odysseus approaches Laertes' garden, Dolios and the other servants are nowhere to be seen, having gone in search of stones with which to rebuild the fallen wall:

οὐδ' εὗρεν Δολίον, μέγαν ὄρχατον ἐσκαταβαίνων,
οὐδέ τινα δμώων οὐδ' υἱῶν· ἀλλ' ἄρα τοί γε
αἱμασιὰς λέξοντες ἀλωῆς ἔμμεναι ἕρκος
οἴχοντ', αὐτὰρ ὁ τοῖσι γέρων ὁδὸν ἡγεμόνευε.

Nor did he come upon Dolios as he went down into the great
    orchard (*orkhatos*),
neither any of his slaves nor his sons. But rather
in order to gather stones to be used for the *garden wall*
    (*herkos*)
had they gone off, and that old man was leading the way.

Odyssey 24.222–225

For the Ithakan community to thrive again, the power of Nature must be securely harnessed. Laertes' retreat to the garden, which entails the abandonment of his house in town as well as the implicit refusal to resume control of the state, is really not at all surprising given the fundamental importance of securing the land that will sustain the populace. The garden is where *eunomia* 'good order' in the community begins.

    Just how precarious such good order can be, and how laboriously wrought, is signified by the end of the *Odyssey*. Homer's song does not end as it might have with Odysseus, Laertes, and the faithful servant Dolios sharing a meal as evening falls. Instead, the scene shifts abruptly from that harmonious tableau to a depiction of the swift, citywide course of the news of the suitors' death. The city cries for retribution, but the cry is not unanimous. Medon, the wise herald, and Phemios, noble bard, address the angered masses in hopes that further violence can be avoided. The suitors, they argue, deserved what they got for their reckless, outrageous behavior towards Odysseus and his household. To their minds, the score had been settled. Of course, this pacifistic counsel does not prevail; such is the force of human emotion. Had Athena not intervened, armed with the oaths of Zeus, all may have been lost, for where discord thrives, community can never gain a secure foothold.

Two things, then, would be fundamental to *polis*-building in Odysseus' world: the containment of Nature and the establishment of a system of justice based on an ideology less primitive than "an eye for an eye." The same is also true of Achilles' world in the *Iliad*. Physical containment of the natural world and its potential dangers would have to go hand-in-hand with the constraint of bestial, overly "natural" impulses in humankind. If, as Aristotle states, the *polis* is to be envisioned as a larger version of the household, Odysseus' house, built around the enormous, carved stump of an olive tree, exists as a model— one of several—for the societal restructuring to come.[14] In the case of the *Iliad*, it is the world order portrayed by Achilles' shield that serves as the model for a social (r)evolution, which is even then being precipitated by the poem's hero. The importance of the Shield to the fabric of the *Iliad* cannot be overstated; it is the center and focus of the poem as a whole. The Shield is often read as a poetic device equivalent in function to the similes with which the poem abounds and, accordingly, as a means by which the poet has expanded the experiential world, universalizing the impact of the quarrel between Achilles and Agamemnon.[15] Such an interpretation, however, does not give the Shield its due. Vis-à-vis the story of Achilles, the similes are *parerga*. Like the frame around a painting, similes inform and direct the interpretation of the subject, *ergon*, they surround. This they do by separating the *ergon* "from the whole field of historical, economic, political inscription in which the drive to signature is produced," for "the *parergon* stands out [*se détache*] both from the

---

[14] *Politics* 1252–1253.

[15] See, for instance, Redfield 1994:187 and Stanley 1993. Similarly, though with a new spin, Alden 2000:48–73, who represents the Shield as a para-narrative serving as a commentary on the plot of the *Iliad* and focuses on the issues of fitting compensation and arbitration highlighted in the Shield's cityscapes and their main-plot associations.

ergon (the work) and from the milieu, it stands out first of all like a figure on a ground."[16] Though literally embedded within and surrounded by the fabric of the story, a simile's essence is of the larger context or world in which the story is said to unfold. Still, a simile represents a selective context, as it does not represent the entirety of diachronic experience and must, accordingly, be separate from the *ergon's* larger milieu, the larger universe in which it finds itself. The simile, not the story, is *parergon*. The simile reifies its *ergon*; it gives the latter meaning. Similarly, without the tale of Achilles' struggle to find meaning in a world whose values he has seen as empty, set in the Age of Heroes but shaped by the new age in which the Homeric poems were substantially formed, the Shield cannot be understood except, perhaps, in the vaguest terms. It remains a stunning, wondrous object, whose individual embellishments can easily be recognized, but the interrelation of these same embellishments cannot be fully realized without the surrounding frame. The Shield is *ergon*, and the tale of Achilles, *parergon*.

Achilles' Shield, then, lies at the heart of the *Iliad*; one might even say that it *is* the *Iliad*. The Shield, on which Hephaistos has fashioned the heavens and the Earth, herself embracing two paradigmatic cities, is also a map of utopia (Figure 2).[17] Maps of utopia are, of course, to some extent a contradiction in terms. As utopia is *ou-topos*, no place, it cannot be spatially located with any specificity. Still, utopia is conceived as a template or blueprint for societal betterment, so it must be possible to envision it in concrete terms. If utopia

---

[16] Derrida 1987:61. This line of reasoning, together with the quote, is derived from Derrida's discourse on Kant's definition of *ergon* and *parergon* in the third *Critique*. Further discussion of textual *parerga* can be found in Giesecke 2002, where the focus is a highly referential Virgilian text.

[17] Historically, the circle is the most common representation of ideal states and social orders; it was "intended both to signify and to assist a redemption of society," Rowe 1976:207. The Shield that appears in this text is a critical response to those of Willcock 1984:270 (which, when I juxtaposed it to a map of Classical Athens and its extra-mural gardens, led me to the realization that the Shield is Homer's map of the ideal *polis*) and van Leeuwen 1912:672. Like van Leeuwen, I thought it redundant to depict Earth at the Shield's center and felt that the Dance should be relegated to its own ring as representative of human collaborative efforts to contain Nature, examples of which efforts the "landscapes" of the rings interior to it portray. On my Shield, unlike those of Willcock and van Leeuwen, herdsmen and lions have been representationally opposed as they are in constant competition/tension with respect to control over the cattle and sheep. Further, the lions, which Homer describes as attacking the cattle, are represented here as spatially and thematically aligned with the City at War. Neither van Leeuwen nor Willcock included "Sacrifice" in their schemes, and it is included here (in the position that it is) to signify that killing may, if ritualized, take place peaceably and that sacrifice may be a way of reconciling the Cities at War and Peace. On the Shield's boss, heavenly bodies have been relegated to the centermost position, as they are separate from, "above," sky and sea.

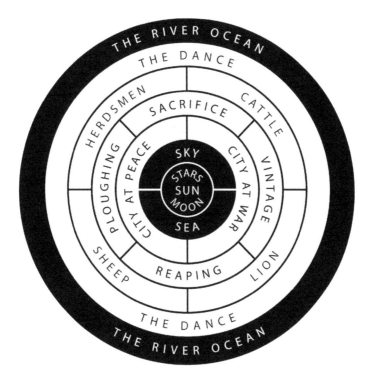

Figure 2. Blueprint of the ideal *polis*. Reconstruction: The Shield of Achilles. Concept by Donald Dunham and Annette Giesecke, drawing by Michael Monahan.

is a blueprint for social re-organization, it is by definition a human phenomenon located in this world, albeit free of coordinates. Further, utopia as a blueprint for social change can be fully conceived only in comparison with what it is not. A map of utopia must also encompass dystopia. For this reason the City at War is paired with the City at Peace. Functionally and structurally, the Shield's utopian map corresponds to the narrative of Odysseus' wanderings, the so-called *apologoi* 'tales', for travel narrative is a form of mapping in that it "transform(s) geographic narrative into discourse."[18] As Louis Marin notes, travel narrative "is the discursive figure of the image that is itself the selection of relations of elements in the world, the construction of the world in the form of an analogic model that covers over reality with the network of its lines and

---

[18] Marin 1984:42.

surfaces."[19] In this way, Odysseus' wanderings also map utopia. As coordinates on this map, the places he visits cannot be physically tracked or found by another, yet they provide both positive and negative models, visions of utopia as well as of dystopia.

The Shield, like its textual frame, presents the city as an ideal but goes further in presenting its audience with an image of the ideal city as well. In a classic essay, "Utopia, The City and The Machine," Lewis Mumford observes that Greek utopias, indeed most utopias from Plato to Bellamy, were "visualized largely in terms of the city."[20] The form of the city, he argues, was particularly well suited to the formulation of utopian visions because it had "the advantage of mirroring the complexities of society within a frame that respected the human scale."[21] The city itself could provide "a glimpse of eternal order, a visible heaven on earth, a seat of abundant life," because it's implicit order was itself modeled on that of the Cosmos.[22] Mumford does not adduce the Shield of Achilles, but the utopian vision it proffers confirms his findings. Simply put, the main components of the Shield's iconographic field are City and Cosmos. Thus the rhythmical description of the Shield's embellishments commences:

> Ἐν μὲν γαῖαν ἔτευξ', ἐν δ' οὐρανόν, ἐν δὲ θάλασσαν,
> ἠέλιόν τ' ἀκάμαντα σελήνην τε πλήθουσαν,
> 485 ἐν δὲ τὰ τείρεα πάντα, τά τ' οὐρανὸς ἐστεφάνωται,
> Πληϊάδας θ' Ὑ   άδας τε τό τε σθένος Ὠρίωνος
> Ἄρκτον θ', ἣν καὶ Ἄμαξαν ἐπίκλησιν καλέουσιν,
> ἥ τ' αὐτοῦ στρέφεται καί τ' Ὠρίωνα δοκεύει,
> οἴη δ' ἄμμορός ἐστι λοετρῶν Ὠκεανοῖο.
> 490 Ἐν δὲ δύω ποίησε πόλεις μερόπων ἀνθρώπων
> καλάς.

> Upon it he wrought the Earth and the sky and the sea,
> both the tireless sun and the full moon.
> 485 And upon it all the stars, those that crown the heavens,
> the Pleiades, the Hyades, and mighty Orion,
> and the Great Bear, whom people also call the Wagon
> and who both revolves in place and keeps an eye on Orion
> and alone takes no part in the baths of Ocean.

[19] Marin 1984:42.
[20] Mumford 1965:3.
[21] Mumford 1965:3.
[22] Mumford 1965:13.

490 And on it he wrought two cities of mortal men,
     beautiful ones.

Iliad 18.483–491

Hephaistos has fashioned the four elements, earth, heaven, water, and celestial fire, all bound by concentric figured rings.[23] Four major constellations also inscribe the heavens. The Cosmos has established a rhythm of fours, and it is in fours that the subsequently detailed cityscapes unfold. The Cosmos, Nature writ large, is the frame for all human action, the scenery against which the human drama transpires. At the same time, the success of the human endeavor embodied by the *polis* depends directly upon the success of the populace in establishing boundaries to separate it from the natural environment. Put somewhat differently, the ultimate success of the *polis* depends on observing the ordering principles of the Cosmos and applying them to the physical and spiritual makeup of the city in an effort to control what is deemed dangerous and unpredictable in Nature. The frame, *parergon*, exerts a considerable degree of control over its *ergon*. While the Cosmos is, by definition, a frame for the human endeavor, the Homeric texts reveal deep concern, even anxiety, about the very real danger of being overwhelmed by the force of the cosmic frame. It is for this reason that the Homeric political ideal envisages the creation of an intervening frame through human intellect and technical skill, symbolized on the Shield by the ring of youths and maidens dancing hand in hand "around" the cityscapes, contiguous to the streams of Ocean that run along the Shield's outer rim.[24] Here collaborative humanity forms a barrier against the elemental.

    Not surprisingly, the scenes depicted on the Shield are replete with references, some more overt than others, to limits and boundaries in the world of

---

[23] This pattern of fours is observed by Hubbard 1992:28. According to Hubbard, there are four main vignettes within the Cities at War and Peace complex: the wedding, the trial, the city besieged, and the ambush. These images are followed by four agricultural scenes, each selected in accordance with the passage of seasons, and by the dance sequence, in which four sets of participants, dancers, spectators, a bard, and acrobats, appear.

[24] As Edwards 1991:200–233 points out, the reconstruction of Homer's poetic masterpiece is fraught with difficulties arising from the simple fact that the poet is not describing an actual object. While it is the case that realizing a "true" graphic representation of the Shield is beyond the audience's grasp, Homer's syntax in describing the various scenes coincides with archaeologically attested representation in concentric bands. As for the dancers, they must necessarily constitute the "outermost" of the earthly images—whether the audience perceives them physically or metaphysically "located"—on the grounds that they are the last group of humans whom the poet describes. In van Leeuwen's reconstruction (1913:672), they inhabit their own "ring" contiguous to Ocean.

the *polis*. Nowhere in the *Iliad* are descriptions of human interaction with the natural environment more concentrated, and as in the case of the *Odyssey*, the natural world is not abstractly conjured as a pleasant reverie but as a force to contend with. Human activities in this environment must be mediated by boundaries, physical and otherwise. Starting cartographically at the point of greatest remove from the city center and spiraling gradually inward, we, the audience, behold *nomoi* 'pastures' for cattle and sheep (*Iliad* 18.587). Pastures constitute Nature inscribed by virtue of human use or presence and not necessarily by the fabrication of physical boundaries. It is in such places, particularly when unbounded, that humanity is most vulnerable, since these are fundamentally wild places, more open to view, certainly, than forests, but still full of potential menace. Such menace descends upon the cowherds in their pasture by the river (*Iliad* 18.573–586). Two stealthy lions attack and then greedily devour one of their bulls, and, ultimately, nothing the herdsmen or their terror-stricken dogs can do will prevent it. While beyond a doubt a grisly scene, its gore is instructively rivaled by another, which likewise takes place in a pasture, specifically at a watering hole (*Iliad* 18.520–532). In this rival or "companion" scene, an army of "bestial" men, not predatory animals, sets upon herds and herdsmen alike. Humanity appears particularly susceptible to bestial behavior in wild, unbounded places. As the Shield here and elsewhere vividly demonstrates, human nature or impulse must also be held in check.

Proceeding inward we see a beautiful vineyard heavily laden with grapes (*Iliad* 18.561), its splendor enhanced by the harmonious song and dance of the harvesters. This is a space in which domesticated plant and human alike can thrive, *and* it is not once but *doubly* bounded, by *kapetos* 'ditch' as well as *herkos* 'fence' (*Iliad* 18.564–565). It should be noted that the slaughtered herdsmen were also singing, but their artful song was not sufficient defense against humanity's baser instincts. Alongside the thriving vineyard lies a *temenos basilēion* 'chieftain's estate' (τέμενος βασιλήϊον, *Iliad* 18.550). Here, as in the vineyard, crops and workers thrive. This too is a bounded place, a piece of land marked off or, more literally, cut off from common holdings.[25] The reaping and binding of grain is finely orchestrated and proceeds without a hitch, a sight that pleases the estate's owner. Within the chieftain's estate, apart from the field itself, another ox is slaughtered. But this noble creature falls prey neither to ravening beasts nor bestial men. In this place, where the ideology of the

---

[25] The word *temenos* (τέμενος) 'a piece of land cut off', is, of course, lexically bound to the verb *temnō* (τέμνω) 'to cut'.

polis prevails, rituals of sacrifice ensure that the ox is duly honored for the precious gift of its life. Meanwhile, in the city's nearby fields, the fertile land is plowed in measured stages. Inscribed by communal effort, the land will yield its bounty to the populace.

At last the mind's eye alights on the contours of the Shield's two cities (*Iliad* 18.490–540). At least one of them, the City at War, is specifically described as surrounded by a *teikhos* 'wall' (*Iliad* 18.514). The wall is no less a barrier than a fence around a field or vineyard. Like the *herkos*, which is defined as 'fence, wall, barrier' and 'defensive armor', walls serve to separate humanity from the threats of Nature.[26] Significantly, the timeless moment captured by Hephaistos depicts not Nature's but rather a rival polity's assault upon the city. The wall, a product of human technical skill, also necessarily serves as a defense against savage and unenlightened behavior. Against such dangers, however, the City at Peace offers another form of defense, the incorporeal yet resilient boundary of justice. As Aristotle vehemently declares, justice is fundamental to the health of the community and the cohesion of the *polis*:

ὥσπερ γὰρ καὶ τελεωθεὶς βέλτιστον τῶν ζῴων ὁ ἄνθρωπός ἐστιν, οὕτω καὶ χωρισθεὶς νόμου καὶ δίκης χείριστον πάντων. χαλεπωτάτη γὰρ ἀδικία ἔχουσα ὅπλα· ὁ δὲ ἄνθρωπος ὅπλα ἔχων φύεται φρονήσει καὶ ἀρετῇ, οἷς ἐπὶ τἀναντία ἔστι χρῆσθαι μάλιστα. διὸ ἀνοσιώτατον καὶ ἀγριώτατον ἄνευ ἀρετῆς, καὶ πρὸς ἀφροδίσια καὶ ἐδωδὴν χείριστον. ἡ δὲ δικαιοσύνη πολιτικόν. ἡ γὰρ δίκη πολιτικῆς κοινωνίας τάξις ἐστίν, ἡ δὲ δικαιοσύνη τοῦ δικαίου κρίσις.

For just as a human is the best of animals when perfected, so too when removed from law and justice, he is the worst of all. For injustice is most grievous when armed, and humanity is born with weapons to use for prudence and virtue, but which can be used for quite the opposite. Therefore, without virtue he is most unholy and wild, and with respect to sex and food, the basest. And a sense of right is suited for the life of the *polis*. For justice is the means of ordering the common weal, and justice the judgment of what is fair.

Politics 1253a31–39

Laying down arms and establishing a system of justice sets apart human from beast. The City at Peace signifies an essential harmony not only by the wedding, but also by the "containment" of violent crime within the elders'

---

[26] See Cunliffe 1963:158 on the applications of the term *herkos*.

sacred circle (ἱερῷ ἐνὶ κύκλῳ, *Iliad* 18.504).[27] This circle seeks to limit the endless cycle of bloodshed through deliberations centered on boundaries.[28] The elders are gathered here to establish a *peirar* 'limit' to the penalty of revenge or ransom that can or should be exacted for a particular incidence of homicide. Viewed more broadly, their task is to establish legal limits inherent in a system of justice, the only effective means by which to contain the "beast" within.

The magnitude and universality of the concern with establishing boundaries and limits in the Greek world throughout its gradual emergence from the chaos of the Dark Age is evidenced by the traditional, orally-based texts attributed to Hesiod, the bard of Ascra. The degree of thematic overlap between Homer's Shield and the Hesiodic poems, both the *Works and Days* and the *Theogony*, is quite remarkable, so remarkable that it cannot be coincidental.[29] Of the Hesiodic poems, the *Works and Days* contains the most striking parallels to the Shield: this epic is in its entirety motivated by a quarrel—though it is a quarrel over inheritance rather than over the slaying of a man—and focuses on the establishment of justice effected through true rather than crooked judgments. Once again the audience is presented with a paradigm of two cities, the City of *Dikē* 'Justice' and the City of *Hubris*, corresponding respectively to the Shield's Cities at Peace and War. The lot of Hesiod's Iron Age humanity is a difficult one, their existence consigned to toil on an Earth that has ceased to share her bounty spontaneously. Therefore, in the City of Justice tools are employed to cultivate the land, though not in pursuit of violence, so this city flourishes free from famine and grievous disaster. In Hesiod's words, the City of Justice "blooms," *tethēle*, and its people "flower," *antheusin* (*Works and Days* 227). Justice, the most effective means by which to limit human behavior, is thus inextricably linked to inscription of the land; in this world, moral and physical boundaries are both necessary and complementary. Justice, as the *Theogony* reinforces, stems from Zeus and elevates the little that is godlike in humanity. As Aristotle would later affirm, it is Justice that sets apart human from beast and prevents humankind from savaging one another. Contrarily, while the City of Justice thrives, the City of *Hubris*, steeped in cruelty and outrage, falls victim to famine and plague. It becomes

---

[27] In the City at Peace, the elders with whom judgement in this trial rests are described as seated on smoothed stones arranged in a sacred circle. Each arises in turn from his seat when he pronounces his judgement (*Iliad* 18.503–506).

[28] For a discussion of the setting of limits for penalty and compensation, see Nagy 2003:72–87.

[29] This is noticed and amply elucidated in Nagy 1990 (especially 53–80), upon which the points in this paragraph are based.

"sterile and poor," its walls shattered by the ravages of war and the full force of Zeus' storms.[30]

The dicta of the Shield are as clear as they are profound: the city as an ideal and the ideal city are founded on the containment of dangerous, threatening impulses of and in the natural world. This notion pervades the fabric of the *Odyssey*, but in the *Iliad* it seems, at first glance, limited to the *ergonal* Shield. While it is true that the tale of Achilles is relatively devoid of straight-narrative allusion to the environment, the "secondary" *parergonal* field of similes, itself activating the Achillean frame, is largely dedicated to it. At least four interconnected groups of prevalent *topoi* can be identified amidst the plethora of the *Iliad*'s similes: atmospheric and other natural phenomena, views into the experiences of hunters and herdsmen, the interaction of creatures in the wild, and technical manipulation of the Earth's produce.[31] For example, Diomedes in his destructive fury on the battlefield is likened to a river, flowing with winter force, that overleaps its banks and, unhindered by dikes and vineyard walls laboriously constructed by human hands, sweeps away everything in its path:

> θῦνε γὰρ ἄμ πεδίον ποταμῷ πλήθοντι ἐοικὼς
> χειμάρρῳ, ὅς τ᾽ ὦκα ῥέων ἐκέδασσε γεφύρας·
> τὸν δ᾽ οὔτ᾽ ἄρ τε γέφυραι ἐεργμέναι ἰσχανόωσιν,
> 90 οὔτ᾽ ἄρα ἕρκεα ἴσχει ἀλωάων ἐριθηλέων
> ἐλθόντ᾽ ἐξαπίνης, ὅτ᾽ ἐπιβρίσῃ Διὸς ὄμβρος·
> πολλὰ δ᾽ ὑπ᾽ αὐτοῦ ἔργα κατήριπε κάλ᾽ αἰζηῶν·

> For he rushed through the plain like a river swollen
> in winter, and which, flowing swiftly, has overleapt the
>   embankments,
> and neither can closely constructed barriers hold it back
> 90 nor, indeed, do the walls of the burgeoning vineyard stay it
> as it comes on a sudden, when the rain of Zeus falls in abun-
>   dance,
> and many are the lovely works of mortals that are destroyed
>   by it.

> *Iliad* 5.87–92

Torrential rivers, forest fires, earthquakes, thunderbolts, whirlwinds, dense clouds of dust, thick fog, and snow all appear in the world of the similes. These

---

[30] For the quote, see Nagy 1990:73.

[31] These thematic categories are detailed in Redfield 1994:188–189. Redfield 1994:188–192 also demonstrates how the similes present Nature as a force threatening the security of humanity.

are all phenomena of the natural world that threaten the precarious security of humans and their hard-won achievements, most of which have been geared towards gaining some sort of control over the hostile world that surrounds them. The Homeric perspective, like Hesiod's, is that "the Earth and sea are full of ills" (*Works and Days* 101) difficult for humans to endure, particularly as "the Earth bears no creature more feeble" (*Odyssey* 18.130–131).[32] This same sensibility pervades the similes centering on the lives of those who work the fields, tend the flocks, and range the wilderness in search of prey. Goatherds in the mountains shiver and quickly herd their flocks into a cavern when they spy the ominous approach of a cloud sure to bring ill weather (*Iliad* 4.275–279). Shepherds fear what dangers may be hidden in a mountain mist (*Iliad* 3.10–12), likely some predatory beast, perhaps a lion so ravenous that it will stop at nothing to penetrate the folds enclosing their flocks (*Iliad* 12.299–306). Such men must frequent the vast spaces beyond the city walls, where they have occasion to observe animals in their natural habitat. The sight that recurs in every corner of the wilderness is that of hunter and hunted. Accordingly, nearly all the similes located in the animal kingdom represent predator and prey.[33] Those witnessing the demise of one animal in the jaws of another in the wild would know how easily their flocks, and even they themselves, could be substituted for the predator's more usual fare. Human prosperity and safety depends on securing the subservience of the natural world, an endeavor bearing inevitably mixed results. As another group of similes demonstrates, humanity is most successful when manipulating things like timber, wool, and metal, which have been derived from the natural environment but are not alive or "immediately" life sustaining.[34]

There are certainly similes in the *Iliad* that defy simple classification as representations of the overtly hostile aspect of Nature. Here Nature may be viewed as awe-inspiring, beautiful, and even illustrative of phenomena or behaviors in the human realm. So, for instance, the Trojan elder statesmen, feeble in body yet possessing resonant voices, are compared to cicadas whose chirruping carries through the forests (*Iliad* 3.150–152).[35] Bees and wasps that

---

[32] πλείη μὲν γὰρ γαῖα κακῶν, πλείη δὲ θάλασσα· *Works and Days* 101 (West 1978:99 *ad loc*). οὐδὲν ἀκιδνότερον γαῖα τρέφει ἀνθρώποιο, *Odyssey* 18.130.

[33] Redfield 1994:192. See also Edwards 1993:34–37 on categories of subject matter in the similes.

[34] See Redfield 1994:283n60 for a list of these sorts of similes. They include images of women working ivory and wool as well as images of men shearing, cutting wood, and building.

[35] I have adopted Kirk's definition, 'chirruping', of the problematic word *leirioessan* (λειριόεσσαν) here (1985:283–284). As one who lives in a woodland that resonates with the cicada's voices in the heat of the summer, I find it hard to believe that Homer intended to mock the discourse of

valiantly defend their young in roadside hives provide a parallel for the stalwart resistance of the Greeks (*Iliad* 12.167–172). A poppy, weighed down by a glistening drop of rain, illustrates, in poignant contrast, the terrible beauty of a young man's heroic death and the fragility of human life (*Iliad* 8.306–308). The poppy is merely bent, not destroyed, and the precipitation bearing down upon it will ultimately sustain and nourish it. Such similes abound, varying tremendously in their imagery. They embrace flora and fauna as well as Earth, sky, and sea. Significantly, the similes do not portray a natural world that empathizes with the plight of humanity, nor do they impart any feelings of nostalgia or longing on the poet's part for a less complicated life in total harmony with Nature. Pathetic fallacy and pastoral leanings await another age. Further, when the natural world mirrors humanity, the reflection is never pure. Reflection and reflected must never be assimilated. Should this occur, the results are invariably devastating. Achilles, when he decides to behave like a lion or wolf "recognizing neither pity nor αἰδώς [*aidōs* 'respect for another']," exemplifies this Homeric precept.[36]

The Homeric urban ideal, resting fundamentally on a feeling of "human helplessness" in the face of a natural world filled with dangers and mysteries, was remarkably persistent.[37] Accordingly, the literature of the Archaic and Classical periods is relatively sparing in protracted references to the natural world, and where they do appear, Nature remains at most a frame or scenic backdrop for the human drama. Poetry, particularly "sentimental" lyric, is the genre in which one would most readily expect to find the sustained, passionate reverie of the pastoral dream. However, the pre-Hellenistic, Greek dream world ultimately reveals an essential anthropocentrism.[38] Lyric's most stunning landscapes are those of Sappho, who, purportedly in her own assessment, "so far surpassed other women in poetry as Homer did other men."[39] The fragmentary state of Sappho's soothing words to a heart-broken Atthis does little to detract from the obvious magnitude of her descriptive powers.

---

the elders, however slightly, by means of this comparison. The song of the cicadas is very, very clear, almost deafening at times. It is stunningly impressive, and it is certainly authoritative. Further, its pitch modulates, progressing to an animated crescendo and then falling again. So too must be the speech of the elders as they observe the bloodshed and heroism at the foot of the walls atop which they are seated.

[36] Kim 2000:141.

[37] Segal 1963:20.

[38] On the definition of "pastoral" and "pastoralism" with reference to verbal and visual discourse, see Hunt 1991.

[39] οὔνομα μευ Σαπφώ, τόσσον δ' ὑπερέσχον ἀοιδῶν/ θηλειᾶν ἀνδρῶν ὅσσον ὁ Μαιονίδας, *Palatine Anthology* 7.15.

Here the girl for whom Atthis longs is compared to the "rosy-fingered moon" illuminating the sky and shedding her lovely glow over roses, chervil, and clover in bloom:

> νῦν δὲ Λύδαισιν ἐμπρέπεται γυναί-
> κεσσιν ὥς ποτ' ἀελίω
> 8 δύντος ἀ βροδοδάκτυλος μήνα
>
> πάντα περρέχοισ' ἄστρα· φάος δ' ἐπί-
> σχει θάλασσαν ἐπ' ἀλμύραν
> 11 ἴσως καὶ πολυανθέμοις ἀρούραις·
>
> ἀ δ' ἐέρσα κάλα κέχυται, τεθά-
> λαισι δὲ βρόδα κἄπαλ' ἄν-
> 14 θρυσκα καὶ μελίλωτος ἀνθεμώδης·

> But now she is preeminent among ladies of Lydia,
> 8 like rosy-fingered moon after sunset,
>
> surpassing all the stars; its light extends over the salt sea
> 11 alike and the fields of flowers;
>
> and the dew is spread abroad in beauty, and roses bloom,
> 14 and tender chervil and flowery melilot:
>
> Fragment 96.6–14[40]

Sappho has been said to lose herself momentarily within the frame constituted by her hypnotic simile.[41] This psychic transportation of self would account for the abrupt recollection of, or "reawakening to," her actual subject, a girl for whom another pines, in the fragmentary lines that follow. Yet, if Sappho does enter the frame, she is quick to retreat from it again. The beloved may in some regards resemble the moon, but she is not, and never will be, the moon. The moon reflects her beauty and suggests the degree to which she sustains the life of the one that loves her, but it does not reflect the whole of the girl's person. The moon is ultimately more potent, more distant, and "other." The moon's distance is not infinite, however, and it is herein that the poet's ability to harness or limit the powers of Nature resides. As in Homer, the frame must not overpower that which is framed; the framing member's form and dimensions, the scope of its expressive power, must be controlled. In this fragmentary poem, Sappho has subtly achieved such control by representing the moon as sustaining humanity. The moonlit fall of dew and the bloom of roses,

---

[40] The Sapphic text and its translation are from Page's 1955 edition, 87–88.
[41] Page 1955:92–96.

chervil, and clover is not a scene from wildest Nature. Rather, the dew prompts the growth and blossoming of particular flowering plants, all cultivated by the Greeks for specific purposes. Chervil is an herb possessing medicinal properties, and clover a source of honey. The rose, highly treasured in antiquity, was "the only flower to be intensely cultivated" and a regular inclusion in sanctuary gardens.[42] All of these plants, whether growing in gardens or in the wild, were harvested for the fabrication of garlands and wreaths employed in cultic and other ceremonial contexts.[43] Taking these observations into consideration, the simile assumes not a cosmic but a human scale.

Awareness of Nature's controlled human scale informs the reading of other Sapphic landscapes as well, for instance the lush setting of Aphrodite's epiphany (Fragment 2).[44] In answer to a prayer, Aphrodite is summoned from Crete to a holy temple, her own temple, permeated by the scent of incense and surrounded by luscious groves of apple trees. There is a babbling brook, and a thick, soporific, cover of roses, as well as a meadow, swept by warm breezes, where horses graze and flowers grow. This is not merely a sentimental landscape conjured by a painterly and lovesick imagination. Rather, it is a *temenos*, a sacred space in Nature filled with divinity but inscribed by humankind for the purpose of interaction with the divine. This not a wilderness but a garden that embodies the fertile, life-sustaining essence of Aphrodite.

Judging from the scope of its landscape features, ranging from orchards to meadows for grazing, the *temenos* Sappho describes is a rural sanctuary. *Temenē* such as this played a major part in the attempt to realize Homer's urban ideal. The creation of Greek cities depended on the inscription of Nature, which was accomplished "by claiming a landscape."[45] One method of inscription was the erection of city walls. Another was the establishment of rural sanctuaries, whereby gods inhabiting the countryside could become fully integrated in the city's pantheon.[46] Such inscription also marked agricultural land as belonging to the city and separate from the surrounding wilderness, for rural sanctuaries served as boundaries between inside and outside, framed and frame. They also served to separate one community's arable land from another's.[47] In other words, rural sanctuaries were instrumental in delimiting civic space as well as in creating civic identity. They served to "structure phys-

---

[42] Thompson and Griswold 1982:14. See also Carroll-Spillecke 1989:2.

[43] See Page 1955:91, specifically the note on lines 13–14.

[44] For the poem, see Page 1955:34.

[45] Cole 2000:481.

[46] See Cole 1994:199.

[47] Antonaccio 1994:84 is the source of the quote. See also Snodgrass 1991:18.

ical territory" and to "articulate borders."[48] Rural sanctuaries became *loci* for intercourse and exchange between the local and the foreign, and they became places where conflict, mainly territorial, could be "repeated and ritualized."[49] Eventually a range of rural sanctuaries would develop, some expressing the "territorial sovereignty of a city," others "promoting regional federation," and still others "suitable for interregional or Panhellenic gathering."[50] In essence, the construction of rural sanctuaries was an attempt "to impose some beneficial pattern on happenings outside human control."[51] The process of inscription itself would be laborious yet impermanent. Greece's premier sanctuary, Olympia, demonstrates the vulnerability of such sacred spaces. Situated in an idyllic valley between the Hill of Kronos and the confluence of the rivers Alpheios and Kladeos, Olympia would be buried to a depth exceeding five meters in sand deposited by the eroding hill and the flooding rivers. These *temenē* 'off-cuts' were, after all, once pure wilderness bearing an indigenous "crop." Walls or boundary stones would mark their area, and plantings appropriate to the sanctuary's presiding divinity would replace wild, native flora. Accordingly, oaks were planted for Zeus, laurels for Apollo, olives for Athena, and myrtles for Aphrodite.[52] It is not coincidence that the period in which the Homeric poems and the ideal of the *polis* took shape was also a time marked by sanctuary building, particularly of Panhellenic sanctuaries, in Greece.

The Archaic and Classical impulse to inscribe the natural world, thereby carefully limiting human interaction with wild Nature, manifested itself in various guises, in the visual arts as well as the literary and tectonic. While almost any painted Greek vase dating from this period can be used to demonstrate such inscription, the painterly Red Figure vases of the High Classical period reveal the full gamut of ideological complexities involved in rendering human figures so as to frame them with, not engulf them in, the natural environment. Depictions of landscape are rare in Greek vase painting, and natural settings, even minimally expressed, are worthy of particular note. It is all the more astonishing when the landscape has been portrayed with sufficient detail to enable the viewer to identify a place or, at least, a distinctive type of place. A vase of pivotal importance to our understanding of the evolution of Greek "landscape" painting, the Lykaon Painter's masterpiece, is a *pelikē* 'storage jar'

---

[48] Antonaccio 1994:103.

[49] See de Polignac 1994:3–8 for the exchange and interchange aspect of sanctuaries, and see page 13 specifically for the quote.

[50] de Polignac 1994:15.

[51] Osborne 1994:144.

[52] For the demarcation and planting of sanctuary gardens, see Carroll-Spillecke 1989:34–38.

Figure 3. A landscape "of unusual, even startling interest." Red-figure *pelikē*: drawing of Side A, Odysseus, Elpenor, and Hermes in the Underworld. The Lykaon Painter, ca. 440 BCE. The Museum of Fine Arts, Boston, William Amory Gardner Fund, inv. no. 34.79.

decorated, ca. 440 BCE, with images linked to literature, theater, and mural painting.[53] The so-called A-side of the vase depicts Odysseus, the fully corporeal "spirit" of Elpenor, and Hermes (Figure 3). The artist has located these figures on different levels in a rocky terrain rendered graphically by undulating lines of whitish-yellow paint. Hermes, who is striding towards Odysseus and Elpenor, is spatially closest to the viewer. His eyes fixed upon Elpenor, Hermes advances with his right hand outstretched as if to signal the spirit's appearance to Odysseus. Odysseus himself, sword in hand from the recent sacrifice of two lambs still lying at his feet, sits facing Elpenor, who strains to pull himself out of a chasm in the earth. Surrounding this emerging figure are tall reeds, "their tops waving in the wind."[54] Their presence, it was noted, must

---

[53] For a more thorough discussion of the vase's iconographic content, see Giesecke 1999a. Descriptive material from that essay has been summarized here.

[54] Beazley in Caskey and Beazley 1954:88.

indicate the "proximity of rivers."[55] The *pelikē*'s B-side, more hastily rendered and less spatially complex, portrays Poseidon in pursuit of Amymone. This too is a three-figure group, but all three figures rest on a single ground line. Poseidon, the central figure, advances briskly towards Amymone, who is still carries the *hydria* 'water pot' she had come to fill with water. Gazing back at the god who has ambushed her, her right hand raised in alarm, Amymone is in full flight. She appears to have ample cause for concern, as the god's trident, which he wields, strangely in this context, like a weapon, is less than an arm's length from her. To Poseidon's rear, and likewise glancing back at him, is Amymone's fleeing handmaid. In this scene there is no indication of setting.

Upon the *pelikē*'s arrival to the collection at the Museum of Fine Arts, Boston, Lacey Caskey described the vase as being "of unusual, even startling interest," not only on stylistic grounds but also "because it is the earliest and by far the most impressive representation in ancient art of a famous passage in the *Odyssey*," the journey to the world of the dead, *Nekuia*.[56] Prior to Odysseus' departure from her island, Homer's Circe reveals that it will be necessary for the hero to travel to the ends of the world and enter the House of Hades in order to consult Teiresias regarding the details of his homecoming. In her words, this meeting will take place at the point, marked by a rock, where Puriphlegethon and Kokytos, a branch of the river Styx, flow into Acheron (*Odyssey* 10.513–515). It is here that the dread goddess directs him to dig a carefully measured pit and to pour libations around it (*Odyssey* 10.517–518). After consulting Teiresias, Odysseus sacrifices two sheep whose throats he cuts over the pit. Attracted by the flowing blood, a throng of spirits approach. First among them is that of Odysseus' comrade Elpenor (*Odyssey* 11.35–51). The two sit for some time, as Odysseus later recounts, "exchanging regrets, I with my sword held out stiffly across the blood-pool and the wraith of my follower beyond it, telling his tale" (*Odyssey* 11.81–83).[57] The Lykaon Painter's fidelity to Homer is indeed remarkable. The only alteration he made to the Homeric scene was the addition of Hermes, a figure who serves to balance the composition and is a logical symbolic addition because he facilitates passage into, and on rare occasions out of, the underworld.

Admittedly, the natural scenery depicted on this vase is relatively minimal. "Sketchy" is how Caskey described it.[58] Still, these few landscape features, rocky ground and stand of reeds, evoke not a general "wilderness"

---

[55] Beazley in Caskey and Beazley 1954:88.
[56] Caskey 1934:40.
[57] The translation here is Beazley's from Caskey and Beazley 1954:87.
[58] Caskey 1934:43.

setting but a specific type of place: rocky and very wet. These details are enough to set the stage for the figures, all of them identified with labels, who inhabit the space and who, through their disposition towards one another, define its precise location at the confluence of the underworld's rivers. Further, for all its sketchiness, the scenery on this vase is at the same time "unusually elaborate."[59] It is elaborate, at least, when viewed against the full spectrum of Greek vase painting—and Greek art generally—produced prior to or contemporaneously with it, notably excepting that issuing from the Bronze Age island cultures of Minoan Crete and the Cyclades. In the world of Bronze Age Greece it was the Minoans, together with the inhabitants of the Cyclades, who took the lead in producing technically and iconographically sophisticated artifacts in a variety of media, including clay, ivory, stone, precious metals, and paint. Minoan and Cycladic art of the Bronze Age is characterized by a tangible stylistic ease and freedom, a certain exuberance, and an evident closeness to, or union with, the natural world. Octopodes gracefully wrap their tentacles around the surfaces of Minoan vases; stags butt antlers on carved gems; monkeys pick crocus flowers in a Nilotic landscape on painted walls; steatite is transformed into the head of a magnificent bull; and, on the surface of golden seal rings, celebrants, male and female, clutch altar-topping trees that represent an elusive Nature deity. The Minoans and their neighbors in the Cyclades appear to have embraced Nature. To this extent, the great Minoan palaces were apparently left unfortified.[60] No barriers were deemed necessary to deter hostile forces in Nature or other humans who had succumbed to a lower, bestial nature. Human and beast were seemingly on a par, both noble creatures sharing the gifts, as well as the challenges, presented by Mother Earth.

The second half of the fifteenth century, the later Bronze Age, manifested dramatic changes in the Aegean. Mainland Greeks, taking control of Minoan colonies, trade routes, and administrative centers, became the dominant power, and their anthropocentric, often violent or belligerent sensibilities began quite unsubtly to infiltrate Aegean art.[61] On the palace walls at Knossos, humans, stiff, large in scale, and portrayed against schematized backgrounds, eclipsed the older, exuberant naturescapes. In the so-called Corridor of the Procession, for instance, male and female figures bearing gifts or offerings

---

[59] Caskey 1934:43.

[60] Evidence of fortifications on Minoan Crete, largely deemed Protopalatial in date, is controversial.

[61] I follow Immerwahr 1990:159–160 and 1977, as well as Vermeule 1964 here. For a survey of the arts in the Bronze Age, see Hood 1978, and for fresco painting specifically, see Immerwahr 1990.

march towards what may be a goddess. Meanwhile, on the Campstool Fresco, robed figures sit frozen, rigidly engaged in an exchange of cups. Images such as these have stylistic parallels in Mycenaean palaces where naturescapes, ebullient or otherwise, are conspicuous in their absence. Here processions, hunters with their dogs, and soldiers armed for battle have won the day. The Mycenaeans did, to be sure, possess an appreciation for Minoan art and for the Minoan artistic sensibility. The "aristocratic" shaft graves at Mycenae and other Mycenaean gravesites were filled with characteristically Minoan objects: animal head rhyta, butterfly "buttons," a crystal duck, golden goblets depicting marine life and scenes of bull-leaping, seal-rings portraying "vegetable" worship, and the like. However, Mycenaean graves also yielded objects crafted in a Minoan style yet bearing scenes closer to the mainland heart. Such, for instance, are the famous gold ring embellished with a "battle in the glen," and the delicately wrought "Lion Hunt Dagger" made of bronze inlaid with gold and silver against a niello background. In the end, the evolution, or de-evolution, of representation inspired by the natural world in Bronze Age Greece may best be illustrated by the fate of the octopus, which remained a favorite subject for vase painters. In the hands of Minoan artisans, the octopus veritably defined the shape of the vase it adorned with its strong, far-reaching tentacles. In the twelfth century, octopodes hailing from Mycenaean workshops are all googly eyes and limp tentacles. They float listlessly on the surface of the vase rather than wrap themselves around it. Later in that century, the octopus was reduced to an enervated squiggle, and finally, as Greece plunged into the Dark Age, it disappeared entirely, replaced by an even more basic ornamental repertoire of circles, triangles, and tired wavy lines. A true reflection of an intensifying anthropocentric tendency in the social ideologies of Greece, renewed and committed artistic interest in the natural world would have to await the passing of Alexander and the coming of Rome.

As the Dark Age drew to a close, decorative schemes on vases turned towards abstract geometric ornament applied to increasingly well-proportioned vases in such a way as to reveal and emphasize the structural components (neck, shoulder, belly, and foot) of the vases themselves.[62] Concentric circles and semicircles, together with wavy lines and a limited range of rectilinear motifs, were a favorite. The concern now was with the establishment of control and harmony on the part of a populace wishing to promote order in place of chaos. For those striving for a sense of permanence in a mutable

---

[62] Surveys of the Geometric Style in Greek vase painting include: Benson 1970; Biers 1987:105–125; Boardman 1998:7–82; Coldstream 1977:25–271; Hurwit 1985:71–124; and Robertson 1975:14–21.

universe, mimesis of unpredictable Nature's forms would not be a primary impulse. When a recognizable life-form did appear—a rare occurrence on these Protogeometric vases—it was often that most prized of domesticated animals, a long-legged horse with arching neck and spine rendered in a curvilinear hand, standing timidly in, and utterly engulfed by, a field of confining, linear bands.[63]

Tendencies towards abstraction of animate forms intimated on Protogeometric vases were greatly amplified in the pursuant style known as the Geometric. Around 900 BCE there was a distinct shift from circular to rectilinear ornament, and the desire on the part of the artist to create an ordered design was exceptionally pronounced. The new Geometric vases were covered, head to foot, with registers or bands of repetitive ornaments including meanders, zigzags, triangles, chevrons, checkerboards, and dots, all patterns probably reflecting forms in the natural world but abstracted to a degree that their origins cannot easily, or unambiguously, be traced. The ultimate graphic control over Nature is abstraction. So great was the concern with controlling Nature as Greece emerged from its Dark Age that, after the birth of the Geometric style, a century would pass before recognizable figures drawn from the natural world began to appear with some regularity. The horse reappeared, now notably accompanied by its owner or handler, under bridle or pulling a chariot. Horses and their human masters were joined by a few other life forms, particularly deer or antelope and waterfowl, all of them, like human and horse, reduced to their essence expressed clearly and "simply" as a complex of "rationalized" geometric forms, bereft by abstraction of vital autonomy.[64] Horse and human made a tentative appearance at first, relegated to less than prominent zones, but by the high point of this style, they had shifted to center-stage. Deer and birds, meanwhile, remained relegated to subsidiary zones, their forms endlessly repeating just like the other bands of strictly "inanimate" ornament; they were bound, framed by bands that contained them, and at the same time, they themselves served as frames for increasingly popular scenes of war, hunt, and burial, all scenes reflecting the basic human struggle for survival. Ultimately, the Geometric style could be described as one of hysterical control. If nothing else, it was compulsively obsessive about the

---

[63] On the appearance of "living" forms on Geometric vases, see especially Boardman 1983.

[64] In Pollitt's words, the approach of Geometric artists was to "pare away details which seemed inessential in a form in order to bring out its underlying geometric structures and then to reassemble these structures into a new proportional harmony that was independent of form as it appeared in nature" (1985:98).

establishment of boundaries or limits, thereby reflecting the organizational principles of the nascent *polis*.

The Geometric style prevailed when the Homeric poems were substantially formed, and it shares with the poems not only a formulaic mentality but also an impulse to create order in human life by striving to impose order on Nature. Admittedly, a few isolated expressions of "landscape" can be found: for instance, two deer rear up heraldically on either side of a tree on a *hydria* from Chalcis, and an Argive *kratēr* 'mixing bowl' fragment depicts a bridled horse that stands on a speckled shore above a field of zigzagging waves, "surrounded" by his rider, a bird, two fish, and a group of spectators.[65] Still, the Geometric is not a style that strove for naturalism of any kind. Natural forms, when they do appear, are consistently limited in type and are methodically abstracted so that they can be controlled, confined, and, consequently, understood. The strict control that gave this style stability would, however, also serve as its undoing, for excessive rigidity ultimately constricts creativity.

As Greek contact with the Near East and Egypt increased, a new painting style developed under the influence of imported objects.[66] This new seventh-century style, the Orientalizing, provided artists with fresh possibilities: polychromy and a reconstituted repertoire of pictorial motifs. Rectilinear patterns yielded increasingly to more pliant ornaments such as intertwined cables, running spirals, "tongues," rosettes, lotuses, and palmettes. These ornaments were vastly less abstracted than their Geometric predecessors, intended for a consumer base more settled and secure, less threatened by the environment— less threatened but threatened nevertheless, for a palpable concern with creating boundaries to constrain Nature lingers on throughout this period. Animals favored by Orientalizing painters, including the panther, lion, boar, goat, dog, and rooster, which amble rhythmically round and round the vases they embellish, are certainly much more "true to life" than those portrayed by Geometric artists, yet they remain strictly confined to registers, thus prevented from roaming over the picture field. Now too, as in the Geometric style, there is little vacant space; rosettes and other ornaments are sprinkled around and between the strolling herds. Far from being realistic renderings of animals in space, Orientalizing decorative schemes, particularly the best Corinthian, are pure, tapestry-like ornament, an impression enhanced by the

---

[65] These examples appear in Coldstream 1977; the Argive *kratēr* fragment is figure 45b on page 143, and the Chalcidian *hydria* is figure 61b on page 193.

[66] For surveys of post-Geometric vase painting Archaic through Classical, see Hurwit 1985:125–248, Boardman 1998 and 1974, and Robertson 1975:21–33 and 120–139. On the appearance of Oriental influences generally, see Burkert 1992 (especially 9–40).

fact that beasts drawn from the mythological sphere, such as the sphinx, siren, and griffin, frequently join creatures from the wild.

Heroes derived from the realm of myth would also make an appearance under Eastern influence, and it was their deeds, as well as deeds of more ordinary men and women, that ultimately captured the imagination of both painter and patron, now less attracted to genre scenes focusing on "survival" in the face of menacing Nature than their eighth-century counterparts. This was the case particularly in Athens, where a uniquely dynamic and experimental Orientalizing style was forged. Vases painted in this Protoattic style retain some features characteristic of the Geometric such as multiple bands of decoration, human figures rendered in silhouette but with frontal torso, and a pronounced *horror vacui* 'dread of vacant space', especially in early examples. However, figures, both human and animal, have a more organic appearance, and artists painted them not only in solid silhouette but also in silhouette combined with incision and outline, sometimes filled with white. Bold figured scenes, primarily inhabiting the vases' prominent belly and neck zones, toy with the limiting authority of the bands that enclose them; a horse's ear, a hoof, a hand, or a foot may break through such linear barriers. Still, these protective barriers remain, and they separate figured scenes from the registers of ornamental spirals, cables, rosettes, and leaves that constitute their frame. Strikingly, vegetable and other "natural" motifs became stylistically "frozen" both in appearance and in decorative application, while painters strove to render the human (and super-human) form ever more realistically. It is true that the odd chubby shrub or spiky tree appears in Protoattic figure scenes amid the general flutter of filling ornament from which it is sometimes nearly indistinguishable, and in such cases it serves as a sort of "shorthand" indicating that the scene represented is taking place out of doors. Most organic forms, however, would remain confined within ornamental bands or in relatively obscure zones such as those beneath a given vase's handle or handles, serving in both instances as frames for the figured scenes that dominate the vase's picture field. As the Greek *poleis* continued to define themselves spatially, politically, and ideologically, it was evidently perceived that humanity could flourish, human society could continue to evolve, only if Nature were held at bay.

Athens, the *polis* most confident in individuals to shape their own destiny in an adequately restrained environment, came to dominate the production of vases. Although the Black Figure technique was born in Corinth, it flourished in the hands of Athenian painters who wholeheartedly adopted it as the seventh century drew to a close. It is the Black Figure style that replaced the

Protoattic. Characteristic of this style are figures painted in black silhouette enlivened by means of incised linear details and judiciously applied accents of red and white. Though elegant and distinctive, this technique had its limitations, and, as a result, Athenian vase painters created the splendid Red Figure style, which was in full swing by the last decades of the sixth century.[67] The new style involved the drawing of figures in outline and the use of black paint in dilution, whereby pictorial possibilities were greatly enhanced. Figures could more readily move in space and, through hatching and shading, could be given greater depth. In vases of both styles, artists concentrated their efforts on human and divine subjects, and increasingly lifelike figures continued to be framed by severely restricted intimations of the natural world. Ornamental vegetable borders persisted, as did the Protoattic landscape shorthand, and both were prevented from participating in the human activities that were the painters' focus.[68]

When minimal landscape elements such as trees and boulders appear in the primary picture field, they tend to serve a limited number of representational purposes. On the most basic level, they are employed to set the scene outdoors, but they may also be used to specify a myth, to symbolize abstractions such as victory or immortality, or to serve as attributes of the gods.[69] Thus a burgeoning vine can often be found in depictions of Dionysus, and a serpent-guarded tree appears in illustrations of Heracles' encounter with the Hesperides. A landscape feature may also set the scene for an everyday human activity; olive trees are a logical and necessary component in scenes of olive picking, and it is helpful for the sea to be included in portraits of fishermen. In all instances, it remains the case that the landscape elements, even at their most "expressive" or extensive are permitted to do nothing more than set the stage for the human drama.

Apparent exceptions to Nature's confined role include two famous vases, one Black Figure and the other Red. The former, painted by Exekias ca. 530 BCE, represents Ajax crouching to plant the sword onto which he will presently throw himself (Figure 4). On his left stands the armor of Achilles, which, given to Odysseus rather than himself, motivates his suicide. On his right, slightly bent to mirror the disposition of Achilles' armor, stands a solitary palm. On the second vase, dating to ca. 480 BCE, the Red Figure Kleophrades Painter has

---

[67] For surveys of the Classical Red Figure style, see Boardman 1975 and 1989, as well as Robertson 1975:214–270, 322–327, and 1992.

[68] On natural forms and the border in Greek vase painting, see Hurwit 1977 and 1992.

[69] This categorization is Hurwit's 1991:43.

Figure 4. Alone in the realm of Nature. Attic black-figure *amphora*: the suicide of Ajax. Attributed to Exekias, ca. 530 BCE. Collection du Château musée de Boulogne sur mer, inv. no. 558. Photo, courtesy of the Château musée de Boulogne sur mer.

Figure 5. The storm of war. Attic red-figure *hydria: Iliupersis*. The Kleophrades Painter, ca. 500-450 BCE. Naples, Museo Nazionale Archeologico, inv. no. H2422. Photo, courtesy of the Museo Nazionale Archeologico.

illustrated the various atrocities attending the fall of Troy (Figure 5). Here, in a many-figured scene, King Priam, fruitlessly seeking refuge on an altar and cradling his slain grandson in his lap, is savagely attacked by Neoptolemos. To one side of him Hektor's beloved Andromache heroically attempts to obstruct the hostile assault of the Greeks, and on the other, Cassandra, clutching to the statue of Athena at whose feet she has sought sanctuary, is forcibly removed. Between the tragic scenes representing the death of Priam and the rape of Cassandra is, again, one lone palm. Relatively small, not an imposing natural form, it is dramatically bent to follow the general up-and-down disposition of figures in the scene. Overcome by emotion, we, the viewers, have done what Ruskin cautions we should not and have transferred our own sense of sorrow over Ajax's suicide and the gruesome murder of Troy's citizens to the landscape.[70] Accordingly, both vases are cited as painterly instances of that "pathetic fallacy" in which human emotion is attributed to things that do not

---

[70] See Ruskin 1906, "Of the Pathetic Fallacy."

possess the capacity for experiencing emotion.[71] The Kleophrades Painter's tree is said to weep and Exekias' to be bent in sorrow. However, if we extricate ourselves from the excited state and temporary irrationality occasioned by our own emotional response, other more plausible interpretations present themselves.

It is instructive to bear in mind that there is a fundamental unity of the arts. Thus, for instance, tendencies or trends in painting can likewise be detected in contemporary sculpture and literature. If the painted palms weep and grieve, one would expect to find the natural world communing in the pathos of human life in other artistic media as well. Archaic and Classical sculpture and literature demonstrate nothing of the kind. Even Greek tragedy, a poetic medium designed to elicit pity and fear, yields no examples.[72] The most "pathetically" expressive tragic landscape, that of Sophocles' *Philoctetes*, is a harsh landscape ironically and tragically incapable of consoling him. When Philoctetes describes the caves of the desolate isle on which he had been abandoned as having shared his watches and the mountains as echoing responses to his cries (1452–1460), it serves to emphasize the magnitude of the wrong done to him by his compatriots. Nature does not sympathize with Philoctetes, for this Nature is incapable of doing so. Rather, he has been forcibly, and wrongly, driven out of human society and has, as it were, descended to the level of a beast, thereby becoming a part of the environment. Fortunately for Philoctetes, it is not his destiny to live out his days in desolation and solitude. His own spirit, and the noble spirit of Achilles residing in Neoptolemos, elevates him from his debased existence in the natural world and restores him to the human realm.

Although the *Philoctetes* was composed when Athens was no longer in its prime, the play's lessons may nevertheless be fruitfully applied to the interpretation of Exekias' and the Kleophrades Painter's vases. As he prepares to take his own life, Ajax is not so very different from Philoctetes on the island of Lemnos. Ajax, believing that the Atreidae and Odysseus had stripped him of his honor, deliberately severed himself from his social milieu. He had been denied the prestigious prize of Achilles' armor, and the resulting fit of madness both revealed his human frailty and robbed him of the possibility for revenge. A life thus dishonored was not worth living. So Ajax, like Philoctetes, finds himself isolated from his social milieu, and when he retreats from society, he

---

[71] See, for instance Hurwit 1991:1–53 and, alternatively, Robertson 1975:234 and 1992:63.

[72] This is a reference to Aristotle's view (*Poetics* 1452b32) of the emotive responses appropriate to the well-conceived tragedy.

too stands alone in the realm of Nature. Exekias' composition is stunning in its economy and in the emotion it conveys. The painting reveals everything we, the viewers, need to know. At this climactic moment, we see Ajax alone with only one witness, a solitary palm that is, by its very nature, unfeeling. The palm indicates that Ajax has been driven—or has driven himself—out of his circle of friends into the wild. The desolate wilderness is "where" Ajax is physically and psychologically. He is isolated and utterly alone. Meanwhile, the armor standing before him fleshes out the drama before our eyes; it tells us "why." Nature does not mourn Ajax. This is a human drama played out by a man for an audience of his peers and family. They, and we, experience the weight of his loss.

In the case of the Kleophrades Painter's painting, the viewer is moved again to compassion, sorrow, and even outrage at the brutality of the Greeks against fellow human beings. The Trojan War, like all wars before and after it, was a terrible thing. War brings out the worst in humanity, humanity's bestiality. The *Iliad* demonstrates this fact in no uncertain terms. The solitary palm in the Kleophrades Painter's composition does respond to the savagery brought against the city, specifically to the violent "storm" of war. The storm-battered palm embodies the war-as-storm metaphor; the palm, like the city, is destroyed as the human beast unleashes its fury.[73] In other words, the palm's response is "physical" rather than emotional. As Adam Parry remarks, the very existence of the notion of pathetic fallacy depends on a "disconnect" between human society and the natural world. Fifth-century Greeks may certainly have felt more confident and less afraid than their Archaic predecessors in the face of the environment, but they perceived "no awful gap to be bridged between man and nature."[74] They had not yet forgotten what it was like to feel the constant threat of Nature, and did not long for her influence and presence. Nature was not yet so remote that she was cherished. Neither poet nor painter was compelled to "make contact between himself and nature by attributing his emotions to the latter."[75] By the middle of the fifth century, vase painters were just bold enough to relax their limitations on Nature somewhat, but they were never so bold, so utterly confident in the supremacy of humankind, as to abandon it completely. It was, however, now safe enough to set the stage for the human drama more elaborately.

[73] The phrase "human beast" is borrowed from Zola 1958 (*La bête humaine*), but without specific reference to the content of Zola's work.

[74] Parry 1957:5.

[75] Parry 1957:5.

The traditional explanation for this heightened sense of security and confidence is the Greek victory over the Persian forces at the beginning of the fifth century. The magnitude of the threat to Greece and the sense of validation in the wake of its victory should not be underestimated.[76] To the Greeks, Persia represented all that was brutal, uncivilized, irrational, and uncouth; Persia was very nearly a violent force of Nature. Among those artists inspired by Greece's new confidence was the renowned muralist Polygnotos, who hailed from the island of Thasos. Though Polygnotos, whose floruit is dated between 475 and 450 BCE, was apparently also a sculptor, it is his skill as a painter that brought him public acclaim. Polygnotos' work itself does not survive, but Pausanias' descriptions of his paintings, remarks in the works of the Elder Pliny and Aristotle, and the evidence provided by contemporary vase painting have given us a reasonable impression of the nature of his work. Polygnotos was an innovator, and Pausanias' description of his murals on the walls of the *leschē* 'clubhouse' of the island state of Knidos at Delphi reveals just how he broke new ground. Pausanias describes two murals, one representing "Troy captured and the Greeks setting sail" (Ἴλιος ἑαλωκυῖα καὶ ἀπόπλους ὁ Ἑλλήνων, *Description of Greece* 10.25.2) and the other depicting "Odysseus descended into Hades" (Ὀδυσσεὺς καταβεβηκὼς ἐς τὸν Ἅιδην, *Description of Greece* 10.28.1).[77] A great fan of mythological trivia, Pausanias is interested primarily in the figures populating these murals, but his rambling mythological narratives are interspersed with some invaluable visual impressions. Figures are described as being above or below one another in the picture field. This would seem a small point were it not the case that the vases that are our exemplars of Greek painting prior to the time of Polygnotos were painted in such a way that all figures rest on a single ground line. By placing his figures on different levels, albeit apparently all drawn to the same scale, Polygnotos began to grapple with the problem of perspective and pictorial depth. The painter's interest in the space inhabited by his figures extended also to defining the setting of their actions in more than abstract terms.[78] Pausanias reports that the *Iliupersis* 'destruction of Troy' contained representations of ships, tents, altars, the

---

[76] Pollitt 1985 (especially 100–103), in response to recent efforts at downplaying the impact of the Persian Wars in the development of Greek art, argues for absolute necessity of viewing the wars as a catalyst for artistic achievement.

[77] For simplicity, "Troy captured and the Greeks setting sail" will be referred to as *Iliupersis,* and "Odysseus descended into Hades" as *Nekuia* in the discussion that follows. The Greek text reproduced here is derived from Hitzig's Teubner editions of 1896 and 1907 respectively.

[78] On the innovations of Polygnotos, see Robertson 1992:180–190, 210–215 and Giesecke 1999a:66–67.

walls of Troy, and, most importantly, the sea's pebbly shore. As for the *Nekuia*, Pausanias points to the waters of the Acheron with reeds growing in them and filled with shadowy fish. Upon these waters floats the ferry of Charon, and on their banks the souls of the dead stand in throngs. There are rocks too upon which souls can sit in this underworld landscape, and cliffs such as that whose summit Sisyphos, rolling along his rock, is compelled repeatedly to scale. One gathers from Pausanias that, while figures dominated the murals, there were more than just a few token indicators of landscape and that an effort had been made not just to portray the scenes as out-of-doors but in a specific location. Vase painters followed suit, and there are numerous examples of vases decorated in such a way that they reveal Polygnotos' influence.

Among the best exemplars of the Polygnotan landscape sensibility reflected in vase painting are the Niobid Painter's name vase, which is a *kratēr* now in the Louvre's collection, and the Lykaon Painter's aforementioned *Nekuia pelikē*. The so-called Niobid *kratēr* depicts over a dozen figures ranging up and down the picture field. One side of the *kratēr* represents Artemis and Apollo killing the children of Niobe, and the other may depict Heracles' descent to the underworld. In both scenes the figures' locations in space are "secured" by a series of undulating ground lines indicating a varied terrain. In addition to the terrain itself, a solitary tree has been employed as a suggestion of landscape. That it is Lydia where the slaughter of the children of Niobe is set would be impossible to fathom from the undulating ground and solitary tree. Knowledge of the story is what makes the identification possible. The Lykaon Painter's landscape, by contrast, is more expressive. The clump of reeds and deep crevasse in the rocky ground serve to identify the mouth of the underworld, the particular location where Odysseus performed the sacrifice required to lure the dead. The Lykaon Painter had learned his lessons from Polygnotos well. Indeed, this vase is likely a "copy" of Polygnotos' Delphic *Nekuia*, no slavish copy but an original distillation.[79] The Lykaon Painter has few rivals in fleshing out and particularizing a landscape. Only the Sotades Painter's cups come readily to mind: the apple picker reaching high to grasp her prize amid the branches of a dainty tree, Polyeidos with Glaukos in his cavern tomb, and Aristaeus with a serpent lurking in deep grass.[80] The cups in question, two of them fragmentary, have been decorated with scenes painted on a white ground, a technique more readily suited to adapting the diverse painterly effects of mural painting to the small "canvas" of a vase. Ironically,

---

[79] See my fuller discussion of this issue in Giesecke 1999a:66–68.
[80] Simon 1985:77 describes these as "idyllic landscapes."

the creamy white paint used by the Lykaon Painter for the various features of his landscape and by the white ground painters as a background would prove to be unstable. The white ground technique quickly ceased to be employed in the fabrication of "masterpieces" and was reserved instead for more purpose-fully perishable funerary *lekythoi* 'oil bottles'. On the Lykaon Painter's vase, where it was used only for certain details, the white has all but disappeared, and his landscape is visible only upon closest inspection; his bold scheme contained within itself the seeds of its own destruction.

As inherently unstable and limited in scope as it was, the spatial play within the Lykaon Painter's composition exemplifies painterly techniques that brought to a head what has been called "a crisis in the art of vase-painting," because the spatial effects thereby achieved were "deeply at variance with the traditional Greek concept of what constitutes suitable decoration for a pot."[81] A pot is a solid-walled vessel, and it should look like one. Spatial effects, however, broke down a vessel's three-dimensionality. For this reason, vase painters used such effects with caution, but even then there was a sense that the proper limit had been, or might have been, overstepped. The Meidias Painter and his followers would seek to remedy this philosophical problem. Theirs was a style that staggered figures over the picture field and employed touches of land-scape, but their figures, relatively small and surrounded by agitated swirls of drapery, appear to inhabit an unreal space. That is to say, these petite figurines were staggered less to suggest spatial depth than to cover the entire surface of a given pot ornamentally. In a sense, the old *horror vacui* that had informed the disposition of ornament on Geometric and Orientalizing vases had brought vase painting full circle. In the vase painter's eyes, Nature might aspire to serve as a scenic backdrop for the human drama, but it most appropriately remained an ornamental frame, restricted and contained.

As the Homeric poems reveal, the human instinct to curb and control the potential threat of the natural world in the interest of survival would have to be accompanied by efforts to check that which is "bestial" in the makeup of humankind. From such a perspective, extreme emotion and tendencies such as violence, greed, lewdness, and lawlessness were all base, animal traits, proclivities unworthy of Greeks. Among the notable features of Polygnotos' style was his choice of quiet, reflective moments in the mythological mate-rial that served as the basis for his murals as well as his ability to capture in paint the very essence of an individual's character. For an artist, there could have been no greater challenge than to portray the human spirit or "inner

---

[81] Robertson 1992:180 and 133, respectively.

life" without the hermeneutic crutch of "action." Herein Polygnotos, whom Aristotle describes as *agathos ēthographos* 'good at rendering the inner spirit', was a master, as was the Lykaon Painter.[82] The calm and self-control of Odysseus upon encountering his deceased companion in the latter's composition is almost uncanny, yet the depth of Odysseus' emotion, suggested from his posture, is undeniable. For all its intensity, however, this emotion is thoroughly internalized. The same may be observed in the case of Elpenor who, like Odysseus, would have been overwhelmed by grief and joy but who, in full awareness that he has suffered the consequences of his own immoderate indiscretion, nevertheless stands stoically before the hero. In the sublimation of their emotion, both Odysseus and Elpenor are indistinguishable from the god who bears witness to their encounter. By exercising restraint and self-control, humanity could approximate divinity.

It is telling that the Lykaon Painter's vase is the product of an Athenian workshop and that his *Nekuia* was inspired by a mural decorating a monument ostensibly erected solely by the island state of Knidos, but likely instigated by the prominent Athenian general and statesman Kimon and his circle.[83] As such the Knidian *leschē* could serve both as a thank offering for Kimon's victory over Persia at the Eurymedon River and as a monument to Athens' position of leadership in the Delian League.[84] Of all the Greek *poleis*, it was Athens, particularly in its so-called Golden Age, that most closely embraced and approximated the Homeric ideal of a *polis*-based society secure from the threat of all that was wild, inhuman, and "other." This, at least, is the testimony of the official ideology displayed and disseminated by Athenian monuments and their imagery. Among these monuments is the Knidian *leschē* itself, whose walls had been decorated with scenes from the aftermath of the Trojan War: "Troy Captured" and "Odysseus descended into the underworld." Neither of these scenes is inherently pro-*polis*, pro-Greek, or pro-Athenian, but both were creatively manipulated by Polygnotos in order to satisfy the wishes and needs of his clientele. Polygnotos apparently broke new ground in substituting a morning-after scene for the more familiar *Iliupersis*, destruction of Troy; the devastation of Troy and the slaughter or enslavement of its citizen body was not, after all, Greece's shining hour. The Trojan War was ultimately won through deception, the ruse of the Trojan Horse, and the Greek victory was tainted by sacrilegious crimes that included breach of asylum,

---

[82] ὁ μὲν γὰρ Πολύγνωτος ἀγαθὸς ἠθογράφος, *Poetics* 1450a27–28.
[83] See Castriota 1992:90–132 on the role of Athens in the Knidian project.
[84] Castriota 1992:90. It is Castriota's discussion (1992:90–132) upon which the thematic observations regarding Polygnotos' *Iliupersis* and *Nekuia* are based.

rape, and the desecration of temples. Polygnotos obscured all of this by re-focusing and re-casting the *Iliupersis* so that the Trojans' barbarian other-ness, their breach of *xenia*, their failure to chastise Paris for his extravagant lust—and therefore their condoning of it—would be uppermost in the viewer's mind. The Greeks, meanwhile, were represented as merciful, restrained, even compassionate victors in battle waged for the noblest cause, the preserva-tion of the moderate, divinely sanctioned Greek way of life. Recast in such a way, the Trojan War could serve as a paradigm for the Persian War. As for the *Nekuia*, Polygnotos embellished Homer's vision by adding Theseus, Athens' legendary king, as well as mythological personages from whom individual Athenians and member *poleis* in the Athenian-led, anti-Persian Delian League claimed descent. The *Nekuia* provided a "mythic-genealogical precedent for pan-Aegean identity and solidarity," and, together with "Troy Captured," it promoted "the ancient mythic origins of Athenian commitment and initiative within the larger, collective struggle of the Greeks to defend their ancestral traditions and standards."[85]

The Greek victory over the invading forces of the massive Persian Empire in the early fifth century was the catalyst for the dedication of the Knidian *leschē*, and also the catalyst for Athens' tremendous intellectual and artistic achievements later in the century. Above all, this victory propelled Athens to within virtual striking distance of the Homeric "political" ideal. Realization of Homer's utopian vision would not have appeared beyond Athens, as its citi-zens had long evidenced a marked propensity for its dicta in their social struc-ture, system of justice, cults, arts, and the physical disposition of their city. Through the efforts of statesmen such as Solon, Cleisthenes, and their many supporters, Athens had evolved from citadel to city-state and from kingship to democracy. However limited its scope, the importance of this empower-ment of the people should not be underestimated. Considering, for perspec-tive, the totalitarian nature of the great kingdoms of the Near East and Egypt, the Athenian democratic venture was truly remarkable. Political empower-ment and representation are inextricably linked to the provision of popular access to the law and due legal process. This was clear to Draco, Solon, and Cleisthenes, each in his own right a utopian visionary, and their innovations were all in keeping with Homer's sense of justice, personal responsibility, and collective decision-making.[86]

---

[85] Castriota 1992:94.

[86] I do not wish to imply that Athens had a monopoly on utopian visionaries. I would count as such all the lawgivers and statesmen who worked to improve the lot of the citizen body of their various *poleis*.

It is beyond dispute that the Athenians felt an innate connection to the substance of the Homeric epics; the tradition of the benign and enlightened Athenian tyrant Peisistratos' call not only for the creation of standard editions or transcripts of the Homeric epics, but also for the performance of the epics in the context of the Greater Panathenaia, the city's grand festival held to commemorate the day of its patron goddess's birth, betrays as much.[87] In truth, Athena herself, the symbol and guiding light of Athens, perfectly reflected the Homeric utopian ideology, making her the ideal patron deity for Homer's City at Peace and for Hesiod's City of Justice. Born from the head of Zeus, the virgin goddess Athena signified the dominance of male over female, for by swallowing her mother, Zeus fully appropriated that most miraculous and potentially subversive of female powers, the power of generation. The story of Athena's birth accordingly served as "an ideal paradigm of a social system in which the children are born from the mother but belong to the father."[88] As Aeschylus' *Oresteia* reveals, Athena was the veritable embodiment of Zeus' justice.[89] She played a leading role in the great battle between the Olympian gods and the Giants who threatened Zeus' hegemony, and her support of Zeus' realm would remain unwavering. Hers was a pure wisdom accompanied by technical knowledge, not characteristically female cleverness or trickery. As patron goddess of professional artisans or craftsmen as well as women who worked at home, Athena enabled humankind to control and utilize the natural world. She was the inventor of the plow, the creator of the harness and bridle for horses, the designer of the first ship, and the champion of potters, weavers, and spinners.[90] Fierce and proficient in the art of war, she only drew on her bellicose talents to counter manifest aggression. The olive tree, hardy, noble, and life-sustaining, had been her gift to Athens and, by extension, to humanity. Appropriately, the most sacred cult statue of the goddess in Athens, the Athena *Polias* 'guardian of the city', was carved of olive wood. Both in cult and in myth, Athena was associated with the skilled craftsman Hephaistos who, as the creator of Achilles' wondrous shield, provided the template for the resolution of the *Iliad*'s human crisis. In that epic tale, it is Hephaistos who facilitates the resolution of conflict, both among the gods and among mortals.[91] In the

---

[87] See here Nagy 2002 (especially 7 and 86–98), who notes that Athens, particularly in its celebration of the Panatheneia, played an important role in shaping what would become the definitive "texts" of the *Iliad* and *Odyssey*.

[88] Arthur 1982:77.

[89] See Zeitlin's discussion (1978) of the *Oresteia*.

[90] For a summary of Athena's various powers and prerogatives, see Hurwit 1999:17.

[91] On the role of Hephaistos in the *Iliad*, see Stanley 1993:25 and Hubbard 1992.

city of Athens, the temple of Hephaistos and Athena, built on the low hill that rises up beyond the western edge of the Agora, safeguarded the city's civic and commercial life while Athena watched over the city as a whole from her grand house on the Acropolis.

Under the watchful eye of Athena and Hephaistos, Athens tamed the beast constituted by Dionysus, the deity, perhaps more than any other, associated with wild Nature. In essence a god of vegetation and of "liquid life," he was also the god of release and abandon, the great and potentially terrible equalizer who blurred distinctions between young and old, slave and free, male and female, human and animal. In Athens, the wild abandon that once characterized his worship was artfully contained and ritualized, ultimately transformed into dramatic festivals. In the context of theatrical productions, actors could safely become "other"; the theater would prove to be an effective vehicle by which to comment upon or criticize contemporary society and politics while posing little danger of actually subverting or undermining the existing social order.[92]

Both ideologically and physically, the city of Athens corresponded to the Homeric model for the ideal *polis*. The wild Attic landscape was inscribed and exploited to its best advantage in an effort to ensure the safety and material prosperity of the Athenian people. Great walls surrounded the urban center and secured access, even in times of war, to the port of Piraeus. Outside these walls lay the city's fields and pasturelands, the sustaining countryside.[93] It was here, outside the walls, that the majority of gardens lay, forming part of farms, gymnasia, and sanctuaries (Figure 6). Whether planted with shade trees, vineyards, or flowers, all of these suburban gardens were ultimately utilitarian, designed to enable and enhance both human endeavors and human relations with the gods.[94] Even the wildest places yielded their natural bounty to Athens. Mount Penteli served as a source for marble; Mount Parnes offered hunters an abundance of wild boars and bears; and Hymettos was reputedly the best pasture for bees.[95] Meanwhile, within the city walls, the draining of the swampy area at the north of the Acropolis rendered it the most suitable place for the Agora.[96] Around its central space, a vast array of structures were

[92] See Cartledge 1997 for the social function of the theater, and Henrichs 1990 on Dionysus between the city and wild Nature or "the country."

[93] The importance of the countryside to the city of Athens is discussed in great detail by Osborne 1987 and Tomlinson 1992, both of which are among the works consulted here.

[94] On gardens outside the walls of Athens, see Carroll-Spillecke 1989:passim and 1992:84–101.

[95] So Pausanias *Description of Greece* 1.32.1.

[96] On the problem of dating the draining of the Agora, see Tomlinson 1992:51–52.

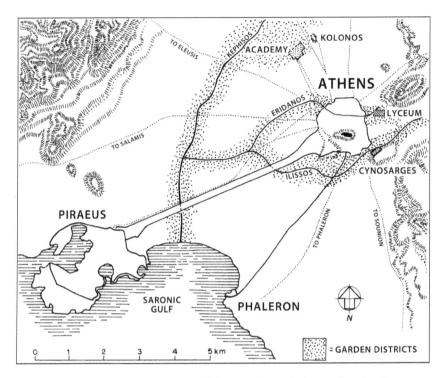

Figure 6. Nature as *parergonal* frame; beyond the walls of Athens and Piraeus, and beyond the long parallel walls that connect them, Nature tamed resides. The garden districts of Classical Athens. Map after Maureen Carroll-Spillecke, *KHΠOΣ: Der antike griechische Garten* (Munich: Deutscher Kunstverlag, 1989), 29, fig. 10.

built including temples, altars, fountain houses, law courts, multi-purpose *stoai* 'detached colonnades', offices of the magistrates, and the meeting hall of the *Boulē* 'council'. Filling the spaces between the city's civic and religious centers was a network of narrow, tortuous streets lined with houses. Judging from their scant remains, these houses essentially conformed to the typical Classical Greek houseplan, based on better-documented and understood archaeological finds at residential sites such as Olynthos. With its nearly impervious exterior façade and room-ringed interior courtyard, the typical house was introspective in the extreme (Figure 7).[97] A refinement of the womb-like cave, the

---

[97] Jameson 1990:183 cites "being invisible to the outside world" as the major aim of the Greek house. For a description of the "typical" Greek house see: Ault 2000, Brödner 1989:298–302, Hoepfner and Schwander 1994, Nevett 1999, Rider 1964, and Wycherly 1978:237–252.

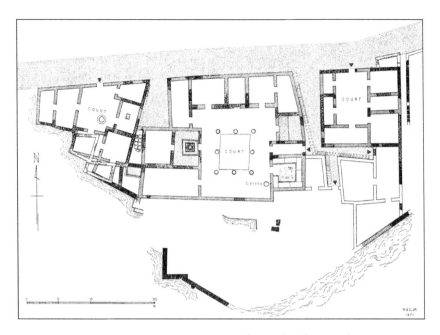

Figure 7. Microcosm of the *polis.* Classical Athenian houses on the Areopagus. Plans after T. Leslie Shear Jr., "The Athenian Agora: Excavations of 1971," *Hesperia* 42 (1973): 148, fig. 4. Reprinted courtesy of The American School of Classical Studies at Athens.

house was a shelter constructed by human hands, consisting of spaces built to conform to human proportions and sensibilities as well as to human needs for security and sustenance in a hostile environment. As such, the house was at once a microcosm of the city and a macrocosm of the human body.[98] Notably, the Classical Greek house contained neither pleasure garden nor horticultural plot, and provisions were made for a separation of the sexes.[99] The female, physically more attuned to the rhythms and mysterious powers of Nature, was kept within the confines of the house while "pure," wild Nature was excluded. By such two-fold constraint, it was hoped, Nature's menace would be rendered impotent. As a result, "the monotony of closely huddled houses and buildings within the city walls was relieved only by scattered sanctuary groves or gardens of varying but rather modest size and by the agora which was ...

---

[98] This line of discourse was inspired by Agrest 1991:173–195, building on Alberti 1965.

[99] As Antonaccio 2000 argues, this separation may have been less architectural than "ideological" or "conventional."

shaded by the planting of trees."[100] Within the city walls, Nature was everywhere held closely in check.

To what degree the Athenian *polis* had achieved dominance over wild Nature is most vividly illustrated by the Acropolis, which "celebrates the breaking of limits, the ready acquiescence of nature to human action, the victory of the polis over everything."[101] This steep mass of stone in the coastal Attic plain, a natural lookout and bastion, was ideally suited for transformation into the citadel and primary sanctuary of the Athenian people. An erstwhile Mycenaean palace center, the Acropolis entered its classic phase under Pericles, who, by sheer force of character, dominated Athenian politics for some thirty years, from 461 until his death in 429. In the wake of the treaty with Persia known as the Peace of Kallias, Pericles successfully proposed to the Athenians that the Oath of Plataia, whereby the Greeks had vowed not to rebuild temples destroyed by the barbarian host, be nullified. The leading city in Greece, the "school of Hellas," would have to look the part.[102] The focus of the so-called Periclean Building Program was, quite naturally, the Acropolis, and its centerpiece, its pièce de résistance, was the new temple of Athena, the Parthenon.[103] This venerable building's complex and much-discussed architectural and iconographic vocabulary is the purest expression of the city's, as well as its first citizen's, utopian vision.[104] The architects' and sculptors' combination of Doric and Ionic features conveyed the idea of Athens as the divinely sanctioned, restrained, and just hereditary leader of the new Greek pan-Ionian alliance. Within Iktinos and Kallikrates' marvel stood the massive, chryselephantine image of the goddess Athena. Virgin "mother" of the Athenian people, she appeared here with winged Victory in hand. Through her heroic efforts, the order of Zeus had survived the challenge of the intemperate Giants, and under her aegis, the Greeks had eliminated the threat of eradication at the hands of a vast barbarian horde. According to the Parthenon's mythology, the Persian Wars were a reenactment of the Battle of the Gods and Giants. They were also shown to be a reenactment of battles between the Greeks and the savage, hubristic forces of Amazons, Centaurs, and Trojans (Figure 8). By linking these various contests and by associating

[100] Carroll-Spillecke 1989:82.

[101] Scully 1991:65.

[102] Thucydides *Peloponnesian War* 2.41.1.

[103] For thorough treatments of the Periclean Building Program, see Camp 2001:72–137, Hurwit 1999:154–221, and Tomlinson 1992:56–61.

[104] Works reviewed in constructing this brief thematic summary include Castriota 1992:134–229, Hurwit 1999:154–245, Pollitt 1972:64–110, Robertson 1975:292–321 and 1981:90–130, and Scully 1991:65–97.

Figure 8. Greek versus beast. Relief *metope* from the Parthenon, Athens. South *metope* no. 27: Lapith and Centaur. British Museum, inv. no. 316. Photo, © Art Resource.

them with Athena's miraculous birth, prominently illustrated on the eastern pediment, the Parthenon represented Athena and her children as the guarantors of a civilized, patriarchal order and of the preeminent justice of Zeus. All this the sculptors rendered with exquisite and idealized "realism" under the guidance of the great Pheidias. It was Pheidias' style, the absolute perfection and self-control infused into both the human and divine, which, perhaps more than any other single feature of the temple, lent credence to the Parthenon's grandiose claim.

The thematic content of the Parthenon sculptures, as well as the Periclean Building Program itself, was unquestionably utopian in essence. Quite apart from visually promoting the ideal of a Hellenic world governed by self-restraint, nobility, and equity, the Program was designed to employ Athenians from a wide range of trades in projects of considerable scope so that all of them might share in the national wealth.[105] Still, as Plutarch reports, it was not without controversy that Pericles appropriated the funds from the purportedly pan-Hellenic and anti-barbarian Delian defense league for the adornment of Athens.[106] Had this man, described as a paragon of courage, moderation, and self-possession, gone too far? To those unaware that the Parthenon represented a fiction even at its inception, the truth would rapidly be revealed. It is deeply ironic that the Athenian state itself became increasingly democratic under Pericles while simultaneously infringing upon the sacred and inviolable self-governance, *autonomia*, of its so-called allies. The adoption of an aggressive imperialistic policy was Pericles' and Athens' grievous error, a classically tragic *hamartia megalē* 'momentous mistake', for it would rapidly lead to the city's and also its charismatic leader's demise.[107] In its dealings with the other members of the Delian League, Athens demonstrated qualities that it had attributed to others, namely the obsessive aggression of the Amazons, the unrestrained fury of the Centaurs, the unbridled covetousness of the Trojans, and the boundless *hubris* of the Persians. However lovely a fiction it was in its physical manifestation, the civic mythology of the Parthenon could never be considered noble. This the memory of Melos, whose adult male population was put to death and whose women and children were sold as slaves, at the very least ensures. Ultimately, unlike Homer's Achilles, Athens was unable to contain the beast within. Had Athens been a city interspersed with pleasure gardens, had it embraced what is inherently benign and nurturing in Nature, in the beast, and in the barbarian, it might have become instead a model of *eunomia* 'good order'. In the eyes of posterity, that distinction fell instead to Sparta.

---

[105] Plutarch *Pericles* 12.

[106] Plutarch *Pericles* 12.

[107] This is, of course, a reference to Aristotle's remarks on the factors that "make" a tragic hero. Among them is a *hamartia megalē* 'momentous mistake' (ἁμαρτίαν μεγάλην, *Poetics* 1453a15–16).

3

Rome and the Reinvention of Paradise

IN 1848, EARTHWORKS ON ROME'S ESQUILINE HILL fortuitously brought to light part of an elegant private house in what was once a fashionable neighborhood in the ancient city's expansive greenbelt. The walls of a *cryptoporticus*, a long vaulted room in the villa's substructure, yielded a most remarkable work of art, an unprecedented example of landscape painting (Figure 9). Dated to the final two decades of the Republic both on the basis of

Figure 9. Landscape as nostalgic dream. The Odyssey Frieze: Section 3, Odysseus and the Laestrygonians. Late 1st century BCE. Originally in a Roman house on the Esquiline Hill, now in the Musei Vaticani. Photo, © Art Resource.

"style" and the appearance of the masonry wall that it adorned, this painting was deemed "the oldest realistic representation of landscape in existence."[1] Those fortunate enough to have seen the fresco in its original context would have been presented with a singularly lovely, sensually gratifying composition. The *cryptoporticus'* interior had been painted to suggest a room enclosed by a double colonnade rendered so as to project illusionistically into the viewer's space. Above a three-quarter height wall beyond the colonnade appeared a rich panoramic vista: bristling crags, shadowy caves, expansive shorelines, wide bays, billowing clouds, windblown trees, minimal architectural features, and a staffage of small figures drenched in morning light. The preponderance of light green and aquamarine hues in this distant landscape would have evoked the expectation of refreshment from a cool sea breeze as one stood to behold—or glanced at in passing—the vista beyond. The viewer's sense of well-being would have been further enhanced by the complementary combination of refuge, the security of an enclosed space, and prospect, the ability to survey one's physical surroundings, afforded by the structure of the composition.[2]

What has traditionally been regarded as the most remarkable aspect of the Esquiline fresco is the composition's success at conveying the impression of a naturalistic landscape to be enjoyed for its own sake. The landscape itself, rather than its minute population, initially captivates the viewer, making the fresco without precedent in Classical art, Greek or Roman. More than a little surprising to the uninitiated, those figures whom one would expect to inhabit this landscape, such as herdsmen pasturing their flocks and fishermen by the sea, are accompanied by Odysseus and his comrades, who reappear several times in what is, in fact, a continuous narration of the hero's encounters with the Laestrygonians, Circe, and the denizens of the underworld. This is the sole surviving exemplar of the "Odyssean wanderings through varied landscapes," *Ulixis errationes per topia,* that Vitruvius recommended as subject matter suitable for painted decoration on walls of *ambulationes* 'spaces of passage'.[3] These Esquiline landscapes, betraying what appears to be at most an incidental interest in Odysseus, his crew, and their harrowing adventures, emblematize

---

[1] For the quote, see Von Blanckenhagen 1963:100 who dates the painting to 50–40 BCE, while Beyen 1960:260–350 presents a slightly larger window, 50–30 BCE. Andreae 1988:282–283 and 2000:242–257 argues for a date close to 30 BCE on the basis of close parallels to room D in the House of Livia on the Palatine.

[2] On the importance of refuge and prospect to the evolution of Roman domestic architecture, see Giesecke 2001.

[3] *De Architecura Libri Decem (Ten Books on Architecture)* 7.5.2. Vitruvius' comment would lead one to believe that such compositions were not without parallel, if not relatively common, in late Republican and Augustan Rome.

the radical differences between Homer's utopian vision, so fully embraced by Classical Athens, and the social dream of first-century BCE Roman Italy. The latter was an essentially nostalgic, pastoral dream of returning to a simpler life in the country, which, from an urban perspective, was *fons et origo* 'fount and origin' of human social organization as well as the repository and historical locus of morality and religiosity. Memory, with its tendency to fabricate and retain images of an idealized past, has a "built-in utopian function" and is consequently the ideal vehicle for constructing visions of an ideal future.[4] Nostalgia, a word itself suggestively replete with Odyssean resonances, is inextricably linked to memory, and it is therefore forward and backward looking at once.

Returning to the Odyssey Frieze specifically, it has been observed that (illusionistically) witnessing Odysseus' life-threatening struggles from a safely removed vantage point inside one's comfortable *domus* illustrates Lucretius' metaphorical comment: "It is a sweet thing for one on land to behold the monumental toil of another when, on the vast sea, winds stir up the waters" (*Suave, mari magno turbantibus aequora ventis, / e terra magnum alterius spectare laborem, De Rerum Natura* 2.1–2).[5] The ideological affinity of the Epicurean poet's dictum and the frieze does not, however, reside in a physical distancing. In other words, removal from hardship, whether achieved physically or metaphysically, does not guarantee a sense of equanimity. On this point Lucretius is unambiguous. One derives pleasure not from witnessing the sufferings of others (*non quia vexari quemquamst iucunda voluptas, De Rerum Natura* 2.3), but from coming to the realization that most, if not all, of what causes toil, hardship, and suffering in human life is avoidable. The Epicurean ideal of *ataraxy*, freedom from all that torments the human psyche, can be achieved by acquiring a knowledge of Nature's workings and by accepting the fact that humanity is an integral part of the natural world, not an entity that is other, removed, and privileged by proximity to divinity. *Ataraxy* is achieved by embracing humanity's place in Nature; to deny this simple truth is to live in constant fear:

> 55 nam veluti pueri trepidant atque omnia caecis
> in tenebris metuunt, sic nos in luce timemus
> interdum, nilo quae sunt metuenda magis quam
> quae pueri in tenebris pavitant finguntque futura.
> hunc igitur terrorem animi tenebrasque necessest

---

[4] As observed by Erlich 2004.
[5] Andreae 1988:283 associates this Lucretian passage with the frieze.

60   non radii solis neque lucida tela diei
     discutiant, sed naturae species ratioque.

55   For just as children quake and fear all things
     in the viewless darkness, thus in the light of day do we fear
     things which are to be feared no more than
     what children shudder at in the darkness and imagine will
        come to pass.
     Therefore, this terror of the mind and this darkness it is
        necessary
60   not for the rays of the sun nor light of day
     to dispel but the aspect and law of Nature.

De Rerum Natura 2.55–61

The pictorial rhetoric of the Odyssey Frieze conveys a sentiment similar to Lucretius'. It is no longer the case, as it was in Classical Athens, that Nature constitutes the frame for human action. Now Nature herself has shifted to center stage. Nature is *ergon,* and humanity, as well as human constructs, *parergon.* Therefore, the wanderings of Odysseus are no longer presented in Homer's anthropocentric, *polis*-oriented terms. The landscapes through which he travels overshadow the Esquiline Odysseus, who is not preoccupied first and foremost with probing the minds and social systems of others. Further, these landscapes, fraught with dangers as they are, have been transformed into landscapes of desire.[6] The transformation has taken place on two fronts, one visually forceful, the other somewhat more subtle. First, the Odyssean *topia* 'landscapes', illusionistically inscribed by architectural members, have been appropriated by the *domus* whose walls they embellish. The pictorial frame of screen walls and pillars would have integrated these landscapes into the fabric of the house and thereby contributed to the deliberate blurring of the "inside" and the out-of-doors that came to characterize Roman domestic architecture. In the Roman world, living in and with Nature became a thing much desired. Inscription, the application of a frame, dissolved the tension between conflicting emotions of fear and longing that wild Nature engenders.

The second means by which Odysseus and the viewer both could aspire to inhabit the landscapes of the wanderings resides in the scenery's population. It has been observed that the creator of the Odyssey Frieze remained remarkably close to Homer with respect to episodic details. For instance, the Laestrygonian scenes represent the daughter of Antiphates, pitcher in hand,

---

[6] For a different perspective on the role of the Frieze's landscape, see Leach 1988:47.

as well as the spring from which she has drawn water. In a landscape of sheer cliffs and projecting headlands, the lofty citadel of the cannibals' king appears, and the wide harbor is filled with Odysseus' ships assailed by giants hurling monstrous rocks from perches on the encircling cliffs or spearing Greeks like fish (*Odyssey* 10.105–124). The most curious aspect of the painter's rendering of the Homeric tale, aside from the disproportionate attention to landscape, is the "intrusion" of singularly disengaged, unruffled, pastoral figures in what is an extraordinarily violent scene.[7] More curious still is the fact that these figures have generally elicited little more than passing comment. A passage from Varro's *De Re Rustica* (*On Agriculture*), a work contemporary with the frieze, provides invaluable insights into late Republican, urbane intellectuals' romanticized attitudes towards "pastoral" figures:

> necesse est humanae vitae a summa memoria gradatim descendisse ad hanc aetatem, ut scribit Dicaearchus, et summum gradum fuisse naturalem, cum viverent homines ex his rebus, quae inviolata ultro ferret terra, ex hac vita in secundam descendisse pastoriciam, e feris atque agrestibus ut arboribus ac virgultis [ac] decarpendo glandem, arbu[s]tum, mora, poma colligerent ad usum, sic ex animalibus cum propter eandem utilitatem, quae possent, silvestria dep<r>enderent ac concluderent et mansuescerent. in quis primum non sine causa putant oves assumptas et propter utilitatem et propter <p>laciditatem. maxime enim hae natura quietae et aptissimae ad vitam hominum. ad cibum enim lacte et caseum adhibitum, ad corpus vestitum et pelles adtulerunt. tertio denique gradu a vita pastorali ad agri culturam descenderunt, in qua ex duobus gradibus superioribus retinuerunt multa, et quo descenderant, ibi processe-runt longe, dum ad nos perveniret.

> It is necessarily the case that from the remotest memory of human life they progressively devolved down to the present time, as Dicaearchus writes, and that the earliest stage was regulated by natural principles, a time when humanity gained their sustenance from those things which the Earth, left unharmed, brought forth on her own accord, and that, from this way of life, they descended

---

[7] It must be noted here that Homer does mention herdsmen (specifically how profitable life there would be for those requiring no sleep) in the physical description of the land of the Laestrygonians (*Odyssey* 10.82–86), though he does not anywhere indicate that such men witness the assault on Odysseus. In Homer, these pastoral figures are very much in the background.

into the second, the pastoral, such that by picking them from wild and uncultivated trees and shrubs, they gathered the acorn, arbut berry, mulberries, and apples for their use, and, similarly, when, for the same advantage, they caught, confined, and tamed those wild animals that they could. Not without reason is it the case that people believe that among these, sheep were first acquired, both because of their usefulness and because of their tameness; for by nature, these are placid and best suited to the lifestyle of humankind, since milk and cheese were adopted for food, and they yielded clothing and fleeces for the body. Finally, in a third step they descended from the pastoral life to the cultivation of fields, and in this stage they retained many aspects of the two earlier stages, and whence they had descended, they then carried on for a long time until coming to our time.

De Re Rustica 2.1.3–5[8]

Varro presents an idealized vision of the past and of humanity's place in the world. In the remote past, humanity, we are told, lived quite effortlessly off an Earth producing her bounty readily of her own accord. From this felicitous state, humanity descended into a second age, a pastoral age, in which people gathered fruit, berries, and acorns, and commenced the domestication of animals. In this pastoral age, the proximity of human and animal was at its greatest. Humans foraged like animals and, through domestication, incorporated animals into their households. In a third, less beatific age, humanity began to till the soil, but even this toilsome age was far removed from, and by implication better than, the present. The Varronian interlocutor goes on to state that "according to the ancients, the most illustrious men were all herdsmen, as both Greek and Latin and the poets of old make clear" (*de antiquis inlustrissimus quisque pastor erat, ut ostendit et graeca et latina lingua et veteres poetae ...*, *De Re Rustica* 2.1.6). This vision unhistorically mythologizes in a way particular to sophisticated urban cultures.[9]

The city, locus of a perspective sufficiently distanced from Nature to incite the wish to reinvent her, is the origin of the pastoral impulse. The figure of the herdsman is ideally suited to the ideological restoration of humanity within the fabric of the natural environment because he transcends historical boundaries. The herdsman's life "is found everywhere and at all periods.

---

[8] The Latin text is from Goetz's 1929 Teubner edition. The translation does not include Goetz's bracketed insertions.

[9] See the valuable discussion of Barrell and Bull 1975:1–9 and also Hunt 1991.

It is a basic form of human existence."[10] Embodying all humanity, the *pastor* 'herdsman' represents the beginnings of human civilization and its future, its salvation, at once. In the persona of the herdsman, as in the act of inscription, the tension between the fear of and the desire for wild Nature dissolves. Aside from hunting, "pastoralism is the only life in nature without arduous labor. In contrast to agriculture, with its year-round drudgery, dependence on the weather, and danger from plant diseases and floods, tending livestock is comparatively leisurely."[11] Accordingly, the herdsman's life appears idyllic, relying as it does on an ostensibly easy symbiosis with Nature. His existence serves as a reminder of the "essential biological kinship" between human and beast as well as a reminder that what once was wild could all too easily become wild again in the absence of human intervention.[12] In the case of the Odyssey Frieze, the shepherds, goatherds, cowherds, and fishermen may be viewed as providing a model for Odysseus and his Roman audience—a model for living within the *topia* of his wanderings rather than striving to forge physical barriers to keep the natural world at bay. The herdsmen, by virtue of what they symbolize, have nothing to fear in the lands of Circe or the Laestrygonians, neither wild Nature herself nor the savage disposition of these lands' inhabitants. Pure and innocent at heart, they also have nothing to fear in death. The desire to reconnect with Nature is a Roman utopian dream, and the herdsman will be a key player in the effort to bring this dream to fruition.

Interestingly, and tellingly, it is in Athens that the source of the pastoral impulse in the Western literary tradition can be found. This source cannot, of course, be found in the flowering of the grand Athenian democratic venture but rather at the commencement of its enduring afterglow, "in the period when disillusion with society became a marked feature of literature: at the end of the fifth and the beginning of the fourth centuries—and in the works of the man who most clearly expressed that disillusion: Plato."[13] Most vividly in the *Phaedrus*, Plato expresses the deleterious effects of too extreme a separation of city from Nature, where an innate beauty and truth reside that are critical links in the acquisition of fundamental human knowledge, knowledge of the self. The opening of the dialogue is all too familiar, but unique in that Plato's Socrates deliberately leaves the city in pursuit of philosophical discourse only in this passage.[14]

---

[10] Curtius 1953:187.
[11] Shepard 1967:74.
[12] See Shepard 1996:161 for the quote.
[13] Parry 1957:15.
[14] Griswold 1986:16.

Socrates happens upon Phaedrus in the middle of a hot summer day as the latter is heading outside the city wall for a walk (πρὸς περίπατον ἔξω τείχους, *Phaedrus* 227a3). When asked where he is headed, Phaedrus remarks that it is healthier to stroll on country roads than within the colonnades and that he needs to stretch his legs after having sat, since sunrise, riveted by the rhetoric of Lysias. Professing to be a person sick with passion for hearing speeches, especially those that are *asteioi* 'refined/urbane' (ἀστεῖοι, *Phaedrus* 227d1) and *dēmōpheleis* 'for the common good' (δημωφελεῖς, *Phaedrus* 227d2), Socrates follows Phaedrus along the Ilissos River to a most pleasant spot in the shade of a tall plane tree. Socrates, overcome by the beauty of the spot, is moved to an impassioned encomium:

> Νὴ τὴν Ἥραν, καλή γε ἡ καταγωγή. ἥ τε γὰρ πλάτανος αὕτη μάλ' ἀμφιλαφής τε καὶ ὑψηλή, τοῦ τε ἄγνου τὸ ὕψος καὶ τὸ σύσκιον πάγκαλον, καὶ ὡς ἀκμὴν ἔχει τῆς ἄνθης, ὡς ἂν εὐωδέστατον παρέχοι τὸν τόπον· ἥ τε αὖ πηγὴ χαριεστάτη ὑπὸ τῆς πλατάνου ῥεῖ μάλα ψυχροῦ ὕδατος, ὥστε γε τῷ ποδὶ τεκμήρασθαι. Νυμφῶν τέ τινων καὶ Ἀχελῴου ἱερὸν ἀπὸ τῶν κορῶν τε καὶ ἀγαλμάτων ἔοικεν εἶναι. εἰ δ' αὖ βούλει, τὸ εὔπνουν τοῦ τόπου ὡς ἀγαπητὸν καὶ σφόδρα ἡδύ· θερινόν τε καὶ λιγυρὸν ὑπηχεῖ τῷ τῶν τεττίγων χορῷ. πάντων δὲ κομψότατον τὸ τῆς πόας, ὅτι ἐν ἠρέμα προσάντει ἱκανὴ πέφυκε κατακλινέντι τὴν κεφαλὴν παγκάλως ἔχειν.
>
> By Hera, the resting place is lovely indeed. For this plane tree is both really wide-spreading and tall, and the chaste tree's height and thick shade are very nice—and look how it is in the prime of its bloom, so as to make the place very fragrant. And, in turn, a stream of very cold water, to judge by my foot, flows most pleasantly beneath the plane. From the statues and gifts, the place would seem to be conse-crated to some nymphs and Acheloos. And, what's more, if you will, how delightful and exceedingly pleasant is the breeziness of the place. It resounds summery and shrill with the singing of cicadas. And what is most pleasant is the grass, namely how it grows on the gentle slope perfect for reclining one's head to rest.
>
> *Phaedrus* 230b2–c5

The beauty of the place affects, indeed enthralls, all the senses. Lovely, *kalē*, to behold as a whole, this place resonates with the song of the cicadas and is permeated by the sweet smell of a chaste tree in full blossom. Its stream is refreshingly cool to the touch, and the grass just thick enough to rest comfortably on. This is also a place palpably inhabited by rural deities, nymphs and Acheloos, offerings to whom Socrates espies. With the combination of shade, stream, floral perfume, and meadow, Socrates has described a classic *locus amoenus*, the "pleasant place" that will enjoy a particularly rich life in the Roman literary tradition, playing a significant part in shaping the Roman vision of paradise.[15] Though Phaedrus is astonished at the fervor of Socrates' reaction to the spot and declares him *atopōtatos* 'really out of place' (ἀτοπώτατος, *Phaedrus* 230c6), being a person who never ventures beyond the boundary of the city walls (ἐκ τοῦ ἄστεος οὔτ' εἰς τὴν ὑπερορίαν ἀποδημεῖς, οὔτ' ἔξω τείχους ἔμοιγε δοκεῖς τὸ παράπαν ἐξιέναι. *Phaedrus* 230d1–2), only Socrates really has any idea "where" he is and what the true value is of the place in which he finds himself. He realizes that if the rural spaces and the trees are unwilling to proffer their wisdom, it is because the pupil is not sufficiently attuned, being instead roused to a counterfeit "enthusiasm" by the teachings of men in the city (*Phaedrus* 230d3–5). Socrates, equipped with a heightened sense of awareness, moves within the dialogue "from an embodiment of sobriety," through possession by divine madness in the form of Bacchic frenzy issuing from the Muses, "to an embodiment of philosophy."[16] The stages of his metamorphosis are all prefigured in the landscape: the *locus amoenus* is marked by the presence of a chaste tree (*vitex agnus castus*), which is sacred to Hera and representative of sobriety, while the plane tree is associated with Dionysus, quintessential Nature deity and regular consort of the nymphs.[17]

The polish of Lysias' speech, when read to him by Phaedrus, does not suffice to elevate Socrates to the realm of highest truth. In order to reach this he must at least temporarily transcend the *polis*, where opinion, rather than truth, resides, and with Nature functioning as a "medium," pass from an impassioned madness to wisdom. The essential link between Nature and philosophy could not be clearer. However, the magical spot along the Ilissos where Phaedrus and Socrates dangle their feet in the refreshing waters and recline in the shadow of a lofty tree is not "wild" Nature. This spot has been inscribed, demarcated and separated from the general landscape, by virtue of being designated sacred, complete with votive statuettes, to the nymphs and the local river god. Phaedrus and Socrates further inscribe this locale by specifically choosing it as a resting place, thereby privileging it. Their seemingly casual intervention in the landscape is in fact a deliberate act of place-

---

[15] For a survey of the *locus amoenus* topos, see Hass 1998.
[16] Dorter 1971:281.
[17] See Dorter 1971:279–288 for a discussion of landscape imagery in the dialogue.

making, a creation of "milieu."[18] What they have done is create a garden, and the garden, it has been said, "is the ultimate pastoral creation, the organization by man of nature into art."[19]

Socrates' shift of philosophizing from the Agora to the garden is prefigured and paralleled by the transformation of the great Athenian gymnasia from facilities dedicated primarily to the fortification of the body—and this, in the main, for the purposes of military training—to places where philosophical schools would grow and thrive.[20] The Academy, like the Lyceum and the Cynosarges, was itself a garden, a mediated, inscribed landscape, and all three were originally sites of cults of considerable antiquity.[21] Like the Lyceum and Cynosarges, the Academy was situated in something of a natural greenbelt sustained by river water.[22] A large wood or grove sacred to the hero Akademos/Hekademos lying to the west of the city in the Outer Kerameikos near Kolonos Hippios, the Academy received a circuit wall in the sixth century BCE at the bidding of Hipparchos, son of the tyrant Peisistratos.[23] Plutarch reports that the next great step towards embellishing the Academy was made by Kimon, as a result of whose initiative this formerly waterless and dry area became "a kind of suburban park" equipped with fine tracks for racing and shady walks.[24] It is little wonder that in the fifth century this pleasant place, teeming with Athenian youths, would attract sophists who, it may be assumed, contributed significantly to its increasingly intellectual climate. Socrates himself was no stranger to the Academy, and this gymnasium park would become the site of Plato's school early in the fourth century.[25] According to information provided by Diogenes Laertius, Plato's school operated both in the gymnasium, where he dedicated a *temenos* sacred to the Muses, and in his private house and garden, which were located in the vicinity of Kolonos Hippios.[26] In other words, Plato's

---

[18] On defining the garden and the concepts of place-making and milieu, see Hunt 2000 (especially 2–29).

[19] Barrell and Bull 1975:225.

[20] A particularly engaging account of the growth of the philosophical schools is provided by Wycherley 1961 and 1962.

[21] On the "exploitation" of the countryside for rural sanctuaries and gymnasia, see Osborne 1987:168–169.

[22] The Academy lay off the Kephisos River, the Lyceum off the Eridanos, and the Cynosarges off the Ilissos.

[23] For the archaeology of the Academy, see Travlos 1971:42–43.

[24] The quote stems from Wycherley 1962:3. For Kimon's transformation of the Academy, see Plutarch *Kimon* 13.7.

[25] On the presence of Socrates in the Academy, see, for instance, Plato's *Lysis* 203a.

[26] See Diogenes Laertius *Lives of Eminent Philosophers* 3.5 and 3.25 as well as 4.1.1 and 4.3.19.

pupils assembled in a garden, either in the gymnasium or in the master's own garden.

In late fifth- and early fourth-century Athens, the life of the mind became ever more closely associated with life in the garden; the extra-mural garden, both the gymnasium park and the private garden, could be seen as a locus for spiritual reconstitution. Plato's pupils may well have tended his garden plot, but the extant evidence suggests that Plato, and presumably his students, withdrew to his garden for didactic and reflective purposes. Gardens now could feed the body and/or the soul. Apparently Epicurus felt the pastoral urge even more strongly than Plato and Aristotle, both of whom had withdrawn from the hubbub of the city to the amenities of gymnasium gardens. In Epicurus' view, even the suburban gymnasia were too bustling and crowded for serious philosophical reflection, and in what was by all accounts an unprecedented and undeniably demonstrative move, he created a spiritual oasis for himself and his "disciples" within the dense urban fabric of Athens. The Elder Pliny tells of this in a lively condemnation of pleasure-garden estates within the city of Rome:

> iam quidem hortorum nomine in ipsa urbe delicias agros villasque possident. primus hoc instituit Athenis Epicurus oti magister. usque ad eum moris non fuerat in oppidis habitari rura.

> Now, indeed, under the name of "gardens" people possess the luxuries of farms and great estates within the city itself. It was Epicurus, the master of undisturbed leisure, who first instituted this practice in Athens; until his time it had not been customary for the countryside to be inhabited inside towns.
>
> *Natural History* 19.19.50–51[27]

Pliny's pronouncement has not been free of controversy.[28] Primarily on the basis of Epicurus' will, as "preserved" by Diogenes Laertius, and the opening of Cicero's *De Finibus Bonorum et Malorum*, it has been argued that Pliny overstates his case. As the will makes separate mention of Epicurus' house in the deme of Melite and the Garden, it has been assumed that the house and garden were not only separate properties but that the garden, which housed Epicurus' school, was in an entirely different deme and was, furthermore, located beyond the Dipylon gate *outside*, not inside, the city wall. Cicero appears to substantitate this theory. After listening to a lecture by Antiochus, the current head of the Academy, at the inner city gymnasium known as the

---

[27] The text is from Jan's 1878 Teubner edition.
[28] See, for instance, Clarke 1973 and Wycherley 1959.

Ptolemaion, Cicero and a group of his friends decide to take an afternoon stroll in the Academy. The friends pass through the Dipylon Gate and, once arrived at their destination, they comment on the "personal" associations of various landmarks. In this context, Cicero's companion Pomponius remarks that they just passed (*modo praeteribamus, De Finibus Bonorum et Malorum* 5.1.3) the Garden of Epicurus. If *modo* is to be taken literally as 'just now', Epicurus' garden, it is argued, would lie not in Melite but on the very fringes of the Academy. Neither bit of evidence, however, need be fatal to the veracity of Pliny's assertion. For instance, Cicero's stroll to the Academy vividly sets the stage for a philosophical discussion but certainly does not purport to be a cartographically infallible text. What's more, *modo* may be used to mean 'only recently' as well as 'just now', and in the course of what was in all likelihood a fifteen or twenty minute walk from Piso's house to the Academy, something seen at any point along the way would qualify as something seen "only recently." As for Epicurus' so-called will, if it does actually treat the house in Melite and the Garden as separable pieces of property, the location of the house in Melite may simply distinguish this house from others owned by Epicurus and his school.[29] Ultimately, whether the Garden was in Melite, "a large and populous deme, including industrial districts as well as the houses of a number of wealthy and notable citizens," or in Kerameis, either just within or just outside of the Dipylon Gate, Pliny's observation remains equally true; Kerameis, which straddled the city wall, was as "urban" as the inner city demes of Melite, Kydathenaion, Koile, Kollytos, and Skambonidai.[30]

The fourth-century "withdrawal" of philosophy into the garden, both extra- and intra-mural, vividly signifies the gradual deconstruction of the city wall as the physical and ideological safeguard of the Athenian *polis*, a process accelerated, and precipitated, by the encroachments of Philip, Alexander, and, ultimately, Rome.[31] In the eyes of Lucretius, the extreme anthropocentrism of fifth-century Athens, the hubristic privileging of humanity over Nature, had all too easily turned into the most nefarious egocentrism, and Pericles' great city had revealed itself not to be an approximation of utopia but a violent, covetous dystopia. The political upheavals that commenced with the Peloponnesian War and continued into the second century BCE stimulated the desire, vari-

---

[29] Epicurus' will, incidentally, is suspiciously similar to that of Theophrastus; see Diogenes Laertius *Lives of Eminent Philosophers* 10.17 and 5.2.51–57 respectively.

[30] For the quote, see Wycherley 1959:74, and for the character of the urban and sub-urban demes, see Whitehead 1986:26.

[31] On walls as one of the definitive elements of the *polis*, and the waning over time of their importance, see Camp 2000.

ously manifested, to break down the artificial barriers between humanity and Nature. At least for some, in an increasingly impersonal, difficult, cosmopolitan world, it would become a comfort to embrace Nature. Emblematic of the spirit of this new age, the Bacchante, fashioned by the illustrious fourth-century architect and sculptor Skopas of Paros but known to us only through literary description and an Imperial Age copy, is radically different from the staid, self-possessed figures that appear on the Parthenon (Figure 10). Having given herself over entirely to wild Nature, the Bacchante embodies sheer abandon. With head thrown back and lips parted to utter the Bacchic cry, she virtually envelops the spectator in the whirlwind of her frenzied dance. In her image,

> ... stone, while retaining its natural form, seems to escape the natural law that governs stones. What appeared was in actuality an image, but art had transformed the imitation into reality ... The hair was stirred by the wind and was separated to show the quality of each strand ... not only that, but it also showed the hands in action—for she did not brandish the *thyrsos*, but she bore a sacrificial victim and seemed to shout the Bacchic cry, a more piercing symbol of her madness.
>
> Kallistratos *Eikones* 2[32]

Dance, especially the Bacchic dance, is irresistibly "catching."[33] Mimicking entrancing, rhythmic motions observed in the animal kingdom, dance is perhaps the purest, oldest means by which to "cross the boundary between human and animal" and, in a blatantly nostalgic act, recover the "essential biological kinship" that human and animal possess.[34] It is little wonder that devotion to Dionysus in the post-Classical Greek world remained undiminished, spreading instead both in "territory" and intensity. Following in the footsteps of his devotee Alexander, the god returned from Greece to the Near East, where he was readily associated with a host of foreign deities. In the Hellenistic world, his worship experienced a renaissance in the guise of a true mystery religion, complete with initiation and purifying salvation, and from the Hellenistic East, Dionysus would "burst upon Rome" itself, as that city searched for deliverance from seemingly endless socio-political turbulence.[35]

---

[32] This translation of the *Eikones* (*Images*) is derived from Pollitt 1990:97.

[33] Shepard 1996:158.

[34] The quotes have been taken from Shepard 1996:159 and 161 respectively, which is the general source for the comments on dance.

[35] See Turcan 1996:291–327 for Dionysus in the Hellenistic East and Rome. The quote is from page 293.

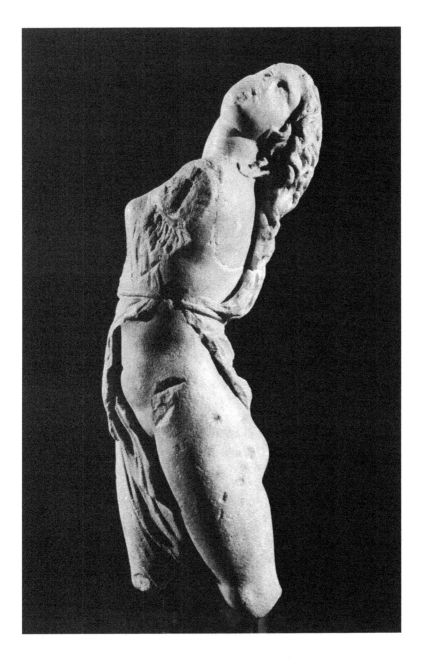

Figure 10. Wild abandon. Dancing Bacchante. Roman marble copy of a mid-4th century BCE original by Skopas. Dresden, Staatliche Kunstsammlungen, Albertinum, inv. no. 133. Photo, © Art Resource.

In Roman Italy Dionysus would come to rest, among other places, in the arms of his bride Ariadne in Pompeii's Villa of the Mysteries.

While the pastoral impulse stirred some in Alexander's new *oikoumenē*, the new "Hellenized" world, to turn to Dionysus, others joined Epicurus whose cult, in turn, "followed" in the footsteps of Dionysus. Owing to the extraordinary missionary zeal of his disciples, Epicurus' doctrines infiltrated and flourished in Asia Minor, Syria, Judaea, Egypt, Italy, and thence, Roman Africa and Gaul. Such was the appeal of shedding irrational, unnecessarily stressful worries and fears in the face of a readily perceptible, fundamental, "physical" association of all animate and inanimate entities in the Cosmos that Epicureanism became "the first world philosophy," accepted by Greek and barbarian alike.[36] Aesthetic pastoralism in Alexander's new world can be detected in a very large spectrum of the pursuits of humanity, including poetry and art, which manifest a pointed increase in attention to landscape or physical setting. As far as poetry is concerned, landscape features most prominently in Alexandrian works, specifically in the verses of Callimachus, Apollonius, and Theocritus.[37] For example, the bucolic *locus amoenus* of Theocritus' seventh *Idyll* has been rendered in a fullness of enchanting detail that beckons the reader with the persuasiveness of a siren song:

> ... αὐτὰρ ἐγών τε καὶ Εὔκριτος ἐς Φρασιδάμω
> στραφθέντες χὠ καλὸς Ἀμύντιχος ἔν τε βαθείαις
> ἀδείας σχοίνοιο χαμευνίσιν ἐκλίνθημες
> ἔν τε νεοτμάτοισι γεγαθότες οἰναρέοισι.
> 135 πολλαὶ δ' ἄμμιν ὕπερθε κατὰ κρατὸς δονέοντο
> αἴγειροι πτελέαι τε· τὸ δ' ἐγγύθεν ἱερὸν ὕδωρ
> Νυμφᾶν ἐξ ἄντροιο κατειβόμενον κελάρυζε.
> τοὶ δὲ ποτὶ σκιαραῖς ὀροδαμνίσιν αἰθαλίωνες
> τέττιγες λαλαγεῦντες ἔχον πόνον· ἁ δ' ὀλολυγών
> 140 τηλόθεν ἐν πυκιναῖσι βάτων τρύζεσκεν ἀκάνθαις·
> ἄειδον κόρυδοι καὶ ἀκανθίδες, ἔστενε τρυγών,
> πωτῶντο ξουθαὶ περὶ πίδακας ἀμφὶ μέλισσαι.
> πάντ' ὦσδεν θέρεος μάλα πίονος, ὦσδε δ' ὀπώρας.
> ὄχναι μὲν πὰρ ποσσί, παρὰ πλευραῖσι δὲ μᾶλα
> 145 δαψιλέως ἁμῖν ἐκυλίνδετο, τοὶ δ' ἐκέχυντο
> ὄρπακες βραβίλοισι καταβρίθοντες ἔραζε·
> τετράενες δὲ πίθων ἀπελύετο κρατὸς ἄλειφαρ.

[36] De Witt 1954:8.
[37] Williams 1991:317.

... but both I and Eukritos to Phrasydamos'
did we turn, and also handsome Amyntas, and on deep
beds of sweet rushes did we recline
and on freshly cut vine leaves, rejoicing.
135　And overhead rustled a multitude
of poplars and elms. And nearby the sacred water
splashed as it flowed down out from a cave of the Nymphs.
And on the shady sprays, smoky brown
cicadas kept busy chirruping. And the tree frog
140　from a distance was croaking in the dense thorns of the
brambles.
Larks and finches were singing, and the turtledove was
cooing,
and about the spring humming bees were flying all around.
Everything smelled of corn harvest most abundant, smelled
of the fruit crop.
Pears by our feet, and by our sides apples
145　were rolling in great abundance. And hanging down
all the way to the ground were branches weighed down with
peaches.
And the four-year-old seal was loosened from the mouths of
the wine jars.

Idyll 7.131–147[38]

At a time when cities were growing in size and number, a degree of nostalgia and yearning for escape to the unspoiled countryside must have contributed to the amplified poetic awareness of the natural world, but it would be an oversimplification to state that it was the only, or even the primary, factor.[39] The Hellenistic poets' "pastoralist" leanings are commingled with a host of distinctly urbane and academic concerns. Alexandrian poetry in particular strives for novelty and polish as well as smallness of scale paired with mythological, ethnographic, geographical, and all other forms of "scientific" erudition. It also evidences a new interest in realism, exoticism, and individualism, both in the emotional life of the individual and in his or her "place" in an increasingly impersonal world. A closer look at the Theocritean *locus amoenus* and the context from which it has been drawn quickly reveals the astonishing compositional complexity and polish of a poem that, at first

---

[38] Gow 1950:166–167 reads "sloes" in place of "peaches" at line 146.
[39] As cautioned by Hutchinson 1988:3.

glance, appears disarmingly simple, accessible, and familiar. Grounded, on the one hand, in "a solid, well-known reality based on the rural economy of Greece and southern Italy," the seventh *Idyll* is surprisingly far-ranging, moving from the small, local Burina spring on Cos to the divine, poetically inspirational Castalian waters of Parnassus, and from wintry Thrace to sweltering Ethiopia.[40] Emotionally, the poem is just as far-reaching, celebrating life and death, love and loss, humanity and divinity, as well as Nature and art. This seemingly "homely," spontaneous singing match between herdsmen in the fields is rendered so realistically that the audience, in a sense, becomes an "eye-witness." However, this proximity is counteracted by a numenistic mysticism and allusive "subversion" that marks the poem as an *epos* 'epic poem' totally unlike any other.[41] Marked textually by Homeric cadences and epithets, the match between Simichidas and the goatherd Lycidas has roots in the meeting between Eumaios and the goatherd Melanthios in the *Odyssey*. But the Homeric encounter, hallowed in its antiquity, will affect the fate and order of a society, while the bucolic singing contest points the way to individual happiness. In the end, the *Idyll*'s manifold thematic tensions, which have by no means been dealt with exhaustively here, dissolve in Nature and in song. In the Theocritean world, Nature is the source of creativity, and through her, humanity may discover "the secrets of their own strengths and weaknesses."[42]

A different sort of landscape altogether may be found in Apollonius' *Argonautica* (*Voyage of the Argo*), touched on briefly here to present a somewhat fuller picture of the representational "scope" of landscape in the hands of Hellenistic poets:

> ἠῶθεν δ', ἀνέμοιο διὰ κνέφας εὐνηθέντος,
> ἀσπασίως ἄκρης Ἀχερουσίδος ὅρμον ἵκοντο.
> ἡ μέν τε κρημνοῖσιν ἀνίσχεται ἠλιβάτοισιν,
> 730 εἰς ἅλα δερκομένη Βιθυνίδα· τῇ δ' ὑπὸ πέτραι
> λισσάδες ἐρρίζωνται ἀλίβροχοι, ἀμφὶ δὲ τῇσιν
> κῦμα κυλινδόμενον μεγάλα βρέμει· αὐτὰρ ὕπερθεν
> ἀμφιλαφεῖς πλάτανιστοι ἐπ' ἀκροτάτῃ πεφύασιν.
> ἐκ δ' αὐτῆς εἴσω κατακέκλιται ἠπειρόνδε
> 735 κοίλη ὕπαιθα νάπη, ἵνα τε σπέος ἔστ' Ἀίδαο

---

[40] Segal 1981:213.

[41] On Theocritus and "epic inversion" or "subversion" as a vital component of the bucolic *epos*, see Halperin 1983:passim. For the inversion/subversion of Homeric epic in particular, see especially pages 217–248.

[42] Segal 1981:226.

ὕλη καὶ πέτρῃσιν ἐπηρεφές, ἔνθεν ἀυτμή
πηγυλίς, ὀκρυόεντος ἀναπνείουσα μυχοῖο,
συνεχὲς ἀργινόεσσαν ἀεὶ περιτέτροφε πάχνην,
οὐδὲ μεσημβριόωντος ἰαίνεται ἠελίοιο.
740 σιγὴ δ᾽ οὔποτε τήνδε κατὰ βλοσυρὴν ἔχει ἄκρην,
ἀλλ᾽ ἄμυδις πόντοιό θ᾽ ὑπὸ στένει ἠχήεντος,
φύλλων τε πνοιῇσι τινασσομένων μυχίῃσιν.
ἔνθα δὲ καὶ προχοαὶ ποταμοῦ Ἀχέροντος ἔασιν,
ὅς τε διὲξ ἄκρης ἀνερεύγεται εἰς ἅλα βάλλων
745 ἠοίην, κοίλη δὲ φάραγξ κατάγει μιν ἄνωθεν·
τὸν μὲν ἐν ὀψιγόνοισι Σοωναύτην ὀνόμηναν
Νισαῖοι Μεγαρῆες, ὅτε νάσσεσθαι ἔμελλον
γῆν Μαριανδυνῶν· δὴ γάρ σφεας ἐξεσάωσεν
αὐτῇσιν νήεσσι, κακῇ χρίμψαντας ἀέλλῃ.
750 τῇ ῥ᾽ οἵγ᾽ αὐτίκα νῆα διὲξ Ἀξερουσίδος ἄκρης
εἰσωποί, ἀνέμοιο νέον λήγοντος, ἔκελσαν.

And at dawn, the wind having been lulled in the darkness,
they arrived full of joy at the inner harbor of the Acherusian
    headland.
It, for its part, soars with steep crags
730 facing the Bithynian sea, and below it rocks,
smooth ones, stand fixed, washed by the sea. And around
    them
the wave roars loudly as it rolls along, but above
wide-spreading planes grow upon the topmost point.
And from it farther inland slopes down
735 a hollow glen beneath, where there is a cave of Hades
by woods and rocks over-arched, whence a breath
icy cold, wafting up from its chill recess
continuously, ever makes congeal a ring of bright-shining
    rime,
nor does it melt in the midday sun.
740 And silence never holds that grim headland,
but rather it murmurs constantly from the roaring sea
and the leaves rustled by the vapors from the cavern's
    depths.
And here too come outpourings of the river Acheron,
which from the headland belches forth, casting into the sea

745　in the east, and a cleft ravine brings it down from above.
　　　And in time afterwards, Sailors' Savior was it called
　　　by the Nisaean Megarians when they were setting out to
　　　　　settle
　　　the land of the Mariandyni. For indeed it saved them
　　　ships and all when they had met a baleful tempest.
750　By this way, straight through the Acherusian headland, their
　　　　　ship did these men
　　　put to shore when the wind had only just fallen.

Argonautica 2.727–751

Thick with plane trees though it may be, the Acherusian headland is anything but a *locus amoenus*. Rather, the deafening roar of the wind-swept sea, the shuddering leaves, and the icy breath issuing forth from the cavern of Hades renders this a *locus horrificus*. The vivid description "create[s] a sense of disquiet and anxiety" in the reader, who, with a shiver, will recall just how close the Argonauts came to meeting their end amidst the Clashing Rocks, at the same time being reminded that the mission as a whole is terribly dangerous, sure to claim many lives.[43] Indeed, even at this stage, the tragic death of Idmon is imminent, this very headland the site of his future burial. Here the landscape creates a mood, assists the plot, and draws the reader in. Again, the reader becomes an eyewitness, experiencing "first hand" the terrors that beset the brave Argonauts. Landscape is clearly still the frame for human action, human actors in this drama being the poet's focus. Instructively, the Acherusian passage closes with an obscure geographic detail: the outfall of the Acheron, the poet writes, was named *Soōnautēs*, Savior of Sailors, by grateful Nisaean Megarians. This grim and awesome wilderness will one day be tamed, its thundering waves drowned out by the urban din produced by the grand city of Heraclea ad Pontum.[44]

As in Hellenistic poetry, the pastoral impulse in Hellenistic art is heavily overlaid with the theoretical, intellectualized concerns of the age; humanity, not Nature, is ultimately *ergon*. Among the primary preoccupations of Hellenistic artists striving for realism was the establishment of a discourse between spectator and subject.[45] In other words, artists tried to find ways to draw the spectator into the subject's psychological and physical universe.

---

[43] Williams 1991:149.
[44] See also Williams 1991:148.
[45] Zanker 2004:83 treats both Hellenistic art and literature. See also Webster 1964:56–177.

This could be achieved not only by selecting emotive subjects but also by enhancing the level of the subject's animation and expressing the space that the figure inhabited. Some of the earliest exemplars of this pictorial attention to landscape are the Alexander Mosaic, or rather the painting upon which it is presumably based, and the famous hunt frieze from the façade of Philip's Tomb at Vergina, both conventionally dated to the second half of the fourth century BCE. The muted palette of the compositions, Alexander's stance, and the inclusion of what appears to be the "same" twisted, weather-beaten tree in both led the Vergina tomb's excavator to assign these works to the same artist, the famed Philoxenos of Eretria, or, at the very least, to "a common atelier."[46] Although these landscapes are vastly more expressive of place than any earlier extant Greek artifact, the pictorial space that contains the subjects is "still shallow and dominated by human inhabitants."[47] This is true also of later works exemplifying the inclusion of landscape features in Hellenistic art: the Telephos Frieze from Pergamon; two reliefs in the Munich Glyptotek, one depicting a scene of sacrifice, the other a "rustic" driving a cow to market; a relief in the British Museum representing Dionysus with his entourage visiting a poet at repose in a courtyard; and the mold-made, terracotta "Homeric Bowls."[48] Returning briefly to the Alexander Mosaic and its limited landscape, what little indication of natural setting exists, a bit of desert sand and a gnarled tree, is nevertheless a terribly important signifier (Figure 11). Specifically, the tree's posture, the disposition of its trunk and limbs, has been observed to mimic that of the fleeing Darius and his charioteer, indicating to the alert viewer that the image is to be read as "a visual rhyme"; the decapitated tree is an Iliadic metaphor for the imminent "death and dismemberment" of the Persian king's empire.[49] This tree does not, however, sympathize with Darius any more than the drooping palm on Exekias' *amphora* 'storage jar' weeps at the imminent death of Ajax. In neither instance is there a hint of pathetic fallacy. In the mosaic, Alexander, descendant of great Achilles, with Medusa, the emblem of Athena and, by extension, of Classical Athens, on his breast, plays out the essence of the Homeric social dream, which, in the form of the *Iliad*, he carried with him on his travels. In a campaign of Herculean

---

[46] Andronikos 1992:118. Cohen 1997:54 is skeptical of this conclusion but still thinks it within the realm of possibility. On the Alexander Mosaic and its relation to what is known of the painterly technique of Philoxenos, see also Bruno 1977:75 and Stewart 1993:123–157 where stylistic, historical, and iconographic observations are synthesized.

[47] Pollitt 1986:192.

[48] These examples are all evaluated by Pollitt 1986:185–209 and by Zanker 2004, who adds works such as the Farnese Bull with its rising mound of rocky sculptural base to the discussion.

[49] Stewart 1993:139–140.

Figure 11. "Arboreal rhyme." Mosaic: Alexander and Darius in battle. From the House of the Faun, Pompeii, ca. 100 BCE, probably after a Greek painting of the 4th century BCE. Naples, Museo Nazionale Archeologico, inv. no. 10020. Photo, © Art Resource.

proportions, he would vanquish both vast expanses of wild Nature and the barbarian, to the Greeks the "effeminate other," an anthropomorphized reflection of what was most threatening in Nature herself. Even after the dimming of Athens' Golden Age, its ideology proved remarkably resilient: it was one of Alexander's goals to spread Athenian culture, not abandon it in exchange for retreat into communion with the wild.

A different, much more extensive treatment of pictorial space may be found in the first-century BCE Nilotic mosaic from Praeneste, which, like the Alexander Mosaic, has been presumed to be a copy, or rather an "adaptation," of a post-Classical painting.[50] The Nilotic mosaic appears to exemplify the sort of landscape or, more literally, "place-painting" that Demetrios the Alexandrian *topographos* 'place-painter' practiced.[51] The character of the mosaic is distinctly cartographic, ethnographic, and zoographic, with equal weight given to the works of Nature and those of humanity. While neither the landscape nor its human inhabitants dominate from a strictly pictorial standpoint, the ubiquity of humanity conveys to the viewer that even the wildest realms have not escaped human encroachment. Even in the case of this mosaic, where the scale of the human actor has been much reduced, Nature remains the *parergonal* frame.

The Hellenistic world was sufficiently urban, academically sophisticated, and removed from the "pure" rural existence to foster a tendency to idealize and romanticize Nature. Still, Nature was generally kept at an arm's length. The Romans, however, did more than open their cities' walls to Nature. They embraced her and held her fast. Nowhere is this truth more apparent than in that most intimate of spaces, the dwelling house. Quite unlike its Classical and Hellenistic Greek counterparts, the Roman house strove to bring its occupants into contact with Nature. While the Greek house functioned as a barrier against the penetration of the natural world, the Roman house was built with an eye towards domesticating it. Interior courtyards were characteristic of both Greek and Roman houses, yet these open spaces were radically different (Figure 12a and b). A visitor to a Greek house would first enter this courtyard and then proceed into one of the rooms clustered around it. A welcome source of air and light, the courtyard would have appeared particularly dramatic if the surrounding structure had an upper story, but the experience of entry could never have roused the sense of awe, mystery, and pleasure that stepping into

---

[50] Cohen 1997:61 argues that the Praeneste mosaic is likely an exemplar of adaptation, and the Alexander Mosaic, by contrast, of stricter copying.

[51] On Demetrios, as well as the Nile mosaic and its relation to the Hellenistic tradition of "chorography" (or *topographia*), map illustration, see Ling 1977 (especially 7 and 14).

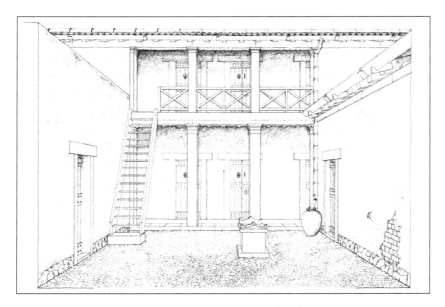

Figure 12a. Nature as "other." House at Olynthos: reconstruction drawing, view into courtyard of house. Drawing after W. Jo Brunner in Wolfram Hoepfner and Ernst-Ludwig Schwander, *Haus und Stadt im klassischen Griechenland* (Munich: Deutscher Kunstverlag, 1994), 98, fig. 76.

Figure 12b. Nature as *ergon*. Peristyle garden, House of the Golden Cupids, Pompeii. Photo, © Art Resource.

a Roman house evoked. Indeed, nearly two thousand years after their destruction by Vesuvius, the spatial experience offered by the houses of Pompeii so affected the twentieth-century Modernist icon, French architect and painter Charles Edouard Jeneret—better known as Le Corbusier—that they became models of particularly effective design in his *Towards a New Architecture*. For Le Corbusier, both a social idealist and architectural utopian, the Pompeiian house was comparable to a soap bubble "perfect and harmonious"; its "exterior ... the result of an interior."[52] Among the houses he singled out was the Casa del Noce (sic), likely the Casa delle Nozze d'Argento, which enthralled his senses with its harmonious rhythms of light and volume and which unambiguously conveyed its intention, the ideological basis of the interior space's constitution. As he stepped through the house door, he was transported to a world of space and light offering escape from what lay beyond its walls:

> Casa del Noce, at Pompeii. Again the little vestibule which frees your mind from the street. And then you are in the Atrium; four columns in the middle (four *cylinders*) shoot up towards the shade of the roof, giving a feeling of force and a witness of potent methods; but at the far end is the brilliance of the garden seen through the peristyle which spreads out this light with a large gesture, distributes it and accentuates it, stretching widely from left to right, making a great space. Between the two is the Tablinum, contracting this vision like the lens of a camera. On the right and on the left two patches of shade—little ones. Out of the clatter of the swarming street, which is for every man and full of picturesque incident, you have entered the house of *a Roman*.

> *Towards a New Architecture* 169

Employing Pompeii and Herculaneum as a basis for generalization, the integration of a garden was an essential ingredient in the success of the Roman house at becoming an urban oasis and providing a locus for respite and reflection. The fact that gardens are to be found almost everywhere in town signifies just how important the garden was to the Pompeiian psyche. Buildings of every size and variety contained them, shops, inns, bath buildings, schools, theaters, and temples included.[53] In fact, it has been remarked that, judging from the excavated area, gardens and cultivated spaces amounted to roughly

---

[52] Le Corbusier 1970:167.
[53] For a detailed discussion of Pompeiian gardens accompanied by an extensive catalog, see Jashemski 1979 and 1993.

seventeen percent of the town's land, nearly the same amount of land as devoted to roads and public squares.[54] In the Pompeiian house, the primacy of the garden asserted itself from the very moment of entry. It became a visual vector that guided the visitor's gaze from the entry through the *atrium* 'entry-court' and beyond the *tablinum* 'library/office' along an axis established by a special feature in the garden such as a fountain or statuette. Moving from the public to the more private spaces in the house, the visitor would still be guided by the garden, beckoned by the sound of water splashing in a fountain and ultimately treated to a sensual feast. Where space allowed for a covered walk, one could stroll around the garden observing the hanging ornaments, aptly called *oscilla*, gently swaying in the breeze as well as a host of wildlife: birds, bees, butterflies, and fish in a basin watched ever so attentively by a cat. Here one might also glimpse a pair of lively pups playing hide-and-seek amid an assortment of statuary: Dionysus and his band of satyrs, Venus at the bath, Mars the erstwhile god of agriculture, herms topped with brightly painted *pinakes* 'tablets', and, lending a bit of philosophical perspective, the godlike Epicurus.[55] The visitor would be enveloped by the sweet scents of lavender, rose, citrus, and thyme in their season, and by a changing spectrum of color supplied by a variety of blossoms, such as marigold, poppy, oleander, cornflower, lily, and periwinkle. At the garden's far end one might recline to dine, converse, and read under the shade of a vine-clad pergola. Even if the weather should turn, the garden would not deny the visitor its various delights, for *triclinia* 'dining rooms' were oriented so as to provide an interesting, even "theatrical," garden view in which painted landscapes playfully mirrored and extended planted compositions or revealed lions hunting in a fictively appended game park. Here Nature is *ergon*, and the *domus*, both its architectural members and its inhabitants, Nature's *parergonal* frame.

The ubiquity of gardens inscribed within extant urban dwellings of Roman Italy is the clear manifestation of a social ideal, a utopian impulse both forward and backward looking. This ideal, succinctly articulated by Martial, is *rus in urbe*, bringing the country landscape into the city.[56] Judging from the comments of Vitruvius and the ground plans of the oldest Pompeiian houses, the "traditional" Italic *domus*, which encompassed within its walls a *hortus* 'kitchen garden' to the rear of the living spaces, evidences an Italic predisposition towards living in close proximity with Nature. Significantly, it was

[54] Conan 1986:349.
[55] The Roman garden is vividly brought to life in Farrar 1998.
[56] *Epigrams* 12.57.21.

a predisposition that manifested itself prior to the arrival of a ready supply of aqueduct-borne water.[57] Still, the old *hortus* is a far cry from a pleasure garden thoroughly integrated into the livng experience (Figure 13). In other words, the traditional Italic house is not representative of a fully developed *rus in urbe* ideal. Rather, this notion of domestic landscape integration stems most immediately from a revolutionary lifestyle development, the cultural phenomenon of the Roman villa that emerged in the first half of the second century BCE but experienced a veritable explosion in the following century. Enriched by foreign conquests as well as by "domestic" opportunities for personal gain, such as failed agricultural reforms, civil war, and proscriptions, wealthy Romans built themselves luxurious country estates that transformed the Italian landscape both physically and spiritually.[58]

Favorite sites for these *villae* were locations on the Tyrrhenian coast from southern Etruria to Campania and the hills in the vicinity of Rome, all places notable for their mild summer climate and splendid views. Here men of means erected *villae maximae ac politissimae*, estates that were extremely large and highly sophisticated, outfitted with Greek or Greek-inspired master-pieces of sculpture, mosaic, and painting.[59] Architectural refinements of the *villae* included exotica such as bedroom antechambers, exercise grounds, changing rooms for bath complexes, covered walkways, aviaries, column-encircled halls, and chambers for storing fruit (*procoetona, palaestram, apody-terion, peristylon, ornithona, peripteron, oporthecen,* Varro *De Re Rustica* 2.prolog 2).[60] Axial symmetry and the visual prominence of the *tablinum* beyond the *atrium*, distinguishing traits of traditional domestic architecture, yielded increasingly to the optical dominance of inscribed Nature; peristyle gardens, as well as "exterior" landscapes that were framed and, accordingly, appropri-ated through a variety of architectural devices, became the intended foci of both public and private spaces, bedrooms, dining rooms, and reception areas alike.[61] On a villa's grounds one might find towers and terraces with walkways built for maximizing views, as well as a variety of water features such as fish-

---

[57] On Pompeiian domestic gardens and their plantings both before and after the construction of the Augustan aqueduct, see Jashemski 1979:16, 32–34, 51–54.

[58] On the evolution of the Roman villa, see D'Arms 1970; McKay 1975; Mielsch 1987; Schneider 1995; Wallace-Hadrill 1994, 1998a, 1998b; and Zanker 1979, 1998.

[59] For the Latin phrase, altered slightly from the original (singular), see Varro *De Re Rustica* 1.13.7. On the villa as a locus for collecting art, see Bartman 1991, Bergmann 1995, Dillon 2000, and Neudecker 1998.

[60] The Latin quotation is from Goetz's 1929 Teubner edition.

[61] On trends in visual axiality, see the important works of Bek 1985 and Jung 1984.

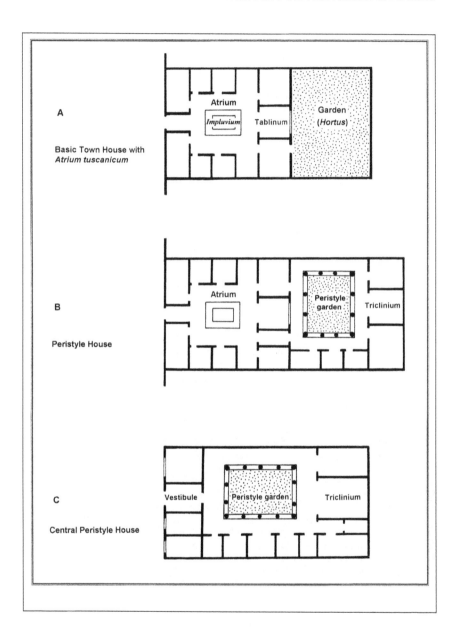

Figure 13. The domestication of Nature. Development of the Roman house. Plans after Linda Farrar, *Ancient Roman Gardens* (Surrey: Sutton Publishing Ltd., 1998), 16.

ponds, fountains, and miniatures of Euripus or Nile flanked by *diaetae*, rooms for dining or relaxing, all set in lushly planted gardens and surrounded by orchards, vineyards, and even hunting *paradeisoi*, enclosed "pleasure parks" modeled on those of the Persian kings, filled with wild boars, gazelles, antelopes, and deer.[62] All of these features and more are attested by the numerous literary descriptions of Roman villas and by physical remains, notably the Villa San Marco and the Villa Arianna at Stabiae, the so-called Villa of Poppaea at Oplontis, the rustic Villa of Publius Fannius Sinistor at Boscoreale, the Villa of Agrippa Postumus at Boscotrecase, and the Villa dei Papiri at Herculaneum.

Overall, the impression persists that the Roman villa afforded its owner and guests luxurious living experientially enhanced by the proximity of the natural environment, yet this impression, however profound or affecting, is but the faintest reflection of the ideological complexity underlying the Roman villa phenomenon. In a culture where the dwelling house had both public and private functions, appearances were everything, and it was of the utmost importance to the elite that their houses unambiguously convey their *dignitas* and *existimatio*, their inherent preeminence and societally determined status.[63] It is little wonder, then, that when material wealth abounded as a result of Rome's expanding territorial dominion, the Roman elite built themselves estates that were "at once a supreme symbol of the individual's power, resources and ability to control the environment and its population, and a place where that power was actively generated through the harnessing of slave and other dependent labour to profitable production."[64] Thus, as befitted the militaristic propensities of their owners, the construction of *villae* was described in the language of dominion. For example, as the poet Statius reports, the villa of Pollius Felix at Surrentum epitomized the victory of *ars* 'art', the Roman equivalent of *tekhnē*, over Nature:

[62] While it has become common practice in works on Roman *villae* to refer to *paradeisoi* as hunting or game parks, the Persian *paradeisos* could nevertheless take a number of forms ranging from orchard and plantation for ornamental trees, or even (in early sources) an enclosure to store produce, to a garden articulated by elaborate water features and pavilions. In other words, as Bremmer 1999 points out, the semantics of "*paradeisos*," a Median loanword introduced into Greek and signifying a walled enclosure, is complex due to the range of the term's application over time. So, for instance, the *paradeisos* is a fragrant Persian garden carefully planted with trees in Xenophon's *Oeconomicus* (*Discourse on Estate Management*) 2.20–25 and a Persian hunting park in Xenophon's *Cyropaedia* (*Education of Cyrus*) 1.3.14 and 8.1.34–38. Meanwhile, one imagines the Babylonian *paradeisos* in which a fever-ridden Alexander sought relief to have been filled with shade trees and cooling waters (Arrian *Anabasis* [*Expedition from Sea to Coast*] 7.25.3), and Lucian (*True History* 2.23) uses "*paradeisos*" to describe Plato's Academy.

[63] On status and the Roman house, see Hales 2003, Howe 2004, Saller 1984, and Wiseman 1987.

[64] Wallace-Hadrill 1998a:43.

30 inde per obliquas erepit porticus arces,
 urbis opus, longoque *domat* saxa aspera dorso.
 qua prius obscuro permixti pulvere soles
 et feritas inamoena viae, nunc ire voluptas;
 qualis, si subeas Ephyres Baccheidos altum
35 culmen, ab Inoo fert semita tecta Lyaeo.
42 ... vix ordine longo
 suffecere oculi, vix, dum per singula ducor,
 suffecere gradus. quae rerum turba! Iocine
45 ingenium an domini mirer prius? haec domus ortus
 aspicit et Phoebi tenerum iubar, illa cadentem
 detinet exactamque *negat dimittere* lucem,
 cum iam fessa dies et in aequora montis opaci
 umbra cadit vitreoque natant praetoria ponto.
50 haec pelagi clamore fremunt, haec tecta sonoros
 ignorant fluctus terraeque silentia malunt.
 his favit natura locis, hic *victa* colenti
 cessit et ignotos docilis *mansuevit* in usus.
 mons erat hic ubi plana vides, et lustra fuerunt,
55 quae nunc tecta subis; ubi nunc nemora ardua cernis,
 hic nec terra fuit: *domuit* possessor, et illum
 formantem rupes *expugnantem*que *secuta*
 gaudet humus. nunc cerne *iugum* discentia saxa
 intrantesque domos *iussum*que *recedere* montem.
60 iam Methymnaei vatis manus et chelys una
 Thebais et Getici *cedat* tibi gloria plectri;
 et tu saxa moves, et te nemora alta sequuntur.

30 From there a colonnade has crawled along the summits,
 a veritable city construction, and with its long roof-line,
   dominates the jagged rocks.
 Where earlier was sunshine mixed with blinding dust
 and the unlovely wilderness of the path, now it is a delight to
   walk.
 It is just as if you should climb Bacchic Ephyre's lofty
35 peak, a covered footway leads from Lyaean Ino.
42 ... For the long array scarcely
 have my eyes sufficed as I am led from one thing to another,
 scarce my steps. What a mass of stuff! Is it the site's
45 or the master's genius that I should marvel at first? To the

east does this part of the house
face and to Phoebus' early rays; his setting does that part
hold prisoner and *refuses to release* his spent light
when the day is already tired, and over the ocean does the
    dark mountain's
shadow fall, and the palace floats on the glassy deep.
50   These chambers groan with the clash of the sea, these others
    of the sounding waves
are ignorant and prefer instead the silence of the land.
Upon these Nature has bestowed her favors; here, *vanquished*
has she *yielded* and, docile, *has become tamed* to unwonted
    tasks.
A mountain was here where you see flat ground; beasts' lairs
    were
55   what you now find as buildings. Where now you see tall
    forests,
here there was no land; the owner *has won dominion*, and in
    him
as he *sculpts* the crags and *overpowers* them, *obediently*
does the earth rejoice. Now behold the rocks learning to
    endure the *yoke*,
and the buildings forging their way in and the mountain
    ordered to retreat.
60   Now let the hands of Methymna's bard and the one and only
    lyre
from Thebes and the fame of the Thracian plectrum *yield* to
    you;
you too move stones, you too do lofty forests follow.

Silvae 2.2.30–62[65]

The villa has overpowered Nature and has demanded acquiescence in its dominion, while Nature, utterly vanquished, has retreated from her position, ultimately assuming the yoke of her new master. Pollius, the villa's owner, is a second Orpheus readily bending Nature to his sway.

By subjugating the wilderness of Italy, the Roman elite could effectively become masters of their own "small" kingdoms, thus rivaling the Hellenistic

---

[65] Deviating from Courtney's Oxford edition, I have substituted *M*'s *intrantes* for Rothstein's *intrantem* at *Silvae (Grove of Poems)* 2.2.59.

dynasts whom they, increasingly exposed to the splendors of the Hellenistic East, were presumably motivated to emulate.[66] Although the degree of influence upon the Roman villa of Hellenistic palaces and estates remains a matter of contention, it is clear that certain aspects of the *villae* have Hellenistic precedents.[67] Literary and archaeological evidence has revealed that Hellenistic palaces, like Roman *villae*, had statue-filled gardens in peristyle courts, pavilions, pools, *nymphaea* 'grottoes', hunting *paradeisoi*, and promenades in parklike grounds, thus manifesting a combination of Greek with Near Eastern and Egyptian influences that, in their pleasurable, "exotic" luxury, approximated the estates' owners to divinity.[68] A favorite comparison for the Roman villa and its grounds is the Ptolemaic *basileia* 'palace' in Alexandria. This royal property, which reportedly covered a quarter of the total area of the city, contained not only a palace complex nestled amidst spacious parks but also a theater, a palaestra, a gymnasium, botanical and zoological gardens, a number of temples and sanctuaries, and the famous Museion.[69] Doubtless, the Hellenistic East provided models for palatial estates in architecturally articulated, landscaped settings. Additionally, the vast agricultural, or "productive," holdings of Hellenistic potentates and nobles should be viewed as parallels to the Roman villa's orchards, vineyards, fisheries, oyster beds, aviaries, rabbit farms, and other manifestations of *pastio villatica* 'farmstead pasturage'.[70] The Roman country estates acted as "centres for the management of the unique resources of the uncultivated environment."[71]

Villae, then, were vehicles by which to display one's power and regal wealth, but they were also places in which to showcase one's taste in art, erudition, and general cultural sophistication. Hellenistic palaces presumably inspired villa owners to outfit their estates with gymnasia, temples, and the like, but Romans certainly also viewed the inclusion of such elements

---

[66] Similarly, Purcell 1987.

[67] For instance, Caroll-Spillecke 1992b:166–175 and Schneider 1995:41 downplay Hellenistic influences while Lauter-Bufe 1975 and Nielsen 1999 (especially 164–171) present Hellenistic estates and palaces as essential influences. Lauter 1998 enumerates known parallels but points out that viewed *in toto*, the Roman villa phenomenon is without Graeco-Macedonian precedent.

[68] On the amalgamation of Greek, Egyptian, and Persian influences in Roman villas and gardens, see Carroll 2003 (especially 54). On Persian gardens specifically, see Bremmer 1999, Kawami 1992, and Moynihan 1979, and for the ornate water features and pavilions of the palatial gardens at Pasargadae, see Stronach 1994. On Egyptian gardens, see Hugonot 1992.

[69] On the Alexandrian *basileia* and the structures it may have contained, see Nielsen 1999:130–138 and Hoepfner and Schwander 1994:235–255.

[70] See Purcell 1995 and Mielsch 1987:32–35.

[71] Purcell 1995:158.

as appropriations of Greek public architecture in form and function, albeit "privatized."[72] In particular, the Roman villa assumed the role of the Greek gymnasium, complete with its statuary and gardens, thus becoming the locus for philosophical discussion as well as for other scholarly or artistic pursuits. So cultured was villa life that the Younger Pliny asserted, "one would think [the owner] were living in Athens, not in a villa" (*Athenis vivere hominem, non in villa putes. Epistles* 7.25.4). In any event, the Roman *villae*'s strong Greek affiliations exposed their owners to censure by traditional moralists—ironically including those who themselves enjoyed such luxuries—as *philograeci* 'lovers of things Greek' corrupted by that *Graia licentia* 'Greek dissoluteness' to which Roman *gravitas* was so utterly opposed.

Quite ingeniously, however, the Roman villa contained within its fabric the means by which to counter charges of excessive Hellenizing luxury, presenting itself as a repository of the hallowed *mos maiorum*, morally superior ancestral tradition.[73] As Varro remarks, life in the country is not only older than life in the city, it is inherently better, for the country has divine, and the city human origins.[74] Specifically, city life resulted from the application of human *artes*, technical and artistic skills. He goes on to say that "all the arts are said to have been discovered in Greece" (*artes omnes dicantur in Graecia ... repertae, De Re Rustica* 3.1.4). From a Varronian perspective, traditional Roman rusticity was superior to the technological urbanity of the Greeks. What is so remarkable about the Roman villa is that it presented itself as, and *was*, a unique blend of the "rustic" and the urban; it was a locus of agricultural activity containing a polished, urbane residence. As Cato's treatise on agriculture discloses, the villa was conceived as having a *pars rustica* 'rustic part' and a *pars urbana* 'urbane part': "The *pars rustica* parades the 'practicalities' and productivity that the 'true' villa is about. The *pars urbana* is a supplement, not obstructing the rustic practicalities but adding 'something more delicate,' urbanity in a rustic setting."[75] In the Italian countryside, these large estates were referred to as *villae urbanae* 'urban villas', and within the city of Rome,

---

[72] For example, Dickmann 1997:123, Carroll-Spillecke 1989:49–65 and 1992b:63–65, Schneider 1995:39, and D'Arms 1970:15.

[73] See Wallace-Hadrill 1998a on the multi-faceted cultural symbolism of the Roman villa.

[74] *Cum duae vitae traditae sint hominum, rustica et urbana, quidni, Pinni, dubium non est quin hae non solum loco discretae sint, sed etiam tempore diversam originem habeant. antiquior enim multo rustica, quod fuit tempus, cum rura colerent homines neque urbem haberent ... quod divina natura dedit agros, ars humana aedificavit urbes, cum artes omnes dicantur in Graecia intra mille annorum repertae, agri numquam non fuerint in terris qui coli possint. neque solum antiquior cultura agri, sed etiam melior, De Re Rustica* 3.1.1–4. Text from Goetz's Teubner edition 1929:113–114.

[75] Wallace-Hadrill 1998a:51.

they were called *horti* 'gardens'.[76] The villa perfectly blended the Greek and the Roman, the rustic and the urbane, Nature and art.[77] It was an ideal signifier representing an ideal reflected even in its nomenclature.

The multi-faceted opportunities for display offered by the villa phenomenon cannot, however, account for its magnitude, either for the fact that so many *villae* were crowded along the Bay of Naples, "that famed crater of luxurious delights," or for the fact that even modest homeowners in the town of Pompeii felt compelled to emulate Roman villa culture. In this emulation they went so far as to enlarge areas dedicated to the garden at the expense of the *atrium* complex that once functioned as domestic core, to furnish gardens with aqueduct-supplied water in preference to latrines, to refurbish peristyle gardens before living quarters after the earthquake of 62 CE, and to decorate their walls with illusionistically painted prospects and floriferous, artfully designed naturescapes.[78] Could the reason for the villa's popularity simply have been demonstrative fashionability?

The answer to this questions lies in the essential difference between the Roman villa and the Hellenistic palace, which, not coincidentally, is also a fundamental point of divergence between the Pompeiian house and the Greek house, Classical and Hellenistic. That difference, simply put, is the obsessive integration of Nature in the domestic environment on the part of the Romans. It is the difference between "domination" and "domestication," which share a linguistic heritage yet describe dissimilar conditions. "Domination" conveys a sense of violent repression or restraint and mastery, while "domestication," predicated on domination, results in the integration of the "subject" in the *domus*, household, of the agent. In the Greek world, humanity remains *ergon*

---

[76] On the use of *horti* as designating an urban estate complete with garden, I follow the Elder Pliny's application of the term (*iam quidem hortorum nomine in ipsa urbe delicias agros villasque possident. Primus hoc instituit Athenis Epicurus oti magister. Usque ad eum moris non fuerat in oppidis habitari rura. Natural History* 19.50–51.). By "urban" I refer to the area both within the Servian Wall and in the "urban" *suburbium*. Purcell 2001 cautions that *horti* are more properly "peri-urban" than "urban" estates, appearing first on the perimeter of Rome, on the urban periphery, but he does acknowledge their appropriation of the old city wall. This appropriation would, in any event, make them an urban phenomenon.

[77] On the blending of nature and art to achieve an ideal, see Bergmann 2002.

[78] For the persuasive argument that the villa provided the inspiration for architectural and decorative developments in Pompeiian houses, see Zanker 1979 and 1998. Zanker 1998:136–137 does, however, believe that what is described here as the domestication of Nature in Roman houses is a direct result of Hellenistic influences, albeit taken in the Roman world to an extreme, the motivation for which extreme is not addressed. The colorful description of the Bay of Naples as *crater ille delicatus* 'that famous crater of luxurious delights' stems from Cicero's *Epistulae Ad Atticum* (*Letters to Atticus*) 2.8.2.

and Nature *parergonal* frame. In the Roman world, where Nature is framed by the *domus*—by the application of *ars*—the situation is ultimately reversed. The domestication of Nature is most readily apparent in the creation of interior garden spaces that were experientially accessible and visually assertive from almost every quarter of the dwelling. The tremendous value of plant life, and the degree to which it was privileged in the Roman house, may be gathered from archaeological sources as well as from any number of literary "anecdotes." These last include accounts of Caesar planting a house's *atrium* with a plane tree subsequently allowed to grow so large that its branches extended over the entire structure and of Vopiscius building his villa around an existing tree that "rose up through the roof and beams to the clear air above."[79] Vopiscius approached the tree occupying the site of his future house very differently from Odysseus, valuing the preservation of the tree's awesome natural force rather than its transformation through the application of "art" into a domestic furnishing, one of the utilitarian objects setting the stage for the human drama.

The domestication of Nature is palpable not only in horticultural tendencies, but also in other aspects of Roman domestic life, for example the keeping of animals. The Romans kept familiar pets, namely dogs, cats, birds, and exotic fish, in addition to creatures such as eels and deer which, together with birds and fish, doubled as part of the villa's industry of market production.[80] The keeping of pets reminds humanity of the communality of life on the planet, crucially aiding in our subconscious, biologically driven "quest for instinctive origins."[81] If animals in the wild are "mediators between us and plants, the rocks and suns around us, the rest of the universe," then forming an intimate relationship with an animal brought into the home is the first step in recognizing and profiting, intellectually and emotionally, from such mediation.[82] Domestic animals, so much a part of human civilization, "are vestiges and fragments of deep human respect for animals, whose abundance dazzled us in their many renditions of life, helping us to know ourselves by showing all that we had not become."[83] Such realizations provide entirely new interpretive possibilities for allusions, both literary and artistic, to the Orpheus myth

---

[79] The quotation is from Statius' *Silvae* 1.3.60, and both anecdotes are collected in Bergmann 2002:93n25.

[80] On the place of animals in Roman life, see Toynbee 1973, particularly page 16 regarding animals kept as pets.

[81] Shepard 1996:161.

[82] Shepard 1996:152.

[83] Shepard 1996:151.

in association with the Roman villa and house. Pollius Felix being compared to Orpheus; the latter appearing on Pompeiian garden walls; and a slave, swarmed by stags, boars, and other creatures of the wild, playing the part of that charmed musician to entertain guests in Q. Hortensius' *paradeisos*, all certainly suggest both imperious and Hellenizing affiliations, mythological and mystic.[84] The figure of Orpheus, however, also embodies an inversion of that stage in remotest antiquity when humanity was willing to learn from the animal kingdom, emulating both their songs and movements. Armed with a tool learned from animals, Orpheus is able to lure them back into proximity, and accordingly primeval unity, with the human.

Finally, the extremity of the Roman desire to embrace the natural world may also be felt in the utter obsession with the creation of framed views of wild Nature, whereby the visually inscribed landscape in itself became a garden. Few extant descriptions of a villa lack some reference to the view or views, while furnishings are generally overlooked.[85] Such was the view's importance that bitter enmities ensued between neighbors over blocked or ruined prospects.[86] For instance, Seneca reports that one man's refusal to remove an offending plane tree prompted his enraged neighbor to retaliate by burning both the offending party's tree and house, and Clodius purportedly threatened Q. Seius, who had refused to sell Clodius his house on the Palatine, with the obstruction of the latter's view.[87] What appears to have fascinated the Romans was not so much a sweeping panorama—though this was certainly highly valued—as a carefully orchestrated, architecturally framed view that not only conveyed a sense of order and variety but also suggested the framed landscape's close integration into the experience of dwelling.[88] Classic examples are provided by the Younger Pliny, who extols a certain room in his Laurentine villa with windows offering views of the sea at his feet, of villas at his back, and forests at his head (*a pedibus mare, a tergo villae, a capite silvae; tot facies locorum totidem fenestris et distinguit et miscet*. 'At one's feet the sea, at one's back country estates, at one's head forests; as many views of different places as it separates and blends in its windows.' *Epistles* 2.17.21). Pliny also points to

---

[84] Pollius Felix is compared to Orpheus in Statius' *Silvae* 2.2.60–62 cited above. Orpheus and a host of exotic animals are depicted in a fresco on the west wall of the garden in the House of Orpheus at Pompeii (VI. 14, 20). The slave's impersonation of Orpheus is recorded by Varro *De Re Rustica* 3.13.3. With the word "mystic," I am alluding to Orphism.

[85] As noted by Schneider 1995:84.

[86] Bergmann 1991:60–66 and 1992:34–42.

[87] These examples are collected in Schneider (1995:85), the first from Seneca *Controversiae* (*Disputations*) 5.5, the second from Cicero *De Domo Sua* (*Regarding His Own House*) 115.

[88] On the preference of framed prospects, see Bergmann 1991 (especially 64).

a dining room that extends to the water's edge, looking out not onto a single vast expanse of ocean but, by means of some artful fenestration, onto three separate seas (*quasi tria maria prospectat*. '... looks out at three seas, so to speak.' *Epistles* 2.17.5). In the Roman villa, framed views of the "exterior" landscape thus complemented carefully orchestrated views of interior garden spaces.

The villa owners' taste for prospects was not, however, limited to "real" architecturally framed views of garden spaces but, in a most interesting development, came to include illusionistically painted faux vistas as well. The earliest identifiable style of painted decoration on Roman walls, the so-called First (Pompeiian) or Masonry Style, is characterized by the emulation of ashlar block work in paint and modeled stucco, complete with decorative veneers and ornate moldings.[89] Based on a structural reality, this style of painting served not only to embellish but also to solidify the wall visually; it was a form of literal illusion. Around 80 BCE the Masonry Style was overshadowed by another, the Second or Architectural Style, in which surfaces literally impenetrable were illusionistically pierced. Armed with painterly devices such as shading, highlighting, and linear perspective, all producing realistic effects, painters in the new style demanded that viewers suspend belief, creating the sensation of being drawn "out" into a landscape variously framed by architectural members. At first, all that might be revealed was a glimpse of sky beyond a screen wall, but later, these illusionistically painted surfaces exhibited elaborate, wall-to-wall vistas of *tholoi* 'circular buildings', grand colonnades, and grottoes. Among the most stunning of the extant examples of Second Style painting is the east wall of *Oecus* 15, a dining or reception room, in the Villa of Poppaea at Oplontis, which depicts a shrub and tree-filled sacred garden dominated by a gleaming bronze tripod (Figure 14). The garden, whose ornate iron gate stands alluringly ajar, is enclosed by a two-tiered peristyle colonnade and is framed by a row of columns "projecting" into the viewer's space. It has been argued that garden vistas such as this, which account for a significant number of the exemplars of the Architectural Style, resulted from the Roman

---

[89] The division of the distinct phases of Roman/Pompeiian fresco painting into four styles (named First, Second, Third, and Fourth Style, respectively) is based on the pioneering work of Mau 1882, and I am adhering to the traditional scheme within this argument. The most accessible and comprehensive recent work on Roman painting remains that of Ling 1991, and Leach's provocative reassessment (2004) of the Pompeiian styles and their "conventional" chronological limits, should not be overlooked. Laidlaw 1985 is still the standard work on the First Style specifically. Clarke 1991:31–77 summarizes recent debates regarding dating shifts of the four styles. Remarks in these pages on the utopics of Roman fresco painting, particularly garden painting, reiterate but also expand upon and re-direct my previous discussion in Giesecke 2001.

Figure 14. Refuge of the sacred garden. Fresco: Second Style prospect. Oplontis, Villa of Poppaea, Oecus 15, ca. 50 BCE. Author's photo.

elite's desire to appropriate aspects of Hellenistic Greek architecture and decor, either public or palatial, for the purposes of self-display, the augmentation of one's public and private persona.[90] Others have argued that the archi-

[90] On Second Style prospects as a vehicle for self-display, see Ehrhardt 1991, and, for a lengthy discussion of the scholarship on this issue as well as the question of Hellenistic influences, architectural, compositional, and "technical," see Tybout 1989.

tectural forms depicted are Roman and not Hellenistic Greek, representative of the elite's fascination with building, specifically with constructing monuments to their exquisite taste and vast resources in every available medium.[91] All of this is doubtless true to some degree, but the fact remains that the characteristic scheme within the Second Style is the prospect, not infrequently a garden prospect, framed by architectural members.[92] Through such painted prospects, Nature inscribed made its presence rather dramatically felt even on the villa's interior walls, on the walls of bedrooms, reception rooms, and dining rooms alike.

The domestication of Nature in the Roman villa, both the extra-urban *villa urbana* and the (intra-)urban *horti*, went far beyond simply providing the means for display of wealth and power; it created a "natural" milieu conducive to physical and mental recuperation from the stresses of urban politics and the difficulties of urban life, such as oppressive summer heat, crowds thronging the streets, and unsanitary conditions. In the Roman world, villa gardens, complete with the deep shade of spreading planes, provided settings for philosophical reflection, duplicating the *locus amoenus* of Plato's *Phaedrus.*[93] By mingling the amenities of the natural world with the benefits of urbanism, the Roman villa became the true successor of Epicurus' Garden. As an urbanized "country" retreat conducive to reflection on the urban condition and the place of humanity in the universe, the villa became synonymous with *otium*, leisure and "withdrawal," though business and politics also had their place within villa grounds.[94] Why the villa and the ideology behind it caught on amongst the members of the elite is not difficult to understand. What could be more ideal than the ultra-soft primitivism, a lifestyle of elegance and leisure rooted in a hallowed agricultural past, that villa life embodied?

Roman villa culture and its distinctive blend of *rus* and *urbs* was not, however, exclusively pursued by the elite: the villa phenomenon had a profound effect on the (re)configuration and decoration of houses owned by persons of lesser means in towns such as Herculaneum and Pompeii. The explanation for the transformation of villa culture from an elite to a much

---

[91] See Kuttner 1998.

[92] My view of what constitutes a garden, namely any inscribed landscape (inscribed by the erection of "barriers" or simply by human "use"), is more liberal than most. Herein I essentially follow Hunt 2000 (especially 1–30). As regards the presentation of Second Style prospects as garden paintings, see also Kuttner 1999.

[93] Cicero *De Oratore* (*On the Orator*) 1.7.28.

[94] For detailed discussions of the manifold resonances of the Roman villa, see D'Arms 1970 and 1998, Frazer 1992, Littlewood 1984, and Purcell 1996.

more widespread "social" phenomenon has everything to do with the sense of security and contentment that the garden, Nature inscribed, has to offer. It is far from coincidental that Epicureanism became extraordinarily popular in Italy at the very moment the garden asserted itself as a ubiquitous presence in Roman domestic architecture. The garden, both the Epicurean Garden and the domesticated landscape, provided a welcome refuge at a time of grievous social and political crisis that ironically issued from the Republic's most notable military triumphs, the destruction of Carthage and Corinth in the middle of the second century BCE. Military triumph brought with it not only prestige and power for the State but also a ready supply of slave labor "employed" at the expense of native Romans and Italians, the replacement of peasant husbandry by capitalist farming, and the emergence of an increasingly wealthy equestrian class that resented more and more the monopoly of political prerogative by the Senatorial order. The gap between rich and poor grew ever wider, and Italian allies clamored for the benefits of Roman citizenship. The new Roman Republic had outgrown its constitution. The conflicts that arose resulted in civil war, the final phase of which played out in the struggle between the republican party, backed by Caesar's heir Octavian, and Mark Antony, Caesar's erstwhile ally and consular colleague. The fall of Antony brought with it the fall of the Republic.[95] In this protracted period of crisis lay the seeds of refuge in the garden as a utopian ideal. Thus it was that the wish of a few became the dream of many.

Rus in urbe, manifested specifically in the domestication of Nature, remained a utopian ideal in the Roman world, but necessarily evolved to suit changes in the realm of politics. Not surprisingly, this ideal underwent its most dramatic adjustment in the course of Rome's own most dramatic reconfiguration, that from Republic to Empire at the hands of Augustus. In the wake of the Battle of Actium, which had purportedly put an end to decades of civil strife, the mood in Rome, particularly among the most wealthy and powerful, was not one of unadultered optimism, for "they saw the civil war and all the other calamities as a consequence of complete moral collapse," itself resulting from a by now deep-seated moral degeneration from which Rome could not hope to recover in the mere blink of an eye.[96] In this climate, Octavian had to tread carefully as he, as an "individual," maneuvered to keep control of the republican constitution he had sworn to save. Accordingly, he instituted a program

---

[95] For lengthier accounts (summarized here) of conditions leading to the collapse of the Republic, see Meier 1990 and Syme 1939.

[96] Zanker 1998:101.

to restore the Republic and to remedy the causes for its decay, "a program to heal Roman society" focusing on the "renewal of religion and custom, *virtus*, and the honor of the Roman people."[97] As part of this initiative, the "August" Octavian proposed legislation that would promote the solidity of the family by imposing penalties for extra-marital relations and rewarding procreation in wedlock. The old Roman virtue of *pietas* 'piety/dutifulness', which entailed devotion not only to family but also to the state and the gods, appropriately became a catchword for the revitalization of the old order.

The villa phenomenon, which combined politically motivated, Hellenizing ostentation with the opportunity for retreat into a life in tune with Nature akin to that of Rome's rural ancestry, provided the Augustan regime with some very interesting challenges and opportunities. In the new atmosphere of traditionally framed moral regeneration, neither personal ambition nor "Epicurean" apolitical withdrawal could be deemed appropriate. It is little wonder then that, as Suetonius reports, Augustus preferred to adorn his villas with seemingly "artless," natural wonders such as terraces and groves as well as with antique "curiosities," such as enormous animal bones and weapons used by the heroes, rather than with costly statues and paintings.[98] The First Citizen of the New Republic needed to appear unpretentious and unassuming, though he owned villas at Capreae, Surrentum, Pausilypon, Baiae, and Nola and certainly participated fully in the villa phenomenon. Therefore, his house on the Palatine, albeit prominently placed adjacent to the Hut of Romulus and contiguous to the Temple of Apollo, was relatively modest, particularly in comparison with the scope of the later imperial palaces. Further, Augustus was not only wary of appropriating land occupied by private houses for such schemes as his forum, but he also recognized the benefit of providing the city's population with public parks. So, for instance, a considerable space around his mausoleum was transformed into "a far-flung public garden, with varied trees and splendid walks."[99] The Augustan approach to the Roman villa's amenities was accordingly one of calculated restraint, and, in a savvy political move, the experience of *rus in urbe* was actively made accessible to the entire population of Rome.

Most interesting of all, however, was the shift in prevalent decorative schemes for walls and the emergence of a new style of fresco painting, the Third, that eclipsed the dramatic prospects so fashionable in the last decades

---

[97] Zanker 1998:101.
[98] *Augustus* 72.3.
[99] Beard 1998:25.

of the Republic. Vitruvius, for one, was horrified by the new style, which replaced realistically depicted architectural elements with structurally impossible, nonsensical, pseudo-architectural monstrosities:

> sed haec, quae ex veris rebus exempla sumebantur, nunc iniquis moribus inprobantur. nam pinguntur tectoriis monstra potius quam ex rebus finitis imagines certae: pro columnis enim struuntur calami striati, pro fastigiis appagineculi cum crispis foliis et volutis, item candelabra aedicularum sustinentia figuras, supra fastigia eorum surgentes ex radicibus cum volutis teneri plures habentes in se sine ratione sedentia sigilla, non minus coliculi dimidiata habentes sigilla alia humanis, alia bestiarum capitibus.

> But these, which were created in imitation of Reality, are now rejected due to our perversion of tastes and ways. For walls are painted with monstrosities rather than truthful representations of definite things: thus in place of columns, fluted reeds appear as structural elements, and in place of pediments decorative attachments adorned with curled and twisting foliage, and also candelabra supporting images of shrines, and atop their roofs clusters of thin stalks and volutes shooting up from their roots [and] in which, quite in defiance of logic, are nestled tiny figures, and frequently too, split tendrils harboring figures, some with human and others with animal heads.

> *De Architectura* 7.5.3[100]

In schemes of the new style, large-scale prospects were eliminated, reasserting the wall as an impenetrable surface. The viewer was thereby denied what might be construed as a "quasi-Epicurean," fictive opportunity for retreat into a garden framed by the architectural accoutrements of demonstrative luxury.[101] In place of a beckoning prospect, the viewer was presented instead with a scheme replicating a *pinacothece*, a gallery displaying framed panel paintings on its walls. One could conceivably argue that the Second Style's large windows into the world beyond were merely minimized, but there is no

---

[100] The text is from Krohn's Teubner edition (1912:159–160) with the exception of the following: *pro fastigiis appagineculi* following *calami*, placed by Krohn after volutes; *plures* in place of *flores*; and *dimidiati* in place of *dimidiata*. These deviations from Krohn's edition are more in keeping with the manuscript tradition.

[101] The phrase "quasi-Epicurean" is employed by Wallace-Hadrill 1998b and has been adapted to this argument. See also Beyen 1938:13ff, Borbein 1975, and Wesenberg 1985 on Epicurean associations of the Second Style prospect.

Figure 15a. Pastoral distancing. Fresco: sacro-idyllic landscape. From Boscotrecase, red cubiculum. Naples, Museo Nazionale Archeologico, inv. no. 147501. Author's photo.

mistaking the "panels" at the center of a Third Style wall with a window onto an "accessible" landscape, even if it *is* a landscape that dominates the picture field.[102] There is a clearly perceptible distance between the viewer and the new landscapes; they are alluring but ultimately impenetrable.

Among the best-known Augustan landscape "panels" are those that once adorned the red bedroom, *cubiculum* 16, in the Villa of Agrippa Postumus at Boscotrecase, a villa that yielded what have been judged "the finest achievements of the early Third Style" (Figure 15a and b).[103] All three landscape panels

[102] See also von Blanckenhagen 1962:31.
[103] Ling 1991:55.

Figure 15b. Pastoral distancing: detail. Boscotrecase fresco. Photo, courtesy of the Museo Nazionale Archeologico.

found in this bedroom share a common theme: they represent a specific form of garden, the sacred grove. These sacred gardens, tantalizingly suspended "in" an unnervingly depthless field of white, consist of one or more trees as well as the shrines and votive statuary erected around them. Somewhat removed from the centrally located groves are clusters of buildings that have variously been interpreted as "modern" and ancient, urban and rustic, secular and sacred, Greek and Roman. Unlike the typical Second Style prospect, these gardens are populated by an array of small figures, male and female, adult and child, goatherds and shepherds, some bearing offerings, others resting in the shade and tranquility of their particular *locus amoenus*. Such figures had appeared on Second Style walls, but generally less prominently, in monochromatic friezes or *pinakes*, illusionistically rendered tiny panel paintings perched on the architectural members framing a grand prospect.[104] They had also appeared, arrestingly so, amidst Odysseus and his men in the Odyssey Frieze, which is, in fact, a Second Style prospect. There, the pastoral figures, in and through whom past and present intersect, invited the viewer to join Odysseus in shaping a new world in an Italian landscape. At Boscotrecase, however, the viewer, distanced by the ambiguous spatiality of the landscape, is forced into the role of spectator. In other words, retreat into the sacred garden is not an option. Yet the spectator *is* invited to reflect on the contemporary resonance of the sacro-idyllic pastoral scenes, on the Augustan effort to revive not only the sacred places but also the religious sensibilities of a bygone era.[105] In these figures, the spectator could find models for *pietas*, a moral life grounded in ancestral tradition.

Pastoral figures play a similar part in the landscapes from another Boscotrecase bedroom, *cubiculum* 19. These landscapes are mythological rather than sacro-idyllic, and their chief means of distancing the viewer is the combination of fathomless background, vivid blue-green in this instance, with "fantastic" subject matter rendered in a continuous narrative, each landscape comprising multiple episodes of the myth portrayed.[106] The specific myths depicted are the rescue of Andromeda at the hands of Perseus and the wooing of Galatea by the Cyclops Polyphemos, both myths rendered in settings that contain elements shared with the sacro-idyllic scenes. Most striking are the

---

[104] Von Blanckenhagen 1962:23–30 provides a catalog of Second Style predecessors to the Boscotrecase landscapes. To this should be added the landscapes from the Villa of Poppaea at Oplontis, for which see Clarke 2000. On the sacred grove in Roman painting, see Bergmann 1992, which deeply influenced my thinking.

[105] See Silberberg-Peirce 1980 on the "politics" of the sacro-idyllic images.

[106] On mythological landscapes generally, see Dawson 1965.

parallels existing between the Polyphemos panel and the sacro-idyllic land-scape from the red bedroom's north wall: a rocky "island" dominated by a votive column and accessed by a curving bridge, a statuette-topped altar, and a flock of milling goats. In place of the red room's herdsman, however, the mythological panel substitutes a pipe-playing Polyphemos, as dedicated and competent a herdsman as any. Because he is presented in Theocritean guise, engaged in a distinctly anti-Odyssean activity, the Cyclops, like the staffage of the sacred groves, has become a figure at once emotionally accessible and elusive. If the pastoral life and the pipe of Pan can tame and humanize even the bestial Polyphemos, then the viewer who embraces traditional, "rustic" values and acknowledges his or her place in the the animate world will like-wise tame the beast within.[107]

The Augustan age saw not only the conception of sacro-idyllic and myth-ological landscape panels but also the birth of the garden painting proper.[108] The earliest and perhaps most stunning example of such garden painting stems from the villa built for the emperor's wife in the village of Rubra, now known as the Villa of Livia at Prima Porta (Figure 16).[109] The garden painting adorned the walls of a rectangular chamber that may have been used for dining. As it covered the room's walls from floor to ceiling, the painting effec-tively dissolved the walls, transforming the space into "a kind of open-sided pavilion set in a paradise forest."[110] Though preternaturally lush and dense, this landscape is no primeval forest; rather, a subtle, carefully calculated sense of balance and order, achieved by rhythmic planting and the application of borders, tempers its apparent wild abundance. As in the Boscotrecase land-scapes, a compositional mechanism asserts itself, frustrating the viewers' inevitable longing to lose themselves in this landscape. As a result, this too is an "Augustan-didactic" landscape, not a landscape of quasi-Epicurean with-drawal. In the Prima Porta garden, the viewer's "barrier" is not so much its low wall, which is a common feature of the Roman garden, as the fact that this garden, realistically rendered though it may be, is unreal, a transparently idealized fiction, both in medium and iconographic content. A garden of such diversity could never, except in the artificial conditions of a greenhouse, trans-

---

[107] On the didactic potential and programmatic content of Roman painting, see Bergmann 1999, Thompson 1960/1961, and Wirth 1983. On decorative programs in the Roman house generally, see Clarke 1991.

[108] For a survey of garden painting, see Michel 1980.

[109] A complete treatment of this garden painting is Gabriel 1955, which served as a basis for descriptive material here.

[110] Ling 1991:150.

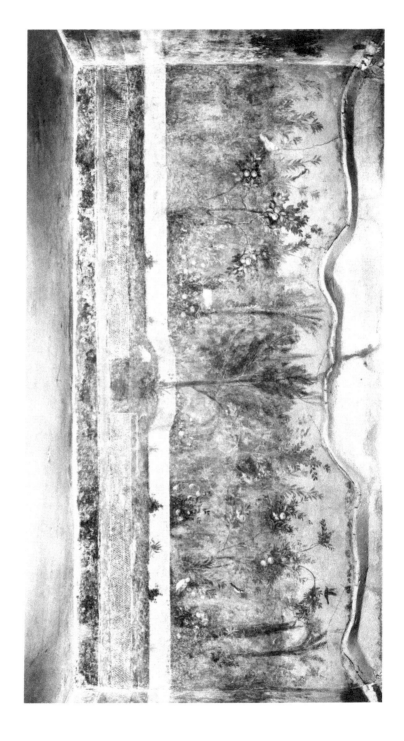

Figure 16. Paradisiacal forest. Garden fresco from the Villa of Livia at Prima Porta, late 1st century BCE. Now in the Museo Nazionale Romano, Rome, inv. no. 126 373. Photo, © Art Resource.

gress the laws of seasonality, thereby "forcing" its manifold plantings to bloom and bear fruit at precisely the same time. Such, however, is the miracle of this garden, a garden veritably pregnant with Augustan arboreal and horticultural mythology.[111] The plant whose presence is most intensely felt in the garden painting is the laurel, the tree sacred to Apollo, god of healing, prophecy, and order, and, significantly, the god who stood at Augustus' side to secure his victory at Actium, to assure vengeance for Caesar's murder, and to issue in a new age of peace and prosperity. As on the Ara Pacis, where the swan constitutes a reference to Apollo, burgeoning plant life signifies the return of a new Saturnian Golden Age to Italian soil, an age of primordial fertility, order, and peace. To some degree, every subsequent garden painting, whether in grand villa or modest house, preserved these associations, and it is therefore little wonder that this genre of fresco painting became the most enduring of all.

Hope is fundamental to, veritably embedded in, the concept of the garden. Were there no hope that plants would ultimately thrive and grow, the planting of seeds and laborious tending of seedlings would be futile and thoroughly unappealing. In their time of crisis, it was the garden to which Romans turned, and *rus in urbe* became a social dream. Gardens, Nature inscribed, infiltrated every aspect of Roman life by penetrating virtually every part of the dwelling; illusionistically painted gardens were even permitted to blend with the substance of the very walls that contained them. As in Classical Athens, the physical constitution of the dwelling house mirrored that of the city, and in keeping with the inscription of Nature on the domestic front, Rome itself became a garden city.[112] Together with public parks, no fewer than sixty *horti*, garden villas, are known to have formed part of the urban fabric, and the extent to which inscribed Nature penetrated the city is nowhere more apparent than in the famous *horti* of Maecenas straddling the Servian Wall.[113] In the Roman world, security and contentment were sought and found in the garden embraced both by city wall and private dwelling. Drawing on traditions preserved by the Italic house as well as on outside influences such as Epicurus' Garden and Hellenistic estates, modeled themselves on the *paradeisoi* of Persian kings and nobles, Rome created its own utopian garden mythology and thereby reinvented paradise. The walled garden was a place where past and present might collaborate to forge a brighter future. As Joseph Rykwert observes, "Paradise is a promise as well as a memory."[114]

---

[111] On Augustus' "arboreal mythology" and the Prima Porta garden fresco, see Kellum 1994.

[112] The quintessential survey of Roman gardens, public and private, remains that of Grimal 1969.

[113] See Andreae 1996, Boatwright 1998, and Haüber 1998.

[114] Rykwert 1981:192. For a history of "paradise" generally in a literary context, see Giamatti 1966.

4

Nostalgia and Virgil's Pastoral Dream
(On the Dangers of Playing Orpheus)

IRGIL, WE ARE TOLD, "was given a house in Maecenas' gardens on the Esquiline with the hope of enticing him to Rome."[1] With this in mind, it would be tempting to identify the Esquiline villa in which the Odyssey Frieze was found with Virgil's Roman house, particularly since the painting may, on many levels, be viewed as a reflection, a pictorial distillation, of the poet's collected works. The artist responsible for the frieze's conception and execution found him or herself within a structure, a house, presumably inscribing, framing, one or more gardens.[2] The painter's illusionistic opening of the wall and fictive appropriation of an "external" landscape complemented the villa's architectural domestication of Nature, its efforts to bring the countryside, *rus*, into the City. Among the bristling crags and luminous shores of this illusionistically "borrowed" Italianate landscape the artist has placed both pastoral figures, in whom the past, present, and future can find common ground, and Odysseus, an epic hero born in a remote Greek past but whose nostalgic journey symbolizes the eternal human quest for a utopian society.[3] Viewed in its original physical and cultural context, the Odyssey Frieze would have forcefully suggested that environmental reintegration, not urban sublimation, was the key to achieving human happiness. Not unlike the artist of the Esquiline frieze, Virgil fashioned landscapes: three gardens painted in words, populated with herdsmen and farmers, and formally contained or framed by the epic genre. These gardens, the landscapes of the *Eclogues*, *Georgics*, and *Aeneid*, constitute the *loci* of his utopian probings. Of these offer-

---

[1] Frank 1922:141.

[2] For the sake of conceptual clarity I have referred to a single artist, though fully aware of the likelihood of both the involvement of multiple hands and the influence of the patron.

[3] The journey is nostalgic in the sense that it is literally driven by painful yearning (*algos*) for homecoming (*nostos*).

126

ings, the *Aeneid*, the seminal work that more than any other would be associated with Rome's glory, marked and defined what was Rome's "great" utopian moment under Augustus, the Republic's second founding and the birth of a new Saturnian Golden Age on Italian soil. Fittingly, it was at this historical moment that, in his tale of Aeneas' travails, Virgil reiterated the wanderings of Odysseus in order to define Rome's social dream.

While the identity of the painter of the Odyssey Frieze, whether Greek or Roman, slave or free, continues to elude us, we do know that Virgil was a farmer's son born in a rural district near Mantua. In other words, Virgil was a true son of rural Italy, and an accordingly "deep and abiding affection" for the country pervades his poetry.[4] Virgil was born into what R. D. Williams eloquently describes as "a period of disastrous and appalling civil war, a period in which all that Rome had achieved through the long centuries of her history appeared likely to vanish in carnage and confusion."[5] Virgil witnessed the birth and disintegration of the First Triumvirate, the invasion of Italy by Caesar and his assassination on the grounds—somewhere in the *porticus* gardens—of Pompey's theater, the elevation of Antony and Octavian, the death of Cicero, the confiscation of large tracts of land throughout Italy earmarked as rewards for a loyal soldiery, and the exhausted collapse, at long last, of the Roman Republic. He also witnessed the metamorphosis of Octavian from a young man feared, at once sickly and ruthless, into a beacon of hope, *divi filius* 'the son of a god', savior of the Republic, and father alike of countrymen and country, *pater patriae*. This turbulent age, wavering constantly between hope and despair, was fertile ground for utopian musings, and it comes as no surprise that it produced one of Rome's most ardent utopians. An Epicurean in his youth and certainly an Epicurean sympathizer in later years, Virgil, the farmer's son, transported himself into a garden or gardens to reflect on the crises of his time—the troubling connotations of the transformation of Italy and of the larger world into Rome's garden, the fact that as the great city grew, its inscription of the countryside became ever more aggressive. The world, it seemed, was in danger of becoming *rus in Urbe*, a landscape engulfed by and subordinated to the interests of *the* City. The very fine line between propriety and excess in the domestication of Nature to achieve the ideal of *rus in urbe* was becoming increasingly apparent. Any inscription of Nature, whether small or large in scale, whether aimed at the sustenance of the body or the soul, is an act of violence. Even the construction of a modest hut or the

---

[4] Clausen 1994:xix.
[5] Williams 1982:336.

mere planting of a seedling violates a pre-existing environmental condition. Violation of environment and violence are not, however, unique to the human among the Earth's myriad beasts; humans merely possess the greatest capacity for destruction. Nature, conceived in the most general terms, is herself both violent and bounteous, terrifying and beautiful. Constituting an integral part of Nature, humanity necessarily partakes of these qualities, all the while quite falsely believing "that we somehow stand outside, or apart from nature."[6]

The absurd and profound question of humanity's relationship to Nature occupied Virgil as he fashioned the tenuous pastoral landscapes of the *Eclogues*, the fields and pasturelands of the *Georgics*, and the vast geographic expanses of the *Aeneid*. Specifically, he grappled with the implications of the inauspicious birth of the Roman *urbs*; the descent of the Roman race from Venus and Mars, both deities associated with cultivated lands; the inextricable link of the Roman people with the wolf; wishes for a second Golden Age; and the dangers inherent in playing the role of Orpheus. As he embarked on his utopian journey, Virgil was fully aware that he was not treading virgin soil; the august Epicurean poet Lucretius, who reportedly died on the very day that a young Virgil assumed the *toga virilis* 'garment of manhood', had already forged a path through this metaphysical wilderness.[7] In Lucretius Virgil found not just a fellow Epicurean, a man of the Garden, but also a truly kindred spirit—a master poet, a keen and passionate observer of humankind and of the natural environment, a man able to join political assertiveness with political quietism, a man who combined a deep affection for the past with a sense of the imperative of evolution, nostalgia with progressivism—a utopian.[8] In other words, Virgil had found an ideal guide in his own search for a prescriptive means to calm the turbulence and anxiety that relentlessly undermined the potential for equanimity upon which the health of the Roman endeavor depended. In his impassioned, apocalyptic calculus, *De Rerum Natura* (fittingly composed as the Republican regime hurtled towards its cataclysmic end), Lucretius had plainly stated that his purpose was to help humanity by revealing the path to total peace of mind, a beatific state characterized by freedom from the anxieties of an unfounded fear of death, the tyranny of unchecked lust, and empty yearnings for fame and fortune. This untroubled state, which the Epicureans labeled *ataraxy*, could only be attained through a contemplative union and

---

[6] Pollan 2001:xxv.

[7] Bailey 1931:21–22 says of the anecdote (which is drawn from Donatus' *Life of Virgil*) that, regardless of its truth, "there can hardly be anywhere in literary biography a more direct suggestion of the falling of the poet's mantle."

[8] As argued in Giesecke 1999b:11.

physical re-integration with Nature, by realizing that humankind is unquestionably part of the "great reciprocal web that is life on Earth."[9]

Lucretius could not have signaled his ideal audience more directly,
focusing on them particularly, the sons of Aeneas, as his didactic *epos* begins:

> Aeneadum genetrix, hominum divumque voluptas,
> alma Venus, caeli subter labentia signa
> quae mare navigerum, quae terras frugiferentis
> concelebras, per te quoniam *genus omne animantum*
> concipitur visitque exortum lumina solis:

> Mother of Aeneas' sons, joy of men and gods,
> nurturing Venus, beneath the gliding constellations of the sky,
> you who the ship-bearing sea, who the crop-bearing lands
> fill to teeming, since through you is *every species of living thing*
> conceived and, upon its birth, beholds the light of the sun:

De Rerum Natura 1.1–5

Specifically, the poem begins with a reminder that the sons of Aeneas, *all*
Romans, are descendants of Venus, who is not merely the mythological honey
sweetening the bitter truths that must cure what ails the Roman psyche. More
importantly, she is the Epicurean pleasure principle, *hēdonē*, the Earth, and
Natura creatrix, the source of all life. It is she who populates the seas, rouses the
crops, and conceives every animate being (*De Rerum Natura* 1.4), the speechless
beast of the fields as well as the human beast, Roman, Greek, and otherwise.[10]
Venus, Lucretius reveals, does not play favorites. Such is the first jarring truth
presented to the Roman audience. The second is that even at her most munifi-
cent, nurturing, and benign, Venus/Nature is violent in her workings. This is
immediately evidenced by the forceful verbs and participles that punctuate
the remainder of the proem:

> te, dea, te *fugiunt* venti, te nubila caeli
> adventumque tuum, tibi suavis daedala tellus
> summittit flores, tibi rident aequora ponti
> placatumque nitet diffuso lumine caelum.
> 10   nam simul ac species patefactast verna diei
> et reserata viget genitabilis aura favoni,
> aeriae primum volucres te, diva, tuumque

---

[9] Pollan 2001:xxv.

[10] For recent critical and comprehensive discussions of the role of Venus in the *De Rerum Natura*,
see Gale 1994:208–288 and Jenkyns 1998:214–292.

significant initum *perculsae* corda *tua vi.*
inde ferae pecudes persultant pabula laeta
15 et rapidos tranant amnis: ita *capta* lepore
te sequitur cupide quo quamque inducere pergis.
denique per maria ac montis fluviosque rapaces
frondiferasque domos avium camposque virentis
omnibus *incutiens* blandum per pectora amorem
20 efficis ut cupide generatim saecla propagent.

You, goddess, you do the winds *flee*, you the clouds of the sky
and your coming; for you the wonder-working Earth
puts forth sweet flowers, for you laugh the level stretches of
the sea,
and, calmed, the sky glows with spreading light.
10 For as soon as the vernal aspect of the day is unveiled
and, unbarred, the life-giving breeze of the west wind blows
strong,
then first you, goddess, and your coming do the birds of the
air
signal, their hearts *pierced with your might.*
Then herds wildly bound through lush pastures
15 and forge raging rivers; to such a degree *captivated* by your
charm
does each eagerly follow you wherever you set out to lead
them.
Finally, through the seas and mountains and sweeping rivers
and the leafy haunts of the birds and verdant fields,
striking sweet love through the hearts of all,
20 you bring it about that they eagerly propagate their breeds,
each after its own kind.

De Rerum Natura 1.6–20

Venus drives the winds to flight, strikes the breasts of birds and beasts with her irresistible force, and brings about that all creatures, captive to her charm, eagerly join in the endless chain of being. Violence lies at the heart of Mother Nature, at her atomic core. Thus the brute power of stormy gales and rain-swollen torrents destroy the sylvan lairs of boars, lions, deer, and birds and sweep away even the most sturdily wrought human works.[11] Nature sustains

---

[11] *De Rerum Natura* 1.271–294.

cities but can and does bring even the most monumental to its knees, for everything that is created, even the Earth herself, must pass away.[12] So it is, Lucretius states, that the mighty walls of the universe will be stormed and tumble into ruin. In her violence too Nature does not discriminate.

There is an inherent violence, then, in the mother of the Roman race and, consequently, in her offspring. This fact is underlined by Venus' embrace with Mars, whom the potency of her allure has rendered powerless—Mars the guardian of fields and protector of the Earth, Mars the father of Romulus and Remus.[13] In the union of the two, Mars represents the violence in Nature, in human nature, and in Roman nature. The embrace of Venus and Mars also exposes the fine balance that must be maintained between destructive ferocity and bountiful fecundity or nurturing cultivation. Venus is the calming influence on Mars and his irascibility while he, in turn, lends urgency and force to her dissemination of delight.

Ironically, it is the beast equipped with the greatest intellect, the human beast, that demonstrates the greatest inclination to disrupt this balance, ever tempted to tip the scales in favor of annihilating forces. As Lucretius asserts, the Earth is gradually decaying and is destined to pass away, but humanity has the capacity both to retard and to hasten her decline, however slightly. For instance, the cultivation of the soil, an activity necessarily harboring seeds of violence, is a means by which humanity can enhance the fertility of the steadily failing Earth.[14] Human nurturing becomes a gesture that the Earth reciprocates. At the same time, humanity is at greatest risk of negatively upsetting the cosmic balance through the inscription of Nature, the transformation of land to landscape, that urbanism involves. It is here, in the literal and figurative erection of barriers to safeguard against external threat, "environmental" or otherwise, that humankind is most susceptible to erroneously privileging itself over that from which it is attempting separation. Nothing conveys this message more clearly than Rome's foundation myth itself, and although Lucretius does not himself recount the tale, the two appearances of Mars in the poem subtly alert the audience to the association. Mars appears first as lover of Venus, mother of the Aeneidae with whom the Roman race began, and later as metonym for the horror of sanguine, inter-species and "fraternal" or intra-species slaughter, which is the result of human experiments in warfare employing a variety of wild beasts and, as Lucretius declares,

---

[12] *De Rerum Natura* 2.606–607, 1144–1145.
[13] *De Rerum Natura* 1.29–37.
[14] *De Rerum Natura* 1.208–212.

too awful for belief.[15] Such passionate excess, devolving into fraternal blood-shed, forever scarred the rising walls of Rome and, by extension, the urban endeavor of Aeneas' sons. Had Romulus and Remus remained mindful of their debt to the wolf that had nurtured them and of the essential kinship of all life on Earth, rueful fratricide could have been avoided. False fears, resulting from the belief that humanity is somehow above or fundamentally different from other forms of life, foster avarice and ambition, the so-called *vulnera vitae* 'wounds of life' (*De Rerum Natura* 3.63) driving people to turn viciously even against those closest to them:

>   unde homines dum se falso terrore coacti
>   effugisse volunt longe longeque remosse,
> 70   sanguine civili rem conflant divitiasque
>   conduplicant avidi, caedem caede accumulantes;
>   crudeles gaudent in tristi funere fratris
>   et consanguineum mensas odere timentque.

>   Whence people, while they, goaded by false fear,
>   wish to have escaped and have removed themselves afar,
> 70   amass a fortune through civil war, and riches
>   do they multiply eagerly, heaping murder upon murder;
>   cruelly do they rejoice in the sad death of a brother,
>   and the tables of their kin do they abhor and fear.

De Rerum Natura 3.68–73

Ultimately, this was the grievous state of affairs when Athens, paragon of culture and urban accomplishment, fell victim to the plague. How quickly apparent utopias can mutate into dystopia, how perilous humanity's urban quest! Lucretius' dramatic demise of Athens, in which the physical represents a moral contagion spreading not only between humans but also from humans to animals (like the ever-faithful dog) that have special ties to humanity, vividly conveys what can happen if Nature's balance is not maintained.[16] However, like every good utopographer, Lucretius counters his dystopian construct with an image of its opposite, a means by which Romans can meet the challenge of creating an urban experience in sync with the Natural balance of things. Just as every utopia is inherently frangible, containing the seeds of its own disso-

---

[15] *De Rerum Natura* 5.1302–1349. On the "use and abuse of animals," see Shelton 1996, from whose title this quoted phrase is taken, and also Gale 1991.

[16] The interpretations of Bright 1971, Commager 1957, Penwill 1996, and Stoddard 1996 have all informed my understanding of Lucretius' Athenian plague.

lution, every dystopia harbors mechanisms for its redemption.[17] Not surprisingly, then, Athens, however beleaguered and sorely tried, is also the source of Lucretius' remedy for humanity's dystopian tendencies in that it produces Epicurus, the Creator of the Garden. At various stages of its evolution, Athens serves both as dystopian and utopian paradigm.

As for the ideal that Lucretius presents, it is utopian in the truest sense, being located in a good place (*eu-topos*) that defies temporal and geographic boundaries (*ou-topos*). Where Roman society, and human society in general, can achieve a desirable and sublime state of mind defined by freedom from all commotive impulses, is in a pastoral *locus amoenus*. This pleasant place is "located" when- and wherever people embrace the considerable amenities offered freely by the natural world in place of vain materialistic delights:

> cum tamen inter se prostrati in gramine molli
> propter aquae rivum sub ramis arboris altae
> non magnis opibus iucunde corpora curant,
> praesertim cum tempestas arridet et anni
> tempora conspergunt viridantis floribus herbas.

> when, nevertheless, stretched out together in soft grass
> by the water of a stream beneath the branches of a lofty tree,
> they enjoy themselves without great expense,
> especially when the weather smiles upon them and the season
> scatters the green grass with flowers.

De Rerum Natura 2.29–33

In such a *locus amoenus* one may hope to find the means, on a metaphysical level, of returning to the blessed springtime of human existence, a time of relative innocence when people were still willing to be taught by Nature, before ambition, greed, and superstition grew rampant.[18] This place, like every other garden essentially a nostalgic, memory-based construct, bridges the gap between the past and present; it successfully combines the primitive and progressive.[19] For those who have set their sights on the attainment of this ideal, the temptation to aspire to mastery over Nature does not exist, nor do they long for the reconstitution of a postlapsarian Golden Age. They need only be mindful of the fact that they form an integral part of an organic whole. At

---

[17] The frangibility of utopia was noted by Goodman 2003.

[18] This is indicated by the reappearance of the *locus amoenus* in the so-called anthropology at *De Rerum Natura* 5.1392–1396. For a fuller discussion, see Giesecke 1999b (especially 5–9).

[19] See Schama 1995:6–16 and passim.

its core, this ideal is quite literally pastoral, as it evokes and, further, reenacts the "historical" moment when inhabitants of the countryside forged the art of song by imitating clear-toned birds and the whistling of reeds inflated by the breezes:

> At liquidas avium voces imitarier ore
> 1380 ante fuit multo quam levia carmina cantu
> concelebrare homines possent aurisque iuvare.
> et zephyri, cava per calamorum, sibila primum
> agrestis docuere cavas inflare cicutas.
> inde minutatim dulcis didicere querelas,
> 1385 tibia quas fundit digitis pulsata canentum,
> avia per nemora ac silvas saltusque reperta,
> per loca pastorum deserta atque otia dia.

> Now to imitate with their mouths the clear-toned songs of
> the birds
> 1380 came much earlier than, in the singing of smooth-flowing
> songs,
> people could set themselves to practicing and delight their
> ears.
> And the whistling of the west wind, through the hollows of
> the reeds, first
> taught country dwellers to blow into hemlock stalks.
> Then, little by little, they learned the sweet plaints
> 1385 that the pipe pours forth when struck by the players' fingers,
> discovered in the pathless woods, forests, and glades,
> in the solitary haunts of the shepherds and their lovely
> resting places.

De Rerum Natura 5.1379–1387

Lucretius' protreptic, pacifistic cry for humanity to embrace its organic place in Nature resonated in Virgil's creative psyche with tremendous force, a force that has been largely underestimated. Allusions to his work pervade the entire Virgilian corpus. Lucretius' poem of the Earth informs the conception of the tenuous pastoral world of the *Eclogues*, influences the themes and rhythms of the *Georgics*, and underlies the strains of social theorizing that emerge from the magisterial *Aeneid*.[20] Simply put, the *De Rerum Natura*, the Republic's seminal

---

[20] For further presentation of the text as *ergon* and intertexts as *parerga* reifying and directing the interpretation of the allusive (*ergonal*) text, see Giesecke 2002:127–148. Instances of Virgilian

utopian epic, constitutes a primary hermeneutic *parergon*, a crucial intertextual frame, informing the interpretation of each Virgilian text.

Of the three *epē* that constitute the Virgilian *oeuvre*, the last-composed, as earlier noted, provides the closest or most readily apparent parallel to the Esquiline frieze. Virgil sings of "arms and a man" in an unambiguous activation of Homer's *Iliad* and *Odyssey*, together constituting Classical Greece's utopian prescriptive, as fundamental *parerga*. Of the two Homeric works, the latter is structurally prevalent, as the *Aeneid* centers on a journey that is an Odyssean *nostos*, a homecoming that will culminate in a social restructuring and a new urban construct laboriously attained.[21] In the case of the *Aeneid*, it is not, of course, the *polis* generally at issue but a specific city, the great urban venture that was Rome. This fact is signified through the proem's literal framing by Homeric allusion at its opening and by mention of Rome's lofty walls at its close:

> *Arma virumque cano*, Troiae qui primus ab oris
> Italiam fato profugus Laviniaque venit
> litora, multum ille et terris iactatus et alto
> vi superum, saevae memorem Iunonis ob iram,
> 5   multa quoque et bello passus, dum conderet urbem
> inferretque deos Latio; genus unde Latinum
> Albanique patres atque *altae moenia Romae*.

> *Of arms do I sing and of a man* who first from the shores of Troy,
> a fugitive by fate, came to Italy and Lavinian
> shores; much was he harassed both on land and sea
> by the might of the gods, because of savage Juno's relentless
>   anger,
> 5   and many things too did he suffer in war until he could
>   found a city
> and bring his gods to Latium—whence the Latin race
> and Alban fathers and also *the walls of lofty Rome*.

> *Aeneid* 1.1–7

---

verbal imitation of the *De Rerum Natura* in the *Eclogues* and *Aeneid* have been catalogued in Giesecke 2000:183–192. For discussion of the presence of Lucretius in the *Georgics*, see, for instance: Bailey 1931, Farrell 1991, Gale 2000, Horsfall 1995:82–83, Mynors 1990, Nethercut 1973, Vallillee 1968, Wigodsky 1972, and Wöhler 1876:1–21.

[21] This is also noted in Suerbaum 1993. For explicit reminders that the Trojans issue originally from Italy, see *Aeneid* 3.94–96 and *Aeneid* 7.206–208.

As the proem reveals, the foundations of Rome's walls were laid amid violence, amid unbridled passion and conflict introduced to Italy and the Lavinian shores by the Trojan refugees. Aeneas, the ancestor of the Roman race, bears the weapons that will ravage his rediscovered ancestral land. The city, violence, and landscape will be pivotal thematic concerns to Virgil as he avails himself of the medium of heroic epic to reflect on the viability and desirability of a *rus in urbe* ideal sought through force of arms and an excess of violence.

As the prominence of the Homeric epics within the Virgilian complex of *parergonal* texts would suggest, the Shield of Aeneas (*Aeneid* 8.626–731), like that of Achilles, functions as *ergon*, and the tale in which it is embedded as *parergonal* frame (Figure 17).[22] Just as the Shield of Achilles is, in essence, the *Iliad*, so the Shield of Aeneas *is* the *Aeneid*; like its Homeric counterpart, it condenses and sublimates the thematic content of its immediate textual frame, without which the act of interpretation would be severely compromised. In terms of general content, both shields provide a utopian prescriptive, but where Homer envisions the general concept of the *polis*, and therefore a "reality" of multiple *poleis*, as a model for ordering the Hellenic world, Virgil presents one city with a vast inscribed landscape as a model for ordering the world and, further, the Cosmos. That one city, Rome, is described not in physical or structural terms but in terms of the exemplary citizenry upon whom its foundation and continued existence depended. Briefly stated, Virgil's description of the Shield opens with Romulus and Remus suckled by the wolf, a scene presaging the tenacity of the Roman people and their will to survive. Additionally, the rape of the Sabine women appears, together with the subsequent war and peace that marked the evolution of a Roman religious and social consciousness. The execution of the treasonous Mettus Fuffettius is balanced by the bravery of Cocles and Cloelia in their resistance against tyranny. Manlius, alerted by the sacred geese, defends Rome's most sacred ground against the onslaught of the Gauls, and the Salii, as well as the Luperci, safeguard the city's continued prosperity. Scenes in the House of Hades illustrate the fates both of sinners,

---

[22] This diagram is a critical response to that of West 1990:298. The Shield of Aeneas is an unambiguous representation of Rome envisioned in terms of its inscription of the world by means of war; violence lies at Rome's heart if the city's history is to be viewed as culminating with Octavian's triple triumph after the Battle of Actium. The powers of the East (Antony and Cleopatra) are juxtaposed here with the powers of the West (Octavian and Agrippa)—the "barbarian," effeminate, Near East with Rome. Romulus and Remus, together with the Sabines, have been graphically aligned with the powers of the West, and Tarquin, together with Mettus, with the powers of the East. On the Shield's rim, where Homer had depicted Ocean, I have shown all Rome's wars fought in order, *pugnata in ordine bella* (*Aeneid* 8.629), the means by which Rome violently inscribed the entire Earth, the swelling sea included.

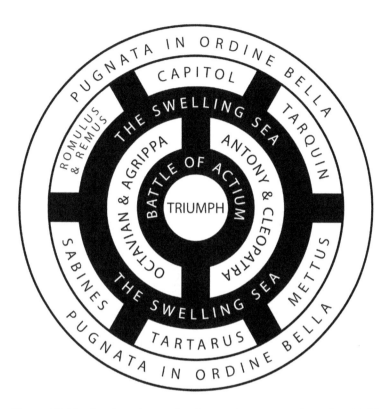

Figure 17. The Earth as Roman landscape. Reconstruction: The Shield of Aeneas. Concept by Donald Dunham and Annette Giesecke, drawing by Michael Monahan.

exemplified by the heinous Catiline, and of the just, whom Cato embodies.[23] Finally, at the Shield's center, the Battle of Actium, the rout of Cleopatra and Antony, and Augustus' triple triumph, which symbolically marked the subjugation of the world, appear. These central themes have been characterized as "the most explicit version which Virgil gives of the goal enunciated by Jupiter in Book I: the establishment of order, peace, and empire. It is the victory of order over disorder, of West over East, of male over female, of civilization over barbarism."[24] The Shield presents a vision that, together with all other Augustan monuments, formed part of a coordinated iconographic and ideological complex enabling the self-fashioning and fabrication of Rome's new

---

[23] See Williams 1973:265–266 for a summation the Shield's main scenes and themes.
[24] Zetzel 1997:199.

Figure 18. Universal fecundity. Marble relief panel from the Ara Pacis
Augustae: goddess variously identified as Tellus, Pax, and Roma. Rome,
ca. 13 BCE. Photo, © Art Resource.

political system.[25] As these monuments so vividly reveal, Augustus' victory
heralds the advent of a new, divinely sanctioned Golden Age of peace, prosperity, and moral rejuvenation hinging on a reconnection with Rome's rural,
georgic past, a return to the garden. The new age would also bring *imperium
sine fine* 'empire without end' (*Aeneid* 1.279), a goal unambiguously achieved
through force of arms. The new Golden Age's diverse associations are, for
instance, encoded in the iconography of the Ara Pacis and the Prima Porta
statue. The former, embellished with a profusion of flora, is a *templum* to Peace
and her promise of universal fecundity (Figure 18). At the same time, it is "a
sacred precinct carved out of the Field of Mars" that functioned as part of a
colossal sundial with an obelisk, itself signifying dominion over Egypt, for the
needle.[26] The Prima Porta statue, in turn, is an honorific representation of the

---

[25] For a concise survey of the Augustan political/cultural program and its physical manifestations, see Wallace-Hadrill 1993.

[26] Galinsky 1996:142. For fuller discussions of the iconography of the Ara Pacis, see the following:
Castriota 1995, Elsner 1995:192–209, Galinsky 1996:139–155, Simon 1968, and Zanker 1988:
passim.

Princeps in his military role (Figure 19). On his cuirass, Mars, accompanied by the famous wolf, retrieves the Roman standards shamefully lost to Parthia, and East and West acquiesce in the new Roman world order, with Sky, Sun, Dawn, and the bountiful Earth bearing witness.[27] A true counterpart to the Ara Pacis, the Prima Porta statue was found within the terrace garden of the villa renowned for its paradise garden fresco and sacred laurel grove.[28] Both monuments, then, sought to wed pastoralism with righteous militarism.

Also characterizing both monuments, a conscious strain of "Attic" Classicism is readily detectable in their polysemic nexus of styles. The famed Doryphoros, the embodiment of the Polykleitan ideal, provided the model for the Prima Porta Augustus, and the friezes of the Ara Pacis bear no small resemblance to the Parthenon's Panathenaic procession. The referential appropriation of Classical Greek art manifested in the Augustan period was no mere by-product of Athens' absorption into the Roman world. Rather, for Augustan "image-makers" such appropriation was "instrumental, a means of achieving an authoritative public presence" by virtue of emanating "the requisite conventions of nobility."[29] It was both "an expression of Roman cultivated taste" and "an exploitation of its image value for purposes of idealization."[30] In particular, High Classical Athenian works were regarded as "paradigms of a New Golden Age."[31] It follows, then, that the language of Augustan monuments cast Rome in the role of fifth-century Athens and the *Princeps* in the role of Pericles. As great a marvel as Periclean Athens was, and while it set sights on Olympian heights, Athens' was *not* an empire without end. By distancing itself too far from what was not actually "other" and misguidedly approximating divinity, Athens sealed its own fate; the Periclean utopia was precisely that, an inherently frangible construct. Ironically, it was Actium that spelled the end both of the Roman Republic and Hellenistic Athens. That city, beloved by Antony and wooed by his consort Cleopatra, would, in Habicht's words, "face harsh times under its new masters and new status as part of the imperium Romanum, until Roman philhellenism reached a new peak under Hadrian

---

[27] See Galinsky 1996:155–164, where it is remarked that Sol is to be identified with Apollo, Aurora with Venus, and Tellus with Ceres, Pax, Venus, and the Magna Mater. See also Elsner 1995:161–172.

[28] For Augustus' personal arboreal mythology and the prevalence of the laurel at this estate, see Kellum 1994. If it is true, as Klynne and Liljenstolpe 2000 propose, that the statue was originally situated in the *atrium* rather than the terrace, the fact remains that the statue would have formed part of an iconographic "program" extending throughout the villa and its grounds.

[29] Brilliant 1994:110.

[30] Brilliant 1994:107.

[31] Brilliant 1994:97.

Figure 19. Sanguinary Golden Age. Marble sculpture: the Augustus of Prima Porta. Early 1st century CE, after bronze original of ca. 20 BCE. Found near the Villa of Livia, Prima Porta, now in the Musei Vaticani, inv. no. 2290. Photo, © Art Resource.

and Antoninus Pius a century and a half later, granting it one more era of late bloom."[32] If Periclean Athens rose anew in the heart of Rome from the ashes of the Republic, would it not be destined to fall again, the gleam of its marbles dulled, when baser instincts inevitably surfaced?

Students of Lucretius—Virgil certainly among their number—could not help but be somewhat skeptical of the Augustan effort to combine pastoral and Atticizing, "Periclean" urban ideals. How could they reconcile the nostalgic inscription of Nature with the belief that a godlike superiority would enable control over her? There is no reason to doubt that Virgil, together with a good part of the war-battered citizenry, earnestly hoped for the fruition of the Augustan promise, but the high degree of intertextual referentiality in the poet's works compels acknowledgement of the works' polyphony.[33] In this throng of voices, the versified sentiments of the numerous poets to whom Virgil's texts allude, those of Lucretius and, through him, of the Garden are among the most resonant. In a given Virgilian text, the voice of Lucretius may be heard in verbal echoes and "borrowed" verses alike, and while it is useful to evaluate individual instances of imitation in terms of having an intertextually validating or polemical effect locally, nevertheless, all allusion to the *De Rerum Natura* ultimately presents the teachings of that text as "alternatives" worthy of consideration. In other words, the importance of employing Lucretius as a hermeneutic guide to the weighty questions Virgil raises regarding the viability of the Augustan take on *rus in urbe* cannot be undervalued.[34] This notion is underscored by the prominence of Lucretius within the multi-faceted *parergonal* framework of Aeneas' shield.

It is worth recalling here the seduction of Vulcan that initiates the Shield's production. As Virgil nowhere indicates that Aeneas requires new armor, this scene, evoking Thetis' entreaty in the eighteenth book of the *Iliad*, is curiously unmotivated by the narrative. Its function is certainly to signal the over-arching Iliadic framework of the battle books, but the language in which the seduction is couched signals a still deeper meaning:

> dixerat et niveis hinc atque hinc diva lacertis
> *cunctantem amplexu molli fovet. ille repente*
> *accepit solitam flammam, notusque medullas*

---

[32] Habicht 1997:365.

[33] On the polyphony of the Virgilian texts, see Lyne 1987.

[34] Among the critics who view the hermeneutic complexity of Virgil as resulting from his posing questions rather than providing answers are Gale 2000, O'Hara 1994, and Perkell 2002.

390   *intravit calor et labefacta per ossa cucurrit,*
       non secus atque olim tonitru cum rupta corusco
       ignea rima micans percurrit lumine nimbos;
       sensit laeta dolis et formae conscia coniunx.
       tum pater aeterno *fatur* devinctus amore:
404   ... ea verba locutus
       optatos dedit amplexus *placidum*que petivit
       coniugis *infusus gremio* per membra *soporem.*

       So she spoke, and with her snowy white arms, on this side
          and on that, did the goddess
       caress him in her soft embrace as he hesitated. Immediately did he
       receive the wonted flame, and his marrow did the familiar heat
390   *penetrate and raced through his relenting bones.*
       Not other than when sometimes, burst in gleaming thunder,
       a fiery crack flies flashing with light through the clouds;
       his spouse sensed it, rejoicing in her deceit and fully aware of
          her beauty.
       Then her lord spoke, *vanquished with everlasting love:*
404   ... having spoken such words
       he gave the desired embraces and sought *tranquil*
       sleep throughout his limbs, *draped in the lap* of his wife.

                           Aeneid 8.387–406

The audience attuned to Virgil's propensity for multi-layered allusion is prompted to relive the seduction of Mars with which Lucretius' prayer to Venus closes:

       effice ut interea fera moenera militiai
30   per maria ac terras omnis sopita quiescant.
       nam tu sola potes tranquilla pace iuvare
       mortalis, quoniam belli fera moenera Mavors
       armipotens regit, in gremium qui saepe tuum se
       reicit *aeterno devictus vulnere amoris,*
35   atque ita suspiciens tereti cervice reposta
       pascit amore avidos inhians in te, dea, visus,
       eque tuo pendet resupini spiritus ore.
       hunc tu, diva, tuo recubantem corpore sancto
       circumfusa super, suavis ex ore loquelas
40   funde petens *placidam* Romanis, incluta, *pacem.*

Bring it to pass, meanwhile, that the savage works of war,
30   over all the seas and lands, slumber and rest.
For you alone, with tranquil peace, are able to help
humankind, since the savage works of war does Mars,
the strong in battle, control, he who often upon your lap
    himself
has cast utterly *vanquished by the eternal wound of love,*
35   and thus, gazing up at you with his shapely neck turned
    back,
feeds his yearning eyes with love, agape, goddess, at you,
and his breath hangs from your lips as he lies back.
May you, goddess, as he reclines upon your hallowed body,
enfolding him from above, from your lips sweet utterances
40   pour forth, celebrated one, seeking *tranquil peace* for the
    Romans.

De Rerum Natura 1.29–40

In both scenes the male deity readily succumbs to the goddess' advances, and in both he is utterly subdued, defeated, by the "wound of love."[35] Unlike her Lucretian counterpart, however, Virgil's Venus seduces her mate not to put an end to war but to promote it, being the means by which Rome's destiny would be won. The painful irony of Virgil's allusion is underscored by the fact that the Lucretian Venus is asked to seek a tranquil and lasting peace, not simply an undisturbed sleep.[36] Virgil's application of yet another Lucretian *parergon*, an empirical discourse on "Jovian" thunder and lightening, further heightens this irony, as it is Jove (denied even his thunder by Lucretius) whom the *Aeneid* presents as the guarantor of Roman glory.[37] From an Epicurean perspective, the destiny of Rome rested instead in its own hands, in the recognition of a collective global destiny. Such, then, is the introduction to Virgil's Shield, an introduction that the ecphrastic verses admonish the audience to acknowledge in the course of interpretation.

It is that "most famous of all Rome's pictorial emblems," Romulus and Remus suckled by the she-wolf, with which Virgil commences his description of Vulcan's wondrous creation:[38]

---

[35] *De Rerum Natura* 1.34 ~ *Aeneid* 8.394.

[36] As I have noted briefly in a previous discussion: Giesecke 2000:76–77.

[37] The *parergonal* passage in question is *De Rerum Natura* 6.279–395. The following contain verbal echoes that signal the *parergon*'s application: *Aeneid* 8.390–392 ~ *De Rerum Natura* 6.282–284.

[38] Williams 1973:267 *ad loc.*

fecerat et viridi fetam Mavortis in antro
procubuisse lupam, geminos huic ubera circum
ludere pendentis pueros et lambere matrem
impavidos, illam tereti cervice reflexa
mulcere alternos et corpora fingere lingua.

He had fashioned also the mother wolf in Mars' green cavern
reclining, and about her teats the twin
boys playfully hanging and mouthing their mother
fearlessly, [while] she, her shapely neck turned back,
caressed them in turn and licked their bodies into shape with
    her tongue.

Aeneid 8.630–634

Here the twin sons of Mars and Venus enjoy salvation from the threat of death
at human hands. Fearlessly—the word is emphatically positioned—they nurse,
"hang playfully about her teats" (*Aeneid* 8.631–632), as the mother wolf, now
their mother, licks them tenderly in the welcome shelter of her verdant cave;
only an external threat is likely to rouse this noble creature to a display of
violence. A more idyllic or suitable beginning for an exposition of Rome's
destiny would be difficult to imagine. At this juncture, with Rome's foundations grounded in harmonious Nature, the inclusion and retention of *rus in
Urbe* would appear a natural development and a constant reminder of the
city's pastoral origins. In due recognition of its primal sanctity, Augustus, the
City's second Romulus, refurbished the wolf's cave below the Palatine. Yet the
multifaceted *parergonal* resonances within Virgil's idyllic scene ripple the ideological canvas enough to blur its optimistically providential clarity, the effect
of the subtle reappearance of the Lucretian seduction in the figure of the
wolf: her smooth neck, like that of Lucretius' love-struck Mars, turned back
in a loving glance (*tereti cervice reflexa, Aeneid* 8.633).[39] This same effect occurs
from the Shield's intertextual echo of the praises of country life with which
the second *Georgic* closes:

interea dulces *pendent* circum oscula nati,
casta pudicitiam servat domus, ubera vaccae
525 lactea demittunt, pinguesque in gramine laeto
inter se adversis luctantur cornibus haedi.
ipse dies agitat festos fususque per herbam,

---

[39] As in *De Rerum Natura* 1.35 cited above.

ignis ubi in medio et socii cratera coronant,
te libans, Lenaee, vocat pecorisque magistris
530   velocis iaculi certamina ponit in ulmo,
corporaque agresti nudant praedura palaestra.

Meanwhile his sweet children *hang* about his kisses,
his chaste house preserves its purity, udders do his
525   cows suspend full of milk, and in the thick grass, his fat
kids spar with horns turned against each other.
The master himself celebrates holidays, and lying in the
grass
where there is a fire in the middle and his friends wreathe
the bowls of wine,
pouring libation to you, Lenaeus, he calls upon you, and for
herdsmen
530   he sets up targets on an elm for the contest of the flying
javelin,
and they bare their robust bodies for the rustic wrestling
match.

Georgics 2.523–531

In the *Georgics* it is the farmer's children who embrace their parent. They hang from his neck, showering him with grateful kisses, as it is his considerable, often less than gentle efforts, coordinated with the rhythms of Nature, that ensure the sustenance of homeland, family, and flocks.[40] Some form of violence may be part and parcel of agriculture, but it is in working the land that violence must stay. In this way rivalries could remain amicable, taking the form of sport. The farmer's mode of life, marked by a Saturnian Golden Age innocence, was embraced by the Sabines as well as by Remus and his brother. Farming also offered the essentially pacifistic lifestyle that fortified Etruria and the walls of Rome:

hanc olim veteres vitam coluere Sabini,
hanc Remus et frater; sic fortis Etruria crevit
scilicet et rerum facta est pulcherrima Roma,
535   septemque una sibi muro circumdedit arces.
ante etiam sceptrum Dictaei regis et ante
impia quam caesis gens est epulata iuvencis,

---

[40] See also *Georgics* 2.514–515.

aureus hanc vitam in terris Saturnus agebat;
necdum etiam audierant inflari classica, necdum
540 impositos duris crepitare incudibus ensis.

Such a life the Sabines of old once lived,
such Remus and his brother, thus Etruria grew strong
indeed, and so Rome became the fairest thing of all,
535 and as one city surrounded her seven hills with a wall.
Even before the sovereignty of the Dictaean king and before
an impious race feasted on slaughtered bullocks,
such a life did Saturn lead on Earth;
nor yet had people heard the trumpet calls be sounded,
    nor yet
540 sword blades ring out when placed upon hard anvils.

Georgics 2.532–540

The Shield, and the *Aeneid* as a whole, discloses the truth behind such noble fiction. Romulus and Remus, their young lives put at risk by the strife existing between their father and *his* brother, ultimately did not heed the lesson of the Lupercal. Instead they re-enacted and amplified their human legacy. Though both were herdsmen and wards of the goodly Faustulus, and therefore innately equipped to live a harmonious pastoral life, they followed in the footsteps of Aeneas' Trojans: murderous discord attended, and followed, the erection of Rome's walls. Remus did not survive to see the walls completed; the rape, *sine more* 'in defiance of civilized behavior' (*Aeneid* 8.635), of the Sabine women marked not the end but the beginning of centuries of blood shed in Rome's struggle with its Italian brothers. The fleeting truce between Aeneas and Latinus and the rent body of Mettus vividly illustrate that what once was whole or sealed can all too easily be broken.[41] The flesh of the treacherous Alban befouled the forest, his blood spattering the foliage in place of morning's welcome dew (*Aeneid* 8.644–645), but it was neither the first nor last indignity the innocent woods and fields would suffer as Rome inscribed its territory.

So, with an "in-organic," misplaced display of violence, the Trojan prince ignites rural passions (*Aeneid* 7.482) and thereby prompts a harvest not of grain but of swords (*Aeneid* 7.526). He has violated a special bond between humanity and the natural environment that predated his arrival, described by Latinus as a "pre-lapsarian, pre-Trojan Eden," and through his errant intervention, the "latent violence of man and nature is tugged to the surface and made the

---

[41] For the treaty between Aeneas and Latinus, see *Aeneid* 12.166ff.

paramount motivator of events."[42] The shooting of Silvia's stag, a wild creature domesticated yet retaining still its soul-sustaining freedom, plants the seed of discord.[43] This stag had been emblematic of the Latins' ideal harmony in Nature.[44] Now shepherds no longer recline on grassy riverbanks but, bearing the dead, stream into Latinus' city in great floods. Ironically, one of the shepherds' own is responsible: Aeneas, disrupting the primal Latin harmony, had been cast as a second Paris (*Aeneid* 7.363), that Phrygian *pastor* who most immediately prompted the demise of his own city. Ominously, Troy ultimately fell as the result of an affront to the natural order, its walls penetrated by a massive horse pregnant, not with foal or filly, but with hostile arms (*feta armis*, *Aeneid* 2.238), a perversion of georgic arts.

Herdsmen, embodying a timeless humanity, are no less susceptible to the violent impulses that pervade the Cosmos than any other beast. While, as Lucretius argues, they provide a direct link to a pre-urban age of greater global harmony, shepherds may also "introduce violence or become its conduit."[45] With Paris and Aeneas as models, is it any wonder that the *pastor* Romulus slew his brother at the inception of the urban effort? Aeneas, after all, had slain his Italian "brother" Turnus. Would Augustus deviate from the path established by Aeneas and Romulus, *his* models, in some aspects yet not in others? Would he be a good shepherd, or turn against the countryside that sustained both the city and the rural populace?

Aeneas, the new Paris, is also the ignorant *pastor* whose arrow mortally wounds the doe-queen of Carthage (*Aeneid* 4.69–73) as that city's walls are rising. Upon his arrival Aeneas marvels at the new Tyrian urban effort. What once had been a cluster of herdsmen's huts is now an impressive mass of buildings linked by roads and in the process of fortification through mural inscription (*Aeneid* 1.421–425).[46] At this critical juncture, the balance between creativity and violence is upset by the ignorant shepherd Aeneas. The Tyrians had been likened to an industrious swarm of bees tending their young, gathering honey, and, indeed, resorting to military action when necessary, yet they abandon their noble tasks as their doe queen, infuriated by the *pastor*'s errant dart, introduces a grim sylvan bacchanal into a nascent urban space

---

[42] Putnam 1998:102.

[43] The "seeds of discord" is a reference to *Aeneid* 7.339.

[44] As Putnam 1998:100 persuasively argues, and, similarly, Vance 1981 on the thematic import of Silvia's stag. Moorton (1989), by contrast, views Italy even prior to Aeneas' arrival as postlapsarian and predisposed towards violence.

[45] Chew 2002:625.

[46] On the identification of the Tyrian *magalia* as shepherds' huts, see Austin 1971:146 *ad loc.*

unsuited to its nefarious excesses (*Aeneid* 4.300–303). *Pastor* Aeneas in his error repeats the transgression of the *Georgics' pastor* Aristaeus (*Georgics* 4.317), *pastor* Apollo's son, who in ignorance has destroyed his once flourishing colony of bees and, in the process, the fine balance between creativity and violence embodied by Orpheus.[47] Through Aristaeus' error, Orphic powers are perverted and the natural order reversed, in this case through the return, albeit briefly, of departed life. In the end, an impassioned Orpheus becomes, like Dido, the victim (in Orpheus' case, literally) of a corrupted bacchanal, its celebrants possessed by their god in his most brutal incarnation. The laying of its walls is a critically vulnerable point in a city's history, considering that the nature of the wall, its physical or ideological permeability, reflects the extent to which its architects wish to separate themselves from the environment. Romulus and Remus, herdsmen both, did not learn from Carthage or from Troy, its fate sealed when the hubristic Laomedon refused payment to Neptune and Apollo for the building of the Trojan walls. In his deficiency as a mentor, *pater* Aeneas, who should have learned from Dido's Carthage and from Troy, fails his sons no less than Daedalus failed Icarus when the latter plied his waxen wings in flight.[48]

Apollo, Dido, and Dionysus all, either literally or symbolically, play a part in the Actian tableau, and therefore reside at the heart of Virgil's Shield. On the surface, the iconography of the scene is clear enough: Apollo, the god of light and clarity, has arrived in support of Augustus, Agrippa, and the Olympian host in their cosmic struggle against Antony, Cleopatra, and the monstrous, hybrid deities of the barbarian East. The outcome will be world dominion for Augustus and victory for the forces of light over darkness, good over evil, and restraint over excess. But nothing is quite what it seems, and hermeneutic clarity is merely an illusion. As "world" conqueror, particularly of the East, Augustus would have been associated, or even identified, with Alexander. This the final image on the Shield reveals (*Aeneid* 8.728); here Augustus has restrained the indignant Araxes, its expanse once straddled by Alexander. However, it was

---

[47] With regard to Apollo as *pastor,* I am referring to his experience as a shepherd in the service of Admetus. Here, Orpheus' musicality, his ability to mimic Nature, is viewed primarily as a means to achieve a "perfect" harmony therein—similarly Bradley 1969. For the more common focus on Orpheus as a poet and his music/poetry as overly-sentimental, potentially subversive, excessively individualistic, sterile, and antiquated in Octavian's new world order, see for example Conte 2001, Gale 2003, Habinek 1990, and Perkell 2001:38–39. The perversion of Orphic powers and reversal of the natural order occur when Orpheus succeeds, albeit briefly, in recalling Eurydice from the dead by virtue of the power of his song.

[48] On the failure of Daedalus, see Putnam's reading (1998:81–82) of the ecphrasis at *Aeneid* 6.14–37.

primarily Antony who modeled himself after Alexander's image.[49] Suddenly the distinction between Augustus and his great rival is blurred. Alexander, in turn, had represented himself as a new incarnation of Achilles, from whom he was allegedly descended, and of Dionysus, with whose orgiastic cult his snake-handling mother was particularly enamored. On the Shield, Antony, as consort of Cleopatra-Isis, has been cast as Osiris-Dionysus, but if Augustus is Alexander, he is likewise Dionysus, the (potentially) disorderly fraternal counterpart to the orderly Apollo.[50] Further, if Augustus is on any level a second Aeneas, he is also closely linked to, and indeed momentously affects the fate of, an Eastern queen who has a deep relationship with the land. So thoroughly is Cleopatra identified with her native landscape that she is shown on the Shield as retreating into the Nile's embrace (*Aeneid* 8.711–713). The mighty river, deeply distraught, offers the vanquished queen the protection that might have been expected of a "moral" Roman conqueror. Cleopatra is meant to recall Dido, confirmed by the tag "blanching at her imminent death" (*pallida/pallentem morte futura*), applied to both as they are sacrificed to the Roman cause.[51] In facing Cleopatra, Augustus(-Aeneas) assumes the role both of *nescius* 'ignorant' *pastor* and of Apollo wrongfully pursuing his sister, since Dido, pursued by Aeneas(-Apollo), is herself likened to Diana, goddess of wild places.[52] In the assumption of either role, Augustus upsets a sacred balance. As Aeneas and Alexander, Augustus is also Achilles encountering his Penthesileia, the value of her life recognized too late. The snare of associations linking and subversively interchanging the actors within the Actium tableau is staggeringly dense, and a picture emerges that Aeneas is perhaps fortunate not to have comprehended. In his battle against Antony, Augustus will ultimately kill his Roman brother, true, in this sense, to the legacy of Romulus. In so doing, Augustus, issuing directly from Aeneas' line, will have turned Troy against itself. This much is implied by the quotation of Ennius' *Andromache* in the description of Antony's forces, a reminder that empire and riches would not suffice to save a second Troy:[53]

> O pater, o patria: o Priami domus,
> Saeptum altisono cardine templum,

[49] On Augustus and Antony as Alexander, see Gruen 1985:68–69.

[50] See Weber 2002 (especially 338), who in this piece stresses Aeneas' own Dionysian associations.

[51] See Putnam 1998:148. *Aeneid* 4.644 ~ *Aeneid* 8.709.

[52] On the similes in which Aeneas and Dido are likened to Apollo and Diana respectively, see Clausen 1987:15–25.

[53] The reference is noted by Conington 1883:153 *ad loc.*

Vidi ego te adstantem ope barbarica
Tectis caelatis laqueatis
Auro ebore instructam regifice.
Haec omnia vidi inflammari,
Priamo vi vitam evitari,
Iovis aram sanguine turpari.

O father, o fatherland, o house of Priam,
sanctuary protected with hinge sounding on high;
I have seen you stand tall with barbarian wealth,
with embossed, paneled ceilings,
with gold, with ivory fitted regally.
All this I saw go up in flames,
the life from Priam by force removed,
Jove's altar with blood defiled.

Andromache Fragment 5.92–99[54]

Further, by presenting the Actian battle as parallel to battles between the Gods and Giants or Greeks and Amazon queens, the ecphrasis moves dangerously close to the iconographic program of the Parthenon, Augustus closer to Pericles. How could Augustus hope to duplicate or surpass the imperialistic feats of Pericles and Alexander while simultaneously advocating pastoralism and the georgic mode? How could cattle slaughtered by the *triumphator* be reconciled with a bloodless Golden Age? Miraculously, it was somehow possible in Evander's "Rome," but unlikely under a Romulean principate. This the characteristically succinct and polished Tibullus confirms:[55]

> Romulus aeternae nondum formaverat urbis
>   moenia, consorti non habitanda Remo;
25 sed tunc pascebant herbosa Palatia vaccae
>   et stabant humiles in Iovis arce casae.
> lacte madens illic suberat Pan ilicis umbrae
>   et facta agresti lignea falce Pales,
> pendebatque vagi pastoris in arbore votum,
30   garrula silvestri fistula sacra deo,
> fistula cui semper decrescit harundinis ordo:
>   nam calamus cera iungitur usque minor ...

---

[54] The text is from Vahlen's 1903 Teubner edition.

[55] Tibullus is described by Quintilian (10.1.93) as *tersus atque elegans*. The Tibullan reference is suggested by Eigler 2002:292.

55   carpite nunc, tauri, de septem montibus herbas
    dum licet: hic magnae iam locus urbis erit.

Of the eternal city had Romulus not yet traced
    the walls, destined not be inhabited by his brother Remus;
25   but then cows still grazed on a grassy Palatine
    and humble huts stood on Jove's height.
Dripping with milk, there was Pan beneath the shadow of the
    ilex
    and Pales fashioned in wood by a rustic's knife,
and on the tree hung the roaming herdsman's offering,
30   a warbling pipe sacred to the sylvan god,
a pipe whose array of reeds becomes smaller bit by bit;
    for each reed is joined with wax to a smaller...
55   Graze the grass now, bullocks, from the seven hills
    while you may; this will soon be the site of a great city.

Tibullus 2.5.23–56

In his view, there would be no cattle grazing and no shepherds piping in the Forum or on the Seven Hills after the construction of Rome's walls.

While it is true that Virgil raises many questions about the viability of Augustan utopics, he does not retreat without providing answers for his audience. As the Shield and its textual frame, pervaded by Lucretian resonances, reveal, the key to *rus in urbe* lies at the heart of Rome. This key comprises the Lupercal, the grotto of Faunus-Lupercus at the foot of the Palatine, and the fig tree, identified with the Ficus Ruminalis, that was grouped with a sacred olive and vine in the Roman Forum.[56] Both the Lupercal and the Ficus provided shade and shelter for the twins and their lupine mother, and both memorialized a moment in Rome's history in which a balance in Nature had been achieved. They were testimony of the common origins of all life, of beasts human and "wild." The language in the Shield's description of the Lupercal is, once again, telling:

fecerat et *viridi* fetam Mavortis *in antro*
procubuisse lupam, geminos huic ubera circum
ludere pendentis pueros et lambere matrem
impavidos, illam tereti cervice reflexa
mulcere alternos et corpora fingere lingua.

[56] On plantings in the Forum, see Andreae 1996:21–22.

> He had fashioned also the mother wolf in Mars' *green cavern*
> reclining, and about her teats the twin
> boys playfully hanging and mouthing their mother
> fearlessly, [while] she, her shapely neck turned back,
> caressed them in turn and licked their bodies into shape with
>   her tongue.
>
> Aeneid 8.630–634

This verdant cavern recalls another, which once sheltered the *Eclogues'* dispossessed herdsman Meliboeus:[57]

> ite meae, felix quondam pecus, ite capellae.
> non ego vos posthac *viridi* proiectus *in antro*
> dumosa pendere procul de rupe videbo;
> carmina nulla canam; non me pascente, capellae,
> florentem cytisum et salices carpetis amaras.
>
> Go along now my once fortunate flock, go my goats.
> You, hereafter, I, reclining *in a green cavern*, will not
> see hanging in the distance from a thorny crag.
> No songs will I sing; not with me pasturing you, my goats,
> will you graze the flowering clover and bitter willow.
>
> Eclogue 1.74–78

A casualty of the Triumvirs' land confiscations, Meliboeus will lose his lands to a soldier whom he describes as impious and barbarian, "impious" because he fought in a civil war, "barbarian" not because he is a foreigner but because he is a "brutal, bloodstained soldier" displacing a civilian from an inherently pacifistic and moral pastoral existence.[58]

The *Eclogues* advocate a gentler form of landscape inscription than Meliboeus' nemesis, steeped in the arts of war, represents. Militarism here is barbarian and "other," a thing to be excluded, *and* it is associated with the City. However, the first *Eclogue* also presents Rome, together with its First Citizen, as a "divine" source of salvation for the Italian countryside, its native arts, and its inhabitants.[59] Rather than imperialism and civil war, acts such as the resto-

---

[57] Putnam 1998:182 makes the connection.

[58] See Clausen 1994:58 *ad loc.*

[59] The reference here is to lines 6–8 of the first *Eclogue*: *O Meliboee, deus nobis haec otia fecit./ namque erit ille mihi semper deus, illius aram/ saepe tener nostris ab ovilibus imbuet agnus.* "O Meliboeus, a god has created this peace for me;/ for indeed to me that man will always be a god, his altar/ often will a young lamb from our folds stain."

ration of Tityrus' land, based on a true understanding of humanity's place in Nature, are what will approximate Octavian to divinity. At this juncture, the pendulum can swing either way; Rome has reached a critical point in its evolution, having grown and evolved to such an extent that the herdsman Tityrus cannot immediately relate to it:

> Urbem quam dicunt Romam, Meliboee, putavi
> stultus ego huic nostrae similem, quo saepe solemus
> pastores ovium teneros depellere fetus.
> sic canibus catulos similes, sic matribus haedos
> noram, sic parvis componere magna solebam.

> The city that they call Rome, Meliboeus, I thought,
> foolishly, to be like this village of ours, where often we
> herdsmen are wont to drive the tender offspring of our
> sheep.
> Thus I knew puppies are like dogs, thus kids like their
> mothers,
> thus I used to compare large with small.
>
> *Eclogue* 1.19–23

The City is in danger of losing its pastoral roots as it forges a new order. To preserve its pastoral underpinnings, that new order must not duplicate the ideals of Classical Athens, that magnificent exemplar of urbanism:

> ... Pallas quas condidit arces
> ipsa colat; nobis placeant ante omnia silvae.

> ... the citadel that she has founded, let Pallas
> herself inhabit; to us may forests above all give pleasure.
>
> *Eclogue* 2.61–62

Rome's utopian ideal, *rus in urbe*, will remain within grasp as long as Rome cherishes the lessons of the Lupercal and the shady Ficus. Both wolf and shade, like every other part of Nature, can be threatening or destructive, but are more likely to be so if approached in ignorance, if abused, or if misunderstood. So Dido regretfully laments her exposure to the Trojans' brand of exclusive urbanism:

> non licuit thalami expertem sine crimine vitam
> degere more ferae, talis nec tangere curas;

It was not permitted me a life free from the marriage bed,
   untainted,
   to lead, like a beast in the wild, and to experience not such
   agonies;

Aeneid 4.550–551

As long recognized, the essence of her sentiments is Epicurean.[60] Accordingly, her urban sensibility is fundamentally "inclusive," as the topography of her city, which is built around a densely shaded grove (*lucus in urbe fuit media, laetissimus umbrae* 'in the midst of the city was a grove abounding in shade', *Aeneid* 1.441), suggests. Tityrus in his good fortune is able to experience the benefits of inclusive urbanism as he reclines in the shade of a spreading beech playing his rustic flute amid the modest, but sufficient, bounty of his fields:

(Meliboeus): Tityre, tu patulae recubans sub tegmine fagi
2   *silvestrem* tenui *Musam* meditaris avena; ...
79   (Tityrus): Hic tamen hanc mecum poteras requiescere
       noctem
   fronde super viridi: sunt nobis mitia poma,
   castaneae molles et pressi copia lactis ...

(Meliboeus): Tityrus, you lying at ease under the cover of a
       spreading beech,
2   practice the *woodland Muse* on your slender reed; ...
79   (Tityrus): Here, nevertheless, you could rest this night with
       me
   upon the green grass; we have ripe apples,
   mealy chestnuts, and an abundance of pressed cheese ...

Eclogue 1.1–2, 79–81

The phrase "woodland Muse" (*silvestrem Musam*, *Eclogue* 1.2), which echoes Lucretius, betrays that the *otium* he has secured from the benign *iuvenis* 'youth' is Epicurean.[61] In fact, the situation of Tityrus replicates that happy state ascribed by the Epicurean poet to humanity at the time when music and poetry were born.[62] The *otium* enjoyed by both Tityrus and Lucretius' "primitive" humanity depends on the availability of sufficient food and upon the

---

[60] See Clausen 1987:49.
[61] *De Rerum Natura* 4.589: *fistula silvestrem ne cesset fundere musam* 'lest the pipe cease to pour forth the woodland Muse.'
[62] *De Rerum Natura* 5.1386–1396.

possibility of relaxation and restoration, both mental and physical, under the shady cover of trees. In other words, it depends upon immersing oneself in the delights of the *locus amoenus* and embracing the landscapes of which one necessarily, biologically, forms a part. Virgil's brand of pastoral *otium*, then, has much in common with *ataraxy*, the Epicurean utopian ideal. The opportunity of achieving this ideal is presented to Aeneas upon his arrival on Latin shores. The Lucretian resonances within Virgil's description tell us this much: now the Trojans recline beneath the limbs of a lofty tree and spread their humble feast upon the grass:

> Aeneas primique duces et pulcher Iulus
> corpora sub ramis deponunt arboris altae,
> instituuntque dapes et adorea liba per herbam
> subiciunt epulis (sic Iuppiter ipse monebat)
> et Cereale solum pomis agrestibus augent.

> Aeneas and his chief captains and fair Iulus
> recline their bodies beneath the branches of a lofty tree
> and set up the meal on the grass and spelt wafers
> do they place beneath the food—Jove himself advised them—
> and heap their wheaten plates with the produce of the coun-
> tryside.

Aeneid 7.107–110

This would prove to be but a fleeting moment of harmony. Soon the Trojans would fall victim to destructive passions, and their descendants would follow suit.[63] Again and again the sons of Aeneas rush to arms.

Judging from the substance of his works, Virgil believed in the resourcefulness of the human beast, and however grim the ending of the *Aeneid*, he was no pessimist, at least no more so than Lucretius, whose epic closes in a similar vein. In each case the ending is, above all, cautionary rather than prophetic. Both endings disclose a fundamental truth about utopian visions: as their socio-political frame changes with the passage of time, utopian visions may become obsolete.[64] Homer's utopian vision, born with the *polis* itself, was not suitable for crisis-ridden Rome. *Rus in urbe*, the quasi-Epicurean ideal that emerged from an urban milieu, could never be reconciled with it.

---

[63] See Johnson 2001 and Lyne 1983 on Virgil's politics of war and the Roman legacy of hostility.

[64] Their essentially static nature is what Hansot 1974:9–10 presents as the key difference between Classical and modern utopias, for the latter "attempt to make change an integral part of utopian reality" (10).

Epilogue
The Medallions and Other Magic Gardens

B ARELY VISIBLE BENEATH A CENTURY'S ACCUMULATION OF GRIME, a limpid lake beckons the viewer, its grassy shores flanked by stands of stately trees, its waters reflecting the clouds that grace a moody sky. On the opposite wall is its pendent, the depiction of a small farmhouse shaded by a grove and accessed by a road winding its way through verdant fields. These pastoral scenes belong to a series of eight oil paintings, known collectively as the Medallions; they are, and would from the first have been, the most visually striking features of the long, dark hallway that they adorn. This space, which admits little natural light, is the first floor and therefore main entrance hallway in the twenty-apartment tenement at 97 Orchard Street in New York City's Lower East Side.

When the hallway was refurbished and the Medallions were painted on its walls at the beginning of the twentieth century, life in this New York tenement must have been similar in many ways to that of the residents of Rome's *insulae*, its apartment complexes. When the pastoral scenes appeared, 97 Orchard Street had become increasingly crowded; the tenement housed seventy-one people in 1870 and one hundred and ten just two decades later. Indeed, in 1903, the Lower East Side was reputedly the most densely populated place on earth, making the city block that contained 97 Orchard Street "the most populated neighborhood in the world" with its residents numbering more than two thousand.[1] Crowded living conditions and the constant, strident surges of activity in the streets outside bring to mind the tirades of Horace, Martial, and Juvenal. As was the case with the emergence, and subsequent explosion, of Roman Italy's villa phenomenon, the Medallions suggest that the urban ideal was giving way to the pastoral. In other words, the garden, not the city, was becoming the utopian paradigm, the substance of the social dream. The introduction of "country" into the city for purposes of physical, intellectual, and

---

[1] Miller and Voulangas 1999:31.

moral health had, in fact, been a concern for some time. These, for instance, were among the goals cited by Andrew Jackson Downing in his 1848 proposal for a People's Park, a much-needed open space that would serve as the "lungs of the city."[2] His vision would be realized in Vaux and Olmsted's Central Park, the largest of this period's environmental efforts. At the same time, environmentally minded reformers saw to it that parks were created on a smaller scale, springing up on land reclaimed from tenements. Thus *rus in urbe* became an ideal also of this epic city.

When they completed their journey to the lower Hudson Valley, the first European settlers reportedly found a second Eden, a land flowing with milk and honey.[3] They were overwhelmed by the raw beauty of the landscape, by the lakes, valleys, forests, and flower-strewn meadows of this relatively untouched land. Whether it is this "unspoiled" landscape, the farm whose orchards ultimately became Orchard Street, or a remote ancestral homeland that the Medallions portray, these are the landscapes of memory, nostalgic in their longing for a past whose idealized conditions were viewed as integral to the ideals of the present. Nostalgia, as well as the creation of gardens, is both forward and backward looking.

The essentially nostalgic and utopian nature of the creation of garden spaces in an urban context is more apparent in some cases than in others, and it is worth considering closely those exemplars that advertise their underlying principles. Such, for instance, are the vibrant gardens that fill reclaimed open spaces in the once crime-ridden, gang-infested Norris Square neighborhood in lower North Philadelphia. One of many successful products of the Pennsylvania Horticultural Society's "Philadelphia Green" urban gardening initiative, Norris Square is no longer an urban jungle. Plantings enhanced by backdrops of garden murals unambiguously evoke the largely Puerto Rican community's rural past. These gardens are both "an improvement to the neighborhood, a form of physical rehabilitation" and a tangible means of preserving a cultural heritage.[4] The gardens provide hope where, for many, there was little or none, and this hope is cradled in memory. Fittingly, Norris Square's first major mural/garden project has been christened "*Raíces*," Roots.

Ideologically, every garden reproduces the physical reality of the plants it encloses. The older and larger the plant, the deeper its roots penetrate the storehouses of the Earth's geological memory. The cycles of seed-production

---

[2] Burrows and Wallace 1999:791.

[3] For the reactions of these early immigrants, see Burrows and Wallace 1999:3.

[4] See Golden, Rice, and Kinney 2002:69 for the quotes and pages 66-77 for Norris Square and its gardens generally.

and of foliage falling and then sprouting anew harbor an eternal promise. They harbor hope. Reflecting on the magnificent garden Adolf Rosengarten began to shape in 1912 on Philadelphia's Main Line, Chris Woods poignantly observes:

> A garden is a bridge between the human race and nature. It translates the chaos of the natural world into a language that is comprehensible and comfortable. It is essential entertainment, giving us sensual pleasure, while at the same time turning our minds to spiritual matters. While it is a complex creation, it reminds us of a more simple existence.[5]

What a garden does, by seducing us with its allurements of texture, scent, and color, is remind us of an essential unity, our essential unity with the natural world. This unity became and remains an ideal conceived in an urban context. Specifically, as manifested in Roman Italy, this ideal is conceived of as such when urban culture finds itself in a crisis or when the disadvantages of urban living begin to overshadow its benefits. In the Roman world, this ideal, described as *rus in urbe*, manifested itself in the flourishing of Epicureanism, a philosophy predicated on the essential atomic unity of life, and in the intense domestication of Nature evidenced by the avid embrace of flora, fauna, land, sky, and sea in the Roman villa as the Republic plunged irrevocably and fatally into civil war. The ideal of *rus in urbe* proved tractable and pliant, adaptable to a new social order and a new regime, and Augustus transformed its soft-primitivist strains into a dream of the Republic restored, the return of a Saturnian Golden Age in the rediscovery of Rome's humble, georgic past. However, utopian dreams, bound as they are to the distinct social conditions from which they rise, are not endlessly capable of mutation. At a critical juncture, they will reveal irreparable rifts and ultimately shatter, later emerging as something altogether new.

As Lucretius and Virgil demonstrate, *rus in urbe* as re-conceived by the Augustan regime was fundamentally irreconcilable with the dream of Pericles, the social dream of Classical Greece. Thoroughly urbanized, imperial Rome could never have become a second Athens, nor should it have wished to be, for the social dream of Pericles was also that of Homer, a dream conceived at the dawning of the urban impulse in Greece, from the post-Dark Age conditions

---

[5] The garden is Philadelphia's Chanticleer, and the quote has been taken from the garden's visitors' guide, "Chanticleer: A Pleasure Garden." Chris Woods, once the estate's head gardener, became the Director and Chief Horticulturalist of Chanticleer when it opened to the public in 1993.

underlying the birth of the *polis*. The *polis*, an ideologically and physically constructed "machine for living well,"—not merely a place in which to survive, a fortress, but a place in which to flourish—*was* this social dream.[6] The *polis* was conceived not only as a center of defense, but also, critically, as a center of habitation, "political" institutions, cults, industry, trade, education, and entertainment. And, as the Shield of Achilles demonstrates, the exclusion of wild Nature was fundamental to its development.[7] The Shield, Homer's utopian blueprint, discloses a world order established by the erection of barriers to check the potentially devastating encroachment of an untamed wilderness, from both within a settlement and without: walls and fences to keep Nature out, and a system of laws to contain the baser instincts of a city's inhabitants.

As Homer's Shield so vividly reveals, both before the birth of cities and in the infancy of the urban endeavor, there was no need to dream of gardens.

---

[6] The phrase "a machine for living well" is a reference both to Aristotle's statement that the *polis* exists in order to promote "good living" (*Politics* 1252b29-30) and to Le Corbusier's conception of a house as "a machine for living" as articulated in *Towards a New Architecture*.

[7] The essential elements of the *polis* are recounted in Hansen 2004:138-143.

Bibliography

Agrest, D. I. 1991. *Architecture from Without: Theoretical Framings for a Critical Practice.* Cambridge, MA.

Alberti, L. B. 1965. *The Ten Books of Architecture* (1485). Reprint from the Leoni Edition of 1755, ed. J. Rykwert. London.

Alden, M. 2000. *Homer Beside Himself: Para-Narratives in the Iliad.* Oxford.

Anderson, M. L. 1987. *Pompeian Frescoes in the Metropolitan Museum of Art.* New York.

Andreae, B. 1988. "Wandmalerei augusteischer Zeit." In *Kaiser Augustus und die verlorene Republik: Eine Ausstellung im Martin-Gropius-Bau, Berlin, 7. Juni–14. August 1988*, ed. M. Hofter, V. Lewandowski, H. G. Martin, J. Schiek, S. Schljapin, and M. Schmitz, 273–290. Mainz am Rhein.

———. 1996. *Am Birnbaum: Gärten und Parks im antiken Rom, in den Vesuvstädten und in Ostia.* Mainz am Rhein.

———. 2000. *Odysseus: Mythos und Erinnerung.* Mainz am Rhein.

Andronikos, M. 1992. *Vergina: The Royal Tombs and the Ancient City.* Trans. L. Turner. Athens.

Antonaccio, C. 1994. "Placing the Past: The Bronze Age in the Cultic Topography of Early Greece." In *Placing the Gods: Sanctuaries and Sacred Space in Ancient Greece*, ed. S. E. Alcock and R. Osborne, 79–104. Oxford.

———. 2000. "Architecture and Behavior: Building Gender into Greek Houses." *Classical World* 93.5:517–535.

Arthur, M. B. 1973. "Early Greece: The Origins of the Western Attitude Toward Women." *Arethusa* 6.1:7–58.

———. 1982. "Cultural Strategies in Hesiod's *Theogony*: Law, Family, Society." *Arethusa* 15.1.2:63–82.

Ault, B. A. 2000. "Living in the Classical *Polis*: The Greek House as Microcosm." *Classical World* 93.5:483–496.

Austin, N. 1975. *Archery at the Dark Side of the Moon: Poetic Problems in Homer's Odyssey.* Berkeley.

Austin, R. G., ed. 1971. *P. Vergili Maronis Aeneidos Liber Primus.* Oxford.

Bachofen, J. J. 1967. *Myth Religion and Mother Right.* Trans. R. Manheim. Princeton.

Bailey, C. 1931. "Virgil and Lucretius." *Proceedings of the Classical Association* 28:21–39.

Barrell, J., and J. Bull, eds. 1975. *A Book of English Pastoral Verse.* New York.

Bartman, E. 1991. "Sculptural Collecting and Display in the Private Realm." In *Roman Art in the Private Sphere: New Perspectives on the Architecture and Décor of the Domus, Villa, and Insula,* ed. E. K. Gazda, 71–88. Ann Arbor.

Beard, M. 1998. "Imaginary *Horti*: Or up the Garden Path." In *Horti Romani: Atti del Convegno Internazionale Roma, 4-6 maggio 1995.* Bulletino della Commissione Archeologica Comunale di Roma, Supplementi 6, ed. M. Cime and E. La Rocca, 23–32. Rome.

Becker, A. S. 1995. *The Shield of Achilles and the Poetics of Ecphrasis.* Lanham, MD.

Bek, L. 1980. *Towards Paradise on Earth: Modern Space Conception in Architecture, A Creation of Renaissance Humanism.* Analecta Romana Instituti Danici IX. Herning.

Benson, J. L. 1970. *Horse, Bird, and Man: The Origins of Greek Painting.* Amherst.

Bergmann, B. 1991. "Painted Perspectives of a Villa Visit: Landscape as Status and Metaphor." In *Roman Art in the Private Sphere: New Perspectives on the Architecture and Décor of the Domus, Villa, and Insula,* ed. E. K. Gazda, 49–70. Ann Arbor.

———. 1992. "Exploring the Grove: Pastoral Space on Roman Walls." In *The Pastoral Landscape.* Studies in the History of Art 36, ed. J. D. Hunt, 21–46. Washington, DC.

———. 1995. "Greek Masterpieces and Roman Recreative Fictions." *Harvard Studies in Classical Philology* 97:79–120.

———. 1999. "Rhythms of Recognition: Mythological Encounters in Roman Landscape Painting." In *Spiegel des Mythos: Bilderwelt und Lebenswelt,* ed. F. de Angelis and S. Muth, 81–107. Wiesbaden.

———. 2002. "Art and Nature in the Villa at Oplontis." In *Pompeian Brothels, Pompeii's Ancient History, Mirrors and Mysteries, Art and Nature at Oplontis, & the Herculaneum 'Basilica',* ed. C. Stein and J. H. Humphrey, 87–120. Portsmouth, RI.

Bergren, A. 1993. "The (Re)Marriage of Penelope and Odysseus Architecture Gender Philosophy." *Assemblage* 21:7–23.

Betsky, A. 1995. *Building Sex: Men, Women, Architecture and the Construction of Sexuality.* New York.

Beyen, H. G. 1938. *Die pompejanische Wanddekoration vom zweiten bis zum vierten Stil.* Vol. I, i. The Hague.

———. 1960. *Die pompejanische Wanddekoration vom zweiten bis zum vierten Stil.* Vol. II, i. The Hague.

Biers, W. R. 1987. *The Archaeology of Greece: An Introduction.* Revised edition. Ithaca.

Blanckenhagen, P. H. von, and C. Alexander. 1962. *The Paintings from Boscotrecase.* Mitteilungen des deutschen archäologischen Instituts, römische Abteilung, sechstes Ergänzungsheft. Heidelberg.

———. 1963. "The Odyssey Frieze." *Mitteilungen des deutschen archäologischen Instituts, römische Abteilung* 70:100–146.

Boardman, J. 1974. *Athenian Black Figure Vases.* London.

———. 1975. *Athenian Red Figure Vases: The Archaic Period.* London.

———. 1983. "Symbol and Story in Geometric Art." In *Ancient Greek Art and Iconography*, ed. W. G. Moon, 15–36. Madison.

———. 1989. *Athenian Red-figure Vases: The Classical Period.* London.

———. 1998. *Early Greek Vase Painting, 11th-6th Centuries BC: A Handbook.* London.

Boatwright, M. T. 1998. "Luxuriant Gardens and Extravagant Women: The *Horti* of Rome between Republic and Empire." In *Horti Romani: Atti del Convegno Internazionale Roma, 4-6 maggio 1995.* Bulletino della Commissione Archeologica Comunale di Roma, Supplementi 6, ed. M. Cime and E. La Rocca, 71–82. Rome.

Borbein, A. H. 1975. "Zur Deutung von Schwerwand und Durchblick auf den Wandgemälden des zweiten pompejanischen Stils." In *Neue Forschungen in Pompeji und den anderen vom Vesuvausbruch 79 n. Chr. verschütteten Städten*, ed. B. Andreae and H. Kyrieleis, 61–70. Recklinghausen.

Bradley, A. 1969. "Augustan Culture and a Radical Alternative: Vergil's *Georgics.*" *Arion* 8:347–358.

Bremmer, J. 1999. "Paradise from Persia, Via Greece, into the *Septuagint.*" In *Paradise Interpreted: Representations of Biblical Paradise in Judaism and Christianity*, ed. G. P. Luttikhuizen, 1–20. Leiden.

Bright, D. F. 1971. "The Plague and the Structure of the *De Rerum Natura.*" *Latomus* 30:607–632.

Brilliant, R. 1994. "Augustus and Hadrian: Classical and Classicizing Modes." In *Commentaries on Roman Art: Selected Studies*, 97–114. London.

Brödner, E. 1989. *Wohnen in der Antike.* Darmstadt.

Bruno, V. J. 1977. *Form and Color in Greek Painting.* New York.

Buitron-Oliver, D., and B. Cohen. 1995. "Between Skylla and Penelope: Female Characters of the *Odyssey* in Archaic and Classical Greek Art." In *The Distaff Side: Representing the Female in Homer's Odyssey*, ed. B. Cohen, 29–58. New York.

Burkert, W. 1992. *The Orientalizing Revolution: Near Eastern Influence on Greek Culture in the Early Archaic Age.* Trans. M. E. Pinter and W. Burkert. Cambridge, MA.

Burrows, E. G., and M. Wallace. 1999. *Gotham: A History of New York City to 1898.* Oxford.

Buschor, E. 1944. *Die Musen des Jenseits.* Munich.

Camp, J. M. 2000. "Walls and the *Polis.*" In *Polis & Politics: Studies in Ancient Greek History*, ed. P. Flensted-Jensen, T. H. Nielsen, and L. Rubinstein, 41–58. Copenhagen.

———. 2001. *The Archaeology of Athens.* New Haven.

Campbell, D. A. 1967. *Greek Lyric Poetry.* Bristol.

Carpenter, R. 1946. *Folktale, Fiction, and Saga in the Homeric Epics.* Berkeley.

Carroll, M. 2003. *Earthly Paradises: Ancient Gardens in History and Archaeology.* London.

Carroll-Spillecke, M. 1989. *ΚΗΠΟΣ: Der antike griechische Garten.* Munich.

———. 1992a. "The Gardens of Greece from Homeric to Roman Times." *Journal of Garden History* 12.2:84–101.

———. 1992b. "Griechische Gärten." In *Der Garten von der Antike bis zum Mittelalter.* Kulturgeschichte der antiken Welt 57, ed. M. Carroll-Spillecke, 153–176. Mainz am Rhein.

Cartledge, P. 1997. "'Deep Plays': Theatre as Process in Greek Civic Life." In *The Cambridge Companion to Greek Tragedy*, ed. P. E. Easterling, 3–35. Cambridge.

Caskey, L. D. 1934. "Odysseus and Elpenor in the Lower World." *Bulletin of the Museum of Fine Arts* XXXII.191:40–44.

Caskey, L. D., and J. D. Beazley. 1954. *Attic Vase Paintings in the Museum of Fine Arts Boston.* Part II. London.

Castriota, D. 1992. *Myth, Ethos, and Actuality: Official Art in Fifth-Century B.C. Athens.* Madison.

———. 1995. *The Ara Pacis Augustae and the Imagery of Abundance in Later Greek and Early Roman Imperial Art.* Princeton.

Chew, K. 2002. "*Inscius pastor:* Ignorance and Aeneas' Identity in the *Aeneid.*" *Latomus* 61.3:616–627.

Clarke, J. R. 1991. *The Houses of Roman Italy 100 B.C-A.D. 250: Ritual, Space, and Decoration.* Berkeley.

———. 2000. "Landscape Paintings in the Villa of Oplontis." *Journal of Roman Archaeology* 13:81–107.

Clarke, M. L. 1973. "The Garden of Epicurus." *Phoenix* 27.4:386–387.

Clausen, W. 1987. *Virgil's Aeneid and the Tradition of Hellenistic Poetry*. Berkeley.

———. 1994. *A Commentary on Virgil: Eclogues*. Oxford.

Clay, J. S. 1981. "The Old Man in the Garden: *Georgic* 4.116–148." *Arethusa* 14.1:57– 65.

———. 1983. *The Wrath of Athena: Gods and Men in the Odyssey*. Princeton.

Cohen, A. 1997. *The Alexander Mosaic: Stories of Victory and Defeat*. Cambridge.

Coldstream, J. N. 1977. *Geometric Greece*. London.

Cole, S. G. 1994. "Demeter in the Ancient Greek City and its Countryside." In *Placing the Gods: Sanctuaries and Sacred Space in Ancient Greece*, ed. S. E. Alcock and R. Osborne, 199–216. Oxford.

———. 2000. "Landscapes of Artemis." *The Classical World* 93.5:471–481.

Commager, H. S. 1957. "Lucretius' Interpretation of the Plague." *Harvard Studies in Classical Philology* 62:105–118.

Cook, E. F. 1995. *The Odyssey in Athens: Myths of Cultural Origins*. Ithaca.

Conan, M. 1986. "Nature into Art: Gardens and Landscapes in the Everyday Life of Ancient Rome." *Journal of Garden History* 6.4:348–356.

Conington, J., and H. Nettleship, eds. 1883. *The Works of Virgil*. Vol. III: *Aeneid VII–XII*. 3rd ed. London.

Conte, G. B. 2001. "Aristaeus, Orpheus, and the *Georgics*: Once Again." In *Poets and Critics Read Vergil*, ed. S. Spence, 44–63. New Haven.

Crane, G. 1988. *Calypso: Backgrounds and Conventions of the Odyssey*. Athenäum Monografien, Beiträge zur klassischen Philologie 191. Frankfurt am Main.

Cunliffe, R. J. 1963. *A Lexicon of the Homeric Dialect*. Norman, OK.

Curtius, E. R. 1953. "The Ideal Landscape." In *European Literature and the Latin Middle Ages*, trans. W. R. Trask, 183–202. London.

D'Arms, J. H. 1970. *Romans on the Bay of Naples: A Social and Cultural Study of Villas and Their Owners from 150 B.C. to A.D. 400*. Cambridge, MA.

———. 1998. "Between Public and Private: The *Epulum Publicum* and Caesar's *Horti Trans Tiberim*." In *Horti Romani: Atti del Convegno Internazionale Roma, 4-6 maggio 1995*. Bulletino della Commissione Archeologica Comunale di Roma, Supplementi 6, ed. M. Cime and E. La Rocca, 33–43. Rome.

Dawson, C. M. 1965. *Romano-Campanian Mythological Landscape Painting*. Rome.

Derrida, J. 1987. *The Truth in Painting*. Trans. G. Bennington and I. McLeod. Chicago.

De Witt, N. W. 1954. *Epicurus and His Philosophy*. Minneapolis.

Dickmann, J.-A. 1997. "The Peristyle and the Transformation of Domestic Space in Hellenistic Pompeii." In *Domestic Space in the Roman World: Pompeii and Beyond*, ed. R. Laurence and A. Wallace-Hadrill, 121–136. Portsmouth, RI.

Dillon, S. 2000. "Subject Selection and Viewer Reception of Greek Portraits from Herculaneum and Tivoli." *Journal of Roman Archaeology* 13:21–40.

Doherty, L. E. 1995a. "Sirens, Muses, and Female Narrators in the *Odyssey*." In *The Distaff Side: Representing the Female in Homer's Odyssey*, ed. B. Cohen, 81–92. New York.

———. 1995b. *Siren Songs: Gender, Audiences, and Narrators in the Odyssey*. Ann Arbor.

Dorter, K. 1971. "Imagery and Philosophy in Plato's *Phaedrus*." *Journal of the History of Philosophy* 9:279–288.

Dougherty, C. 2001. *The Raft of Odysseus: The Ethnographic Imagination of Homer's Odyssey*. Oxford.

duBois, P. 1982. *Centaurs and Amazons: Women and the Pre-History of the Great Chain of Being*. Ann Arbor.

———. 1988. *Sowing the Body: Psychoanalysis and Ancient Representations of Women*. Chicago.

Dyck, A. R. 1981. "The Witch's Bed but Not Her Breakfast." *Rheinisches Museum für Philologie* 124:196–198.

Edwards, A. T. 1993. "Homer's Ethical Geography: Country and City in the *Odyssey*." *Transactions of the American Philological Association* 123:27–78.

Edwards, M. W. 1991. *The Iliad: A Commentary*. Vol. V: Books 17–20 (general ed. G. S. Kirk). Cambridge.

Ehrhardt, W. 1991. "Bild und Ausblick in Wandbemalungen zweiten Stils." *Antike Kunst* 34:28–65.

Eigler, U. 2002. "Urbanität und Ländlichkeit als Thema und Problem der Augusteischen Literatur." *Hermes* 130.3:288–298.

Elsner, J. 1995. *Art and the Roman Viewer: The Transformation of Art from the Pagan World to Christianity*. Cambridge.

———. 1996. "Inventing *Imperium*: Texts and Propaganda." In *Art and Text in Roman Culture*, ed. J. Elsner, 32–54. Cambridge.

Erlich, R. 2004. "Ursula K. Le Guin: Eutopia, Antiutopia, Dystopia." Paper presented at the 29th Annual Meeting of the Society for Utopian Studies, Toronto, October 7–10.

Farrar, L. 1998. *Ancient Roman Gardens*. Phoenix Mill, UK.

Farrell, J. 1991. *Vergil's Georgics and the Traditions of Ancient Epic: The Art of Allusion in Literary History*. New York.

Ferguson, J. 1975. *Utopias in the Classical World*. Ithaca.

Ferriolo, M. V. 1989. "Homer's Garden." *Journal of Garden History* 9.2:86–94.

Filarete. 1965. *Treatise on Architecture (1461-1463)*. Trans. J. R. Spencer. New Haven.

Fine, J. V. A. 1983. *The Ancient Greeks: A Critical History*. Cambridge.

Finley, M. I. 1967. "Utopianism Ancient and Modern." In *The Critical Spirit: Essays in Honor of Herbert Marcuse*, ed. K. Wolff and B. Moore, 3–20. Boston.

———. 1970. *Early Greece: The Bronze and Archaic Ages*. New York.

———. 1979. *The World of Odysseus*. 2nd ed. New York.

———. 1982. *Economy and Society in Ancient Greece*, ed. B. D. Shaw and R. P. Saller. New York.

Foley, H. P. 1978. "'Reverse Similes' and Sex Roles in the *Odyssey*." *Arethusa* 11:7–26.

Foley, J. M. 1997. "Oral Tradition and Its Implications." In *A New Companion to Homer*, ed. I. Morris and B. Powell, 146–173. Leiden.

Frank, T. 1922. *Vergil: A Biography*. New York.

Frazer, A. 1992. "The Roman Villa and the Pastoral Ideal." In *The Pastoral Landscape*. Studies in the History of Art 36, ed. J. D. Hunt, 49–62. Washington, DC.

Gabriel, M. M. 1955. *Livia's Garden Room at Prima Porta*. New York.

Gale, M. R. 1991. "Man and Beast in Lucretius and the *Georgics*." *The Classical Quarterly* n.s. 41.2:414–426.

———. 1994. *Myth and Poetry in Lucretius*. Cambridge.

———. 2000. *Virgil on the Nature of Things: The Georgics, Lucretius and the Didactic Tradition*. Cambridge.

———. 2003. "Poetry and the Backward Glance in Virgil's *Georgics* and *Aeneid*." *Transactions of the American Philological Association* 133.2:323–352.

Galinsky, K. 1996. *Augustan Culture: An Interpretive Introduction*. Princeton.

Giamatti, A. B. 1966. *The Earthly Paradise and the Renaissance Epic*. Princeton.

Giesecke, A. L. 1999a. "Elpenor, Amymone, and the Truth in the Lykaon Painter's Painting." *Bulletin Antieke Beschaving* 74:63–78.

———. 1999b. "Lucretius and Virgil's Pastoral Dream." *Utopian Studies* 10.2:1–15.

———. 2000. *Atoms, Ataraxy, and Allusion*. Spudasmata 76. Hildesheim.

———. 2001. "Beyond the Garden of Epicurus: The Utopics of the Ideal Roman Villa." *Utopian Studies* 12.2:13–32.

———. 2002. "Framing Virgil's Ghosts: Allusion and the Illusion of Rothko's Door." *Helios* 29.2:127–148.

———. 2003. "Homer's Eutopolis: Epic Journeys and the Search for an Ideal Society." *Utopian Studies* 14.2:23–40.

Gleason, K. L. 1994. "*Porticus Pompeiana*: A New Perspective on the First Public Park of Ancient Rome." *Journal of Garden History* 14.1:13–27.

Goetz, G. 1929. *M. Terenti Varronis Rerum Rusticarum Libri Tres.* Leipzig.

Golden, J., R. Rice, and M. Y. Kinney. 2002. *Philadelphia Murals and the Stories They Tell.* Philadelphia.

Goodman, R. 2003. "Utopian Spaces on the Move: Privilege, Loss, and Gain." Paper presented at the 28th Annual Meeting of the Society for Utopian Studies, San Diego, October 30–November 2.

Gothein, M. 1909. "Der griechische Garten." *Mitteilungen des kaiserlich deutschen archäologischen Instituts, athenische Abteilung* 34:100–144.

Gow, A. S. F. 1950. *Theocritus.* 2 vols. Cambridge.

Graham, A. J. 1995. "The *Odyssey*, History, and Women." In *The Distaff Side: Representing the Female in Homer's Odyssey*, ed. B. Cohen, 3–16. New York.

Gresseth, G. K. 1970. "The Homeric Sirens." *Transactions of the American Philological Association* 101:203–218.

Grimal, P. 1969. *Les jardins romains.* 2nd ed. Paris.

Griswold, C. L., Jr. 1986. *Self-Knowledge in Plato's Phaedrus.* New Haven.

Gropengiesser, H. 1977. "Sänger und Sirenen: Versuch einer Deutung." *Archäologischer Anzeiger* 1977:582–610.

Gruen, E. S. 1985. "Augustus and the Ideology of War and Peace." In *The Age of Augustus*, ed. R. Winkes, 51–72. Louvain-la-Neuve.

Habicht, C. 1997. *Athens from Alexander to Antony.* Trans. D. L. Schneider. Cambridge, MA.

Habinek, T. N. 1990. "Sacrifice, Society, and Vergil's Ox-Born Bees." In *Cabinet of the Muses: Essays on Classical and Comparative Literature in Honor of Thomas G. Rosenmeyer*, ed. M. Griffith and D. J. Mastronarde, 209–223. Atlanta.

Hainsworth, J. B. 1988. Commentary on Books V–VIII of the *Odyssey*. In *A Commentary on Homer's Odyssey*. Vol. I, ed. A. Heubeck, S. West, and J. B. Hainsworth, 249–386. Oxford.

Hales, S. 2003. *The Roman House and Social Identity.* Cambridge.

Halperin, D. M. 1983. *Before Pastoral: Theocritus and the Ancient Tradition of Bucolic Poetry.* New Haven.

Hammer, D. 2002. *The Iliad as Politics: The Performance of Political Thought.* Norman, OK.

Hansen, M. H. 1997. "The Copenhagen Inventory of *Poleis* and the *Lex Hafniensis De Civitate*." In *The Development of the Polis in Archaic Greece*, ed. L. G. Mitchell and P. J. Rhoades, 9–23. London.

Hansen, M. H., and T. H. Nielsen. 2004. *An Inventory of Archaic and Classical Poleis.* Oxford.

Hansot, E. 1974. *Perfection and Progress: Two Modes of Utopian Thought.* Cambridge, MA.

Hass, P. 1998. *Der locus amoenus in der antiken Literatur: Zu Theorie und Geschichte eines literarischen Motivs.* Bamberg.

Haüber, C. 1998. "The Esquiline *Horti*: New Research." In *The Roman Villa, Villa Urbana: First Williams Symposium on Classical Architecture held at the University of Pennsylvania, Philadelphia, April 21-22, 1990.* University Museum Monograph 101, Symposium Series 9, ed. A. Frazer, 55–64. Philadelphia.

Henrichs, A. 1990. "Between Country and City: Cultic Dimensions of Dionysus in Athens and Attica." In *Cabinet of the Muses,* ed. M. Griffith and D. J. Mastronarde, 257–277. Atlanta.

Hitzig, H. 1896. *Pausaniae Graeciae Descriptio.* Vol. I, i: Book I, Attica. Leipzig.

———. 1907. *Pausaniae Graeciae Descriptio.* Vol. III, i: Book VIII, Arcadia and Book IX, Boeotia. Leipzig.

Hoekstra, A. 1989. Commentary on Books XIII–XVI of the *Odyssey.* In *A Commentary on Homer's Odyssey.* Vol. II, ed. A. Heubeck and A. Hoekstra, 147–287. Oxford.

Hoepfner, W., and E.-L. Schwander. 1994. *Haus und Stadt im klassischen Griechenland.* Wohnen in der klassischen Polis I. Munich.

Hofstetter, E. 1990. *Sirenen im archaischen und klassischen Griechenland.* Würzburg.

Hood, S. 1978. *The Arts in Prehistoric Greece.* London.

Horkheimer, M., and T. W. Adorno. 1993. *Dialectic of Enlightenment.* Trans. J. Cumming. New York.

Horsfall, N. M., ed. 1995. *A Companion to the Study of Virgil.* Leiden.

Howe, T. N. 2004. "Powerhouses: The Seaside Villas of Campania in the Power Culture of Rome." In *In Stabiano: Exploring the Seaside Villas of the Roman Elite,* ed. A. Pesce, 15–33. Castellamare di Stabia.

Hubbard, T. K. 1992. "Nature and Art in the Shield of Achilles." *Arion* 3rd ser. 2.1:16–41.

Hugonot, J.-C. 1992. "Ägyptische Gärten." In *Der Garten von der Antike bis zum Mittelalter,* ed. M. Caroll-Spillecke, 9–44. Mainz am Rhein.

Hunt, J. D. 1991. "Introduction: Pastoral and Pastoralisms." In *The Pastoral Landscape.* Studies in the History of Art 36, ed. J. D. Hunt, 11–20. Washington, DC.

———. 1992. *Gardens and the Picturesque: Studies in the History of Landscape Architecture.* Cambridge, MA.

———. 2000. *Greater Perfections: The Practice of Garden Theory.* Philadelphia.

Hurwit, J. M. 1977. "Image and Frame in Greek Art." *American Journal of Archaeology* 81:1–30.

———. 1985. *The Art and Culture of Early Greece 1100–480 B.C.* Ithaca.

———. 1991. "The Representation of Nature in Early Greek Art." In *New Perspectives in Early Greek Art,* ed. D. Buitron-Oliver, 33–64. Hanover, NH.

———. 1992. "A Note on Ornament, Nature, and Boundary in Early Greek Art." *Bulletin Antieke Beschaving* 67:63–72.

———. 1999. *The Athenian Acropolis: History, Mythology and Archaeology from the Neolithic Era to the Present.* Cambridge.

Hutchinson, G. O. 1988. *Hellenistic Poetry.* Oxford.

Immerwahr, S. A. 1977. "Mycenaeans at Thera: Some Reflections on the Paintings from the West House." In *Greece and the Mediterranean in Ancient History and Prehistory,* ed. K. H. Kinzl, 173–191. Berlin.

———. 1990. *Aegean Painting in the Bronze Age.* University Park, PA.

Jaeger, W. W. 1966. *Five Essays.* Trans. A. M. Fiske. Montreal.

Jameson, M. 1990. "Private Space and the Greek City." In *The Greek City From Homer to Alexander,* ed. O. Murray and S. Price, 171–195. Oxford.

Jan, L., ed. 1878. *C. Plini Secundi Naturalis Historiae Libri XXXVI.* Vol. III: Libri XVI–XXII. Leipzig.

Janko, R. 1982. *Homer, Hesiod and the Homeric Hymns: Diachronic Development in Epic Diction.* Cambridge.

Jashemski, W. F. 1979. *The Gardens of Pompeii, Herculaneum, and the Villas Destroyed by Vesuvius.* New York.

———. 1993. *The Gardens of Pompeii, Herculaneum, and the Villas Destroyed by Vesuvius.* Vol. II: Appendices. New York.

Jenkyns, R. 1998. *Virgil's Experience. Nature and History: Times, Names, and Places.* Oxford.

Jensen, M. S. 1980. *The Homeric Question and the Oral-Formulaic Theory.* Copenhagen.

Johnson, W. R. 2001. "Imaginary Romans: Vergil and the Illusion of National Identity." In *Poets and Critics Read Vergil,* ed. S. Spence, 3–16. New Haven.

Jung, F. 1984. "Gebaute Bilder." *Antike Kunst* 27.2:71–122.

Kawami, T. S. 1992. "Antike persische Gärten." In *Der Garten von der Antike bis zum Mittelalter.* Kulturgeschichte der antiken Welt 57, ed. M. Carroll-Spillecke, 81–100. Mainz am Rhein.

Kellum, B. A. 1994. "The Construction of Landscape in Augustan Rome: The Garden Room at the Villa *ad Gallinas*." *The Art Bulletin* 76.2:211–224.

Kim, J. 2000. *The Pity of Achilles: Oral Style and the Unity of the Iliad*. Lanham, MD.

King, K. C. 1987. *Achilles: Paradigms of the War Hero from Homer to the Middle Ages*. Berkeley.

King, R. 1979. *The Quest for Paradise: A History of the World's Gardens*. Weybridge, UK.

Kirk, G. S. 1985. *The Iliad: A Commentary*. Vol. I: Books 1–4 (general ed. G. S. Kirk). Cambridge.

Klynne, A., and P. Liljenstolpe. 2000. "Investigating the gardens of the Villa of Livia." *Journal of Roman Archaeology* 13:220–233.

Krohn, F., ed. 1912. *Vitruvii De Architectura Libri Decem*. Leipzig.

Kumar, K. 1991. *Utopianism*. Buckingham.

Kuttner, A. 1998. "Prospects of Patronage: Realism and *Romanitas* in the Architectural Vistas of the 2nd Style." In *The Roman Villa, Villa Urbana: First Williams Symposium on Classical Architecture held at the University of Pennsylvania, Philadelphia, April 21–22, 1990*. University Museum Monograph 101, Symposium Series 9, ed. A. Frazer, 93–108. Philadelphia.

———. 1999. "Looking Outside Inside: Ancient Roman Garden Rooms." *Studies in the History of Gardens and Designed Landscape* 19.1:7–35.

Laidlaw, A. 1985. *The First Style in Pompeii: Painting and Architecture*. Rome.

Langdon, S., ed. 1993. *From Pasture to Polis: Art in the Age of Homer*. Columbia, MO.

Latacz, J. 2001. *Troia und Homer: Der Weg zur Lösung eines alten Rätsels*. Munich.

Lauter, H. 1998. "Hellenistische Vorläufer der römischen Villa." In *The Roman Villa, Villa Urbana: First Williams Symposium on Classical Architecture held at the University of Pennsylvania, Philadelphia, April 21–22, 1990*. University Museum Monograph 101, Symposium Series 9, ed. A. Frazer, 21–28. Philadelphia.

Lauter-Bufe, H. 1975. "Zur architektonischen Gartengestaltung in Pompeji und Herculaneum." In *Neue Forschungen in Pompeji und den anderen vom Vesuvausbruch 79 n. Chr. verschütteten Städten*, ed. B. Andreae and H. Kyrieleis, 169–178. Recklinghausen.

Leach, E. W. 1988. *The Rhetoric of Space: Literary and Artistic Representations of Landscape in Republican and Augustan Rome*. Princeton.

———. 2004. *The Social Life of Painting in Ancient Rome and on the Bay of Naples*. Cambridge.

Le Corbusier. 1970. *Towards a New Architecture.* Trans. F. Etchells. New York.

Leeuwen, J. van. 1913. *Ilias.* Vol. II: Libri XIII–XXIV. Leiden.

Lefkowitz, M. R. 1986. *Women in Greek Myth.* London.

Levitas, R. 1990. *The Concept of Utopia.* New York.

Ling, R. 1977. "Studius and the Beginnings of Roman Landscape Painting." *The Journal of Roman Studies* 67:1–16.

———. 1991. *Roman Painting.* Cambridge.

Littlewood, A. R. 1984. "Ancient Literary Evidence for Pleasure Gardens of Roman Country Villas." In *Ancient Roman Villa Gardens.* Dumbarton Oaks Colloquium on the History of Landscape Architecture X, ed. E. B. Macdougall, 7–30. Washington, DC.

Lord, A. 1960. *The Singer of Tales.* Cambridge, MA.

Louden, B. 1999. *The Odyssey: Structure, Narration, and Meaning.* Baltimore.

Lowenstam, S. 1993. *The Scepter and the Spear: Studies on Forms of Repetition in the Homeric Poems.* Lanham, MD.

Luce, J. V. 1975. *Homer and the Heroic Age.* New York.

———. 1978. "The *Polis* in Homer and Hesiod." *Proceedings of the Royal Irish Academy* 78:1–15.

Lyne, R. O. A. M. 1983. "Vergil and the Politics of War." *The Classical Quarterly* 13.1:188–203.

———. 1987. *Further Voices in Vergil's Aeneid.* Oxford.

Manuel, F. E., and F. P. Manuel. *Utopian Thought in the Western World.* Cambridge, MA.

Marin, L. 1984. *Utopics: Spatial Play.* Trans. R. A. Vollrath. Atlantic Highlands, NJ.

Mau, A. 1882. *Die Geschichte der dekorativen Wandmalerei in Pompeji.* Leipzig.

Mayhoff, C., ed. 1909. *C. Plini Secundi Naturalis Historiae Libri XXXVII.* Vol. II: Libri VII–XV. Leipzig.

McKay, A. G. 1975. *Houses, Villas and Palaces in the Roman World.* Ithaca.

Meier, C. 1990 "C. Caesar Divi filius and the Formation of the Alternative in Rome." In *Between Republic and Empire: Interpretations of Augustus and His Principate,* ed. K. A. Raaflaub and M. Toher, 54–70. Berkeley.

Michel, D. 1980. "Pompejanische Gartenmalereien." In *Tainia: Roland Hampe zum 70. Geburtstag am 2. Dezember 1978,* ed. H. A. Cahn and E. Simon, 373–404. 2 vols. Mainz am Rhein.

Mielsch, H. 1987. *Die römische Villa: Achitektur und Lebensform.* Munich.

Miller, S. and Voulangas, A. 1999. *A Tenement Story: The History of 97 Orchard Street and the Lower East Side Tenement Museum.* New York.

Moorton, R. F. 1989. "The Innocence of Italy in Vergil's *Aeneid*." *The American Journal of Philology* 110.1:105–30.

Morris, I. 1986. "The Use and Abuse of Homer." *Classical Antiquity* 5:94–115.

Moynihan, E. B. 1979. *Paradise as a Garden in Persia and Mughal India*. New York.

Muellner, L. 1976. *The Meaning of Homeric EYXOMAI through its Formulas*. Innsbrucker Beiträge zur Sprachwissenschaft 13. Innsbruck.

Mumford, L. 1961. *The City in History: Its Origins, Its Transformations, and Its Prospects*. San Diego.

———. 1965. "Utopia, The City and The Machine." In *Utopias and Utopian Thought*, ed. F. E. Manuel, 3–24. Boston.

Mynors, R. A. G., ed. 1990. *Virgil: Georgics*. Oxford.

Nagler, M. N. 1977. "Dread Goddess Endowed With Speech." *Archaeological News* 6:77–85.

Nagy, G. 1979. *The Best of the Achaeans: Concepts of the Hero in Archaic Greek Poetry*. Baltimore.

———. 1990. *Greek Mythology and Poetics*. Ithaca.

———. 1996. *Homeric Questions*. Austin.

———. 1997. "The Shield of Achilles: Ends of the *Iliad* and Beginnings of the *Polis*." In *New Light on a Dark Age: Exploring the Culture of Geometric Greece*, ed. S. Langdon, 194–207. Columbia, MO.

———. 2002. *Plato's Rhapsody and Homer's Music: The Poetics of the Panathenaic Festival in Classical Athens*. Hellenic Studies I. Cambridge, MA.

———. 2003. *Homeric Responses*. Austin.

Nethercut, W. R. 1973. "Vergil's *De Rerum Natura*." *Ramus* 2.1:41–52.

Neudecker, R. 1998. "The Roman Villa as a Locus of Art Collection." In *The Roman Villa, Villa Urbana: First Williams Symposium on Classical Architecture held at the University of Pennsylvania, Philadelphia, April 21–22, 1990*. University Museum Monograph 101, Symposium Series 9, ed. A. Frazer, 77–92. Philadelphia.

Nevett, L. C. 1999. *House and Society in the Ancient Greek World*. Cambridge.

Nielsen, I. 1999. *Hellenistic Palaces: Tradition and Renewal*. Studies in Hellenistic Civilization V. Aarhus.

O'Hara, J. J. 1994. "They Might Be Giants: Inconsistency and Indeterminacy in Vergil's War in Italy." *The Colby Library Quarterly* 30.3:206–226.

Osborne, R. 1987. *Classical Landscape with Figures: The Ancient Greek City and its Countryside*. London.

———. 1994. "Archaeology, the Salaminioi, and the Politics of Sacred Space in Archaic Attica." In *Placing the Gods: Sanctuaries and Sacred Space in Ancient Greece*, ed. S. E. Alcock and R. Osborne, 143–60. Oxford.

———. 1996. *Greece in the Making: 1200–478 BC*. London.

Page, D. 1955. *Sappho and Alcaeus: An Introduction to the Study of Ancient Lesbian Poetry*. Oxford.

Parry, A. 1957. "Landscape in Greek Poetry." *Yale Classical Studies* 15:3–29.

Parry, M. 1971. *The Making of Homeric Verse: The Collected Papers of Milman Parry*. Ed. A. Parry. Oxford.

Penwill, J. L. 1996. "The Ending of Sense: Death as Closure in Lucretius Book 6." *Ramus* 25.2:146–169.

Percival, J. 1996. "Houses in the Country." In *Roman Domestic Buildings*, ed. I. M. Barton, 65–90. Exeter.

Perkell, C. 2001. "Pastoral Value in Vergil: Some Instances." In *Poets and Critics Read Vergil*, ed. S. Spence, 26–43. New Haven.

———. 2002. "The Golden Age and its Contradictions in the Poetry of Vergil." *Vergilius* 48:3–39.

Polignac, F. de. 1994. "Mediation, Competition, and Sovereignty: The Evolution of Rural Sanctuaries in Geometric Greece." In *Placing the Gods: Sanctuaries and Sacred Space in Ancient Greece*, ed. S. E. Alcock and R. Osborne, 79–104. Oxford.

Pollan, M. 2001. *The Botany of Desire: A Plant's-Eye View of the World*. New York.

Pollitt, J. J. 1972. *Art and Experience in Classical Greece*. Cambridge.

———. 1985. "Early Greek Art in a Platonic Universe." In *Greek Art: Archaic into Classical*, ed. C. G. Boulter, 96–111. Leiden.

———. 1986. *Art in the Hellenistic Age*. Cambridge.

———. 1990. *The Art of Ancient Greece: Sources and Documents*. Cambridge.

Pomeroy, S. B., S. M. Burstein, W. Donlan, and J. T. Roberts. 1999. *Ancient Greece: A Political, Social, and Cultural History*. New York.

Powell, B. 2002. *Writing and the Origins of Greek Literature*. Cambridge.

Pradeau, J. F. 2000. "Plato's Atlantis: The True Utopia." In *Utopia: The Search for the Ideal Society in the Western World*, ed. R. Schaer, G. Claeys, and L. T. Sargent, 83–91. New York.

Pucci, P. 1979. "The Song of the Sirens." *Arethusa* 12:121–132.

———. 1998. *The Song of the Sirens: Essays on Homer*. Lanham, MD.

Purcell, N. 1987. "Town in Country and Country in Town." In *Ancient Roman Villa Gardens*. Dumbarton Oaks Colloquium on the History of Landscape Architecture X, ed. E. B. Macdougall, 185–204. Washington, DC.

———. 1995. "The Roman Villa and the Landscape of Production." In *Urban Society in Italy*, ed. T. Cornell and K. Lomas, 151–179. New York.

———. 1996. "The Roman Garden as a Domestic Building." In *Roman Domestic Buildings*, ed. I. M. Barton, 121–152. Exeter.

———. 2001. "Dialectical Gardening." *Journal of Roman Archaeology* 14.2:546–556.

Putnam, M. C. J. 1998. *Virgil's Epic Designs: Ekphrasis in the Aeneid*. New Haven.

Raaflaub, K. A. 1997. "Homeric Society." In *A New Companion to Homer*, ed. I. Morris and B. Powell, 624–648. Leiden.

Redfield, J. M. 1994. *Nature and Culture in the Iliad: The Tragedy of Hektor*. Durham, NC.

Rider, B. C. 1964. *Ancient Greek Houses: Their History and Development from the Neolithic Period to the Hellenistic Age*. Chicago.

Robertson, M. 1975. *A History of Greek Art*. 2 vols. Cambridge.

———. 1981. *A Shorter History of Greek Art*. Cambridge.

———. 1992. *The Art of Vase-Painting in Classical Athens*. Cambridge.

Rose, P. W. 1992. *Sons of the Gods, Children of Earth: Ideology and Literary Form in Ancient Greece*. Ithaca.

Rowe, C. 1976. *The Mathematics of the Ideal Villa and Other Essays*. Cambridge, MA.

Ruskin, J. 1906. "Of the Pathetic Fallacy." In *Modern Painters*. Vol. 3, ed. E. Rhys, 145–160. London.

Rykwert, J. 1981. *On Adam's House in Paradise: The Idea of the Primitive Hut in Architectural History*. 2nd ed. Cambridge, MA.

Saller, R. P. 1984. "*Familia, Domus*, and the Conception of the Family." *Phoenix* 38.4: 336–355.

Sargent, L. T. 1994. "The Three Faces of Utopia Revisited." *Utopian Studies* 5.1:1–37.

———. 2000. "Utopian Traditions: Themes and Variations." In *Utopia: The Search for the Ideal Society in the Western World*, ed. R. Schaer, G. Claeys, and L. T. Sargent, 8–17. New York.

Schaer, R. 2000. "Utopia: Space, Time, History." In *Utopia: The Search for the Ideal Society in the Western World*, ed. R. Schaer, G. Claeys, and L. T. Sargent, 3–7. New York.

Schama, S. 1995. *Landscape and Memory*. New York.

Scheid, J. and Svenbro, J. 1996. *The Craft of Zeus: Myths of Weaving and Fabric*. Revealing Antiquity 9. Trans. C. Volk. Cambridge, MA.

Schneider, K. 1995. *Villa und Natur: Eine Studie zur römischen Oberschichtkultur im letzten vor- und ersten nachchristlichen Jahrhundert*. Munich.

Scully, S. 1981. "The *Polis* in Homer: A Definition and Interpretation." *Ramus* 10:1–34.

Scully, V. 1991. *Architecture: The Natural and the Manmade*. New York.

Segal, C. P. 1963. "Nature and the World of Man in Greek Literature." *Arion* 2:19–53.

———. 1968. "Circean Temptations: Homer, Vergil, Ovid." *Transactions of the American Philological Association* 99:419–442.

———. 1981. *Poetry and Myth in Ancient Pastoral: Essays on Theocritus and Virgil.* Princeton.

———. 1994. "The Phaeacians and Odysseus' Return." In *Singers, Heroes, and Gods in the Odyssey,* 12–64. Ithaca.

Shelton, J.-A. 1996. "Lucretius on the Use and Abuse of Animals." *Eranos* 94:48–64.

Shepard, P. 1967. *Man in the Landscape: A Historic View of the Esthetics of Nature.* College Station, TX.

———. 1996. *The Others: How Animals Made Us Human.* Washington, DC.

Sherratt, E. S. 1990. "'Reading the Texts': Archaeology and the Homeric Question." *Antiquity* 64:807–824.

Silberberg-Peirce, S. 1980. "Politics and Private Imagery: The Sacral-Idyllic Landscapes." *Art History* 3.3:241–351.

Simon, E. 1968. *Ara Pacis Augustae.* Tübingen.

———. 1985. "Early Classical Vase-Painting." In *Greek Art: Archaic into Classical,* ed. C. G. Boulter, 66–82, plates 51–73. Leiden.

Snodgrass, A. M. 1991. "Archaeology and the Study of the Greek City." In *City and Country in the Ancient World,* ed. J. Rich and A. Wallace-Hadrill, 1–24. London.

Snyder, J. M. 1981. "The Web of Song: Weaving Imagery in Homer and the Lyric Poets." *The Classical Journal* 76.3:193–196.

Stanley, K. 1993. *The Shield of Homer: Narrative Structure in the Iliad.* Princeton.

Stewart, A. 1993. *Faces of Power: Alexander's Image and Hellenistic Politics.* Berkeley.

Stoddard, K. 1996. "Thucydides, Lucretius, and the End of the *De Rerum Natura.*" *Maia* 48.2:107–128.

Stronach, D. 1994. "Parterres and Stone Watercourses at Pasargadae: Notes on the Achaemenid Contribution to Garden Design." *Journal of Garden History* 14.1:3–12.

Suerbaum, W. 1993. "Der Aeneas Vergils—Mann zwischen Vergangenheit und Zukunft." *Gymnasium* 100:419–447.

Surtz, E., and J. H. Hexter, eds. 1965. *The Complete Works of St. Thomas More.* Vol. 4: *Utopia.* Trans. E. Surtz and J. H. Hexter. New Haven.

Syme, R. 1939. *The Roman Revolution.* Oxford.

Thacker, C. 1979. *The History of Gardens.* Berkeley.

Thomas, C. G., and C. Conant. 1999. *Citadel to City-State: The Transformation of Greece, 1200–700 B.C.E.* Bloomington, IN.

Thompson, M. B., and R. E. Griswold. 1963. *Garden Lore of Ancient Athens.* Excavation of the Athenian Agora 8. Princeton.

Thompson, M. L. 1960/1961. "The Monumental and Literary Evidence for Programmatic Painting in Antiquity." *Marsyas* 9:36–77.

Tomlinson, R. 1992. *From Mycenae to Constantinople: The Evolution of the Ancient City.* London.

Toynbee, J. M. C. 1973. *Animals in Roman Life and Art.* Ithaca.

Travlos, J. 1971. *Pictorial Dictionary of Ancient Athens.* London.

Turcan, R. 1996. *The Cults of the Roman Empire.* Trans. A. Nevill. Oxford.

Tybout, R. A. 1989. *Aedificiorum figurae: Untersuchungen zu den Architektur-darstellungen des frühen Zweiten Stils.* Amsterdam.

Vahlen, J., ed. 1903. *Ennianae Poesis Reliquiae.* Leipzig.

Vallillee, G. 1968. "Lucretius, Virgil, and the Didactic Method." *Échos du Monde Classique* 12:8–12.

Vance, E. 1981. "Sylvia's Pet Stag: Wildness and Domesticity in the *Aeneid.*" *Arethusa* 14.1:127–137.

Van Wees, H. 2002. "Homer and Early Greece." *Colby Quarterly* 38:94–117.

Vermeule, E. T. 1964. *Greece in the Bronze Age.* Chicago.

———. 1979. *Aspects of Death in Early Greek Art and Poetry.* Berkeley.

Vernant, J.-P. 1983. "Hestia-Hermes: The Religious Expression of Space and Movement in Ancient Greece." In *Myth and Thought Among the Greeks*, trans. Routledge and Kegan Paul, 127–175. London.

Vidal-Naquet, P. 1970. "Valeurs religieuses et mythiques de la terre et du sacrifice dans l'Odyssée." *Annales: Économies, Sociétés, Civilisations* 25.5:1279–1297.

Wallace-Hadrill, A. 1993. *Augustan Rome.* London.

———. 1994. *Houses and Society in Pompeii and Herculaneum.* Princeton.

———. 1998a. "The Villa as Cultural Symbol." In *The Roman Villa, Villa Urbana: First Williams Symposium on Classical Architecture held at the University of Pennsylvania, Philadelphia, April 21–22, 1990.* University Museum Monograph 101, Symposium Series 9, ed. A. Frazer, 43–54. Philadelphia.

———. 1998b. "*Horti* and Hellenization." In *Horti Romani: Atti del Convegno Internazionale Roma, 4-6 maggio 1995.* Bulletino della Commissione Archeologica Comunale di Roma, Supplementi 6, ed. Maddalena Cime and E. La Rocca, 2–12. Rome.

Wasserspring, L. 2000. *Oaxacan Ceramics: Traditional Folk Art by Oaxacan Women.* San Francisco.

Ward-Perkins, J. B. 1974. *Cities of Ancient Greece and Italy: Planning in Classical Antiquity*. New York.

Weber, C. 2002. "The Dionysus in Aeneas." *Classical Philology* 97.4:322–343.

Webster, T. B. L. 1964. *Hellenistic Poetry and Art*. New York.

Weinberg, F. M. 1986. *The Cave: The Evolution of a Metaphoric Field from Homer to Ariosto*. New York.

Wesenberg, B. 1985. "Römische Wandmalerei am Ausgang der Republik: der Zweite Pompejanische Stil." *Gymnasium* 92:470–488.

West, D. A. "*Cernere erat*: The Shield of Aeneas." In *Oxford Readings in Vergil's Aeneid*, ed. S. J. Harrison, 295–304. Oxford.

West, M. L., ed. 1978. *Hesiod: Works and Days*. Oxford.

———. 1990. "Archaische Heldendichtung: Singen und Schreiben." In *Der Übergang von der Mündlichkeit zur Literatur bei den Griechen*, ed. W. Kullmann and M. Reichel, 33–50. Tübingen.

Whitley, J. 2001. *The Archaeology of Ancient Greece*. Cambridge.

Whitehead, D. 1986. *The Demes of Attica 508/7– CA. 250 B.C.: A Political and Social Study*. Princeton.

Whitman, C. H. 1958. *Homer and the Heroic Tradition*. Cambridge, MA.

Wigodsky, M. 1972. *Vergil and Early Latin Poetry*. Hermes Einzelschriften 24. Wiesbaden.

Willcock, M. M., ed. 1984. *The Iliad of Homer: Books XIII-XXV*. Basingstoke.

Williams, M. F. 1991. *Landscape in the Argonautica of Apollonius Rhodius*. Frankfurt am Main.

Williams, R. D., ed. 1972. *The Aeneid of Virgil: Books 1-6*. Basingstoke.

———, ed. 1973. *The Aeneid of Virgil: Books 7-12*. Basingstoke.

———. 1982. "The *Aeneid*." In *The Cambridge History of Classical Literature*. Vol. II: *Latin Literature*, ed. E. J. Kenney and W. V. Clausen, 333–369. Cambridge.

Wirth, T. 1983. "Zum Bildprogramm der Räume N und P in der Casa dei Vettii." *Rheinisches Museum* 90.2:450–455.

Wiseman, T. P. 1987. "*Consipicui Postes Tectaque Digna Deo*: The Public Image of Aristocratic and Imperial Houses in the Late Republic and Early Empire." In *L'Urbs: espace urbain et histoire (Ier siècle av. J.C.-IIIe siècle ap. J.C.)*. Actes du colloque international organizé par le Centre national de la recherché scientifique et L' École française de Rome, Rome, 8–12 mai 1985. 393–413. Rome.

Wöhler, R. 1876. *Über den Einfluss des Lucrez auf die Dichter der Augusteischen Zeit*. Greifswald.

Wood, M. 1987. *In Search of the Trojan War*. New York.

Wycherley, R. E. 1959. "The Garden of Epicurus." *Phoenix* 13.2:73–77.

———. 1961. "*Peripatos*: the Athenian Philosophical Scene—I." *Greece & Rome* 2nd ser. 8.2:152–163.

———. 1962. "*Peripatos*: The Athenian Philosophical Scene—II." *Greece & Rome* 2nd ser. 9.1:2–21.

———. 1978. *The Stones of Athens*. Princeton.

Zaidman, L. B. 1992. "Pandora's Daughters and Rituals in Grecian Cities." In *From Ancient Goddesses to Christian Saints*, ed. P. S. Pantel, 338–376. Vol. 1 of *A History of Women in the West*, ed. G. Duby and M. Perrot. Cambridge, MA.

Zanker, G. 2004. *Modes of Viewing in Hellenistic Poetry and Art*. Madison.

Zanker, P. 1979. "Die Villa als Vorbild des späten pompejanischen Wohnge-schmacks." *Jahrbuch des deutschen archäologischen Instituts* 94:460–523.

———. 1988. *The Power of Images in the Age of Augustus*. Trans. A. Shapiro. Ann Arbor.

———. 1998. *Pompeii: Public and Private Life*. Trans. D. L. Schneider. Cambridge, MA.

Zeitlin, F. I. 1978. "The Dynamics of Misogyny: Myth and Mythmaking in the *Oresteia*." *Arethusa* 11.1, 2:149–184.

Zetzel, J. E. G. 1997. "Rome and its Traditions." In *The Cambridge Companion to Virgil*, ed. C. Martindale, 188–203. Cambridge.

Zola, E. 1958. *Autres chefs-d'oeuvre: Pot-bouille, Germinal, La bête humaine*. Paris.

Index of Ancient Authors and Works

General Index

This book was composed by Ivy Livingston
and manufactured by Edwards Brothers, Lillington, NC

The typeface is Gentium, designed by Victor Gaultney
and distributed by SIL International

CPSIA information can be obtained
at www.ICGtesting.com
Printed in the USA
LVHW030747020223
738080LV00002B/11